Math and Vocabulary for Civil Service Exams

LearningExpress®

NEW YORK®

Copyright © 2008 LearningExpress, LLC.

All rights reserved under International and Pan-American Copyright Conventions.
Published in the United States by LearningExpress, LLC, New York.

Library of Congress Cataloging-in-Publication Data:
Math and vocabulary for civil service exams.
    p. cm.
 ISBN 978-1-57685-606-2
 1. Civil service—United States—Examinations—Study guides. 2. Mathematics—Examinations—Study guides. 3. English language—Examinations—Study guides.
 JK716.M24 2008
 513.076—dc22

2007037804

Printed in the United States of America
9 8 7 6 5 4 3 2 1

ISBN: 978-1-57685-606-2

For information on LearningExpress, other LearningExpress products, or bulk sales,
please write to us at:
  LearningExpress
  55 Broadway
  8th Floor
  New York, NY 10006

Or visit us at:
  www.learnatest.com

Contents ▶

Preparing for Your Civil Service Exam

Choosing a career as a government employee can be very rewarding—you'll see respectable salaries, generous benefit packages, and opportunities for significant career advancement. But before you begin your job, you'll probably need to take a civil service exam. This exam requires candidates to score well on all parts of the exam, but the questions that require in-depth math and vocabulary knowledge can be especially nerve-racking if it's been a while since you've used these skills. Arm yourself with this book that will help you dust off your skills as you work your way through the most commonly tested math and vocabulary topics. By making the commitment to practice these difficult questions for the civil service exam, you are promising yourself increased scores and marketability as you enter this career path.

Is your civil service exam months away, or even maybe a few short weeks away? Have no fear—this book will help you prepare for success by working to review and improve your math and vocabulary skills.

Carefully read Chapter 1 to learn about the civil service field. Then, continue on to Chapter 2 (the LearningExpress Test Preparation System), so you can grasp effective test strategies and learn to budget your preparation time wisely. Chapter 2 presents a 30-day study plan and a 14-day study plan. You can decide which of these plans is right for you, or you can create a more personalized plan. Remember to stick as closely as you can to your study plan for the most effective results.

Once you've set a study plan for yourself, look at the table of contents to see the types of math and vocabulary topics covered in this book. The book is organized in five sections:

Section 1—Preparing for Your Civil Service Exam
Section 2—Math Prep for Civil Service Exams
Section 3—Vocabulary Prep for Civil Service Exams
Section 4—Test Time!
Section 5—Helpful Resources

Sections 2 and 3 divide math and vocabulary concepts into compact parts so that you can work on each concept on its own and gain mastery. You may want to read the chapters in sequence, or you may decide to study the chapters that give you the most difficulty early on in your test preparation.

Each chapter in Sections 2 and 3 contains practice questions to drill you on the chapter's main concepts. As you answer the hundreds of practice questions in this book, you will undoubtedly want to check your answers against the answer section at the end of each chapter. If, after answering all the questions in a section you feel you need more practice, reread the questions and try your hand at responding one more time. Repetition is often the key to success as studies show that most repetitive tasks become part of a person's inventory of skills over time.

Section 4 ("Test Time!") includes two practice tests to help you gauge your math and vocabulary skills. These tests will give you the chance to measure what you have learned and review any problem areas you encounter. You may want to take one practice test before you begin Sections 2 and 3 to determine your areas of weakness. Then, you can take the other test after you've reviewed the math and vocabulary topics.

Finally, don't forget about Section 5—the resources at the end of this book. These resources include math words to know, basic math formulas, commonly tested vocabulary terms, and a list of general suffixes, prefixes, and root words. You may consult these resources at any point as you work through this book. One good use of these resources may be to make flashcards or notes about any words or formulas that are new or confusing to you. Then, work with a friend or family member to quiz yourself. You don't even need a partner—try pulling out your flashcards as you wait in line, commute on a bus, or whenever you have a few free minutes.

Always keep your end goal in mind. If you study hard the first time, you will not have to take the civil service exam again—ever! Use this book to get a feel for the math and vocabulary topics presented on the exam. Spend some quality time with these topics, take the practice tests, and then get ready to walk into the exam room with plenty of self-confidence!

1 ▶ Civil Service Jobs

Civil service jobs range from clerical work to forestry, from social work to cartography, and from painting to nursing. The government workforce is diverse with career possibilities in a wide array of specialties and fields, including:

- Accounting
- Administration
- Agriculture
- Air Traffic Control
- Biology
- Budgetary Work
- Cartography
- Chemistry
- Claims Work
- Clerical Work
- Conservation

- Court Work
- Custodial Work
- Defense-related Work
- Drafting
- Educational Service
- Electrical Work
- Engineering
- Finance
- Firefighting
- Health Services
- Human Services

- Information Technology
- Law Enforcement
- Legal
- Machinist Work
- Nursing
- Painting
- Postal Work
- Service Work
- Social Work
- Treasury Work
- Visa Examination

The government is the largest single employer in the United States. Government jobs are secure, have great holiday and vacation schedules, offer health insurance, and provide paid training for employees. Specific benefits include:

- 10 paid holidays a year
- 13 to 26 paid vacation days a year
- 13 sick days a year
- death and disability insurance
- group life insurance
- medical and dental benefits (including healthcare flexible spending accounts, HCFSAs)
- retirement benefits
- alternative work schedules
- government-paid training
- tuition reimbursement

Civilian government employees are grouped by the type of work they do. This is called the *series*. The level of their relative positions (based on difficulty) is called the *grade*. Each grade progresses upward through *steps*. The higher the step, the more money you will earn. Depending on your prior education, you may enter the government pay scale at different grades. For example, high school graduates may enter at GS-2 ("GS" means "General Schedule"), whereas junior college graduates may enter at GS-4.

Unlike jobs in the private sector, government job openings aren't listed in the classified section of your city or local paper. But there are excellent, easily accessible sources of government job information.

The Office of Personnel Management (OPM) updates a list of federal job vacancies daily. You can access this information 24 hours a day, 7 days a week by calling the OPM's automated telephone system, Jobs by Phone, at 703–724–1850. Although this service offers around-the-clock convenience, beware: It may take more than one phone call to find exactly the information you need.

The most user-friendly of the OPM resources, www.usajobs.opm.gov, allows you to search for jobs by region, state, zip code, country, and department. Use this website to print a copy of application forms and access information about pay scales. You can even create a resume online or electronically file your qualifications statement.

FEDERAL PAY SCHEDULES, 2007

GRADE	ANNUAL RATES FOR STEPS (IN DOLLARS)									
	1	2	3	4	5	6	7	8	9	10
1	16,630	17,185	17,739	18,289	18,842	19,167	19,713	20,264	20,286	20,798
2	18,698	19,142	19,761	20,286	20,512	21,115	21,718	22,321	22,924	23,527
3	20,401	21,081	21,761	22,441	23,121	23,801	24,481	25,161	25,841	26,521
4	22,902	23,665	24,428	25,191	25,954	26,717	27,480	28,243	29,006	29,769
5	25,623	26,477	27,331	28,185	29,039	29,893	30,747	31,601	32,455	33,309
6	28,562	29,514	30,466	31,418	32,370	33,322	34,274	35,226	36,178	37,130
7	31,740	32,798	33,856	34,914	35,972	37,030	38,088	39,146	40,204	41,262
8	35,151	36,323	37,495	38,667	39,839	41,011	42,183	43,355	44,527	45,699
9	38,824	40,118	41,412	42,706	44,000	45,294	46,588	47,882	49,176	50,470
10	42,755	44,180	45,605	47,030	48,455	49,880	51,305	52,730	54,155	55,580
11	46,974	48,540	50,106	51,672	53,238	54,804	56,370	57,936	59,502	61,068
12	56,301	58,178	60,055	61,932	63,809	65,686	67,563	69,440	71,317	73,194
13	66,951	69,183	71,415	73,647	75,879	78,111	80,343	82,575	84,807	87,039
14	79,115	81,752	84,389	87,026	89,663	92,300	94,937	97,574	100,211	102,848
15	93,063	96,165	99,267	102,369	105,471	108,573	111,675	114,777	117,879	120,981

Please note that GS pay is adjusted according to your geographic location, so the majority of jobs pay more than the base salary listed in this table. The amount in the Base GS Pay Scale is multiplied by the percentage adjustment and the result is then added to the base pay. Also, certain hard-to-fill jobs, usually in the scientific, technical, and medical fields, may have higher starting salaries. Exact pay information can be found on position vacancy announcements.

Source: U.S. Office of Personnel Management, January 2007.

2 ▶ The Learning-Express Test Preparation System

Taking any test can be tough. But don't let the written test scare you! If you prepare ahead of time, you can achieve a top score. The LearningExpress Test Preparation System, developed exclusively for LearningExpress by leading test experts, gives you the discipline and attitude you need to be a winner.

Getting ready for any test takes work. If you plan to obtain an entry-level civil service position, you will have to score well on your civil service exam. This book focuses specifically on the math and vocabulary skills that you will be tested on—two areas that have proven difficult for many test takers. By honing in on these skills, you will take your first step toward achieving the career of your dreams. However, there are all sorts of pitfalls that can prevent you from doing your best on exams. Here are some obstacles that can stand in the way of your success.

- being unfamiliar with the format of the exam
- being paralyzed by test anxiety
- leaving your preparation to the last minute
- not preparing at all
- not knowing vital test-taking skills like:
  - how to pace yourself through the exam
  - how to use the process of elimination
  - when to guess
- not being in tip-top mental and physical shape
- forgetting to eat breakfast and having to take the exam on an empty stomach
- forgetting a sweater or jacket and shivering through the exam

What's the common denominator in all these test-taking pitfalls? One word: *control*. Who's in control, you or the exam?

Now the good news: The LearningExpress Test Preparation System puts you in control. In just nine easy-to-follow steps, you will learn everything you need to know to make sure you are in charge of your preparation and performance on the exam. Other test takers may let the test get the better of them; other test takers may be unprepared or out of shape, but not you. You will have taken all the steps you need to take for a passing score.

Here's how the LearningExpress Test Preparation System works: Nine easy steps lead you through everything you need to know and do to get ready to master your exam. Each of the steps gives you tips and activities to help you prepare for any exam. It's important that you follow the advice and do the activities, or you won't be getting the full benefit of the system. Each step gives you an approximate time estimate.

Step 1. Get Information	30 minutes
Step 2. Conquer Test Anxiety	20 minutes
Step 3. Make a Plan	50 minutes
Step 4. Learn to Manage Your Time	10 minutes
Step 5. Learn to Use the Process of Elimination	20 minutes
Step 6. Know When to Guess	20 minutes
Step 7. Reach Your Peak Performance Zone	10 minutes
Step 8. Get Your Act Together	10 minutes
Step 9. Do It!	10 minutes
Total	**3 hours**

We estimate that working through the entire system will take you approximately three hours, though it's perfectly OK if you work faster or slower than the time estimates say. If you can take a whole afternoon or evening, you can work through the entire LearningExpress Test Preparation System in one sitting. Otherwise, you can break it up, and do just one or two steps a day for the next several days. It's up to you—remember, *you're* in control.

▶ Step 1: Get Information

Time to complete: 30 minutes
Activities: Read Section 1, "Preparing for Your Civil Service Exam" and Chapter 1, "Civil Service Jobs."
If you haven't already done so, stop here and read Section 1 and Chapter 1 of this book. Here, you'll learn how to use this book, see an overview of the range of civil service jobs, and be presented with a discussion regarding earnings and job searches.

Knowledge is power. The first step in the LearningExpress Test Preparation System is finding out everything you can about the types of questions that will be asked on any math and vocabulary section of the civil service exam. Practicing and studying the exercises in this book will help prepare you for those tests. Math topics that are tested include:

- arithmetic, powers, and roots
- fractions
- decimals
- percents
- number series
- word problems
- charts, tables, and graphs
- algebra
- geometry and measurement

Vocabulary topics that are tested include:

- vocabulary in context
- reading comprehension
- synonyms
- antonyms
- grammar
- spelling

After completing the LearningExpress Test Preparation System, you will then begin to apply the test-taking strategies you learn as you work through practice questions in these topic areas (Chapters 3 through 14). You can see how well your training paid off in Chapters 15 and 16, where you will take two practice civil service tests.

▶ Step 2: Conquer Test Anxiety

Time to complete: 20 minutes
Activity: Take the Test Stress Test
Having complete information about the exam is the first step in getting control of the exam. Next, you have to overcome one of the biggest obstacles to test success: test anxiety. Test anxiety not only impairs your per-

formance on the exam itself, but it can even keep you from preparing! In Step 2, you'll learn stress management techniques that will help you succeed on your exam. Learn these strategies now, and practice them as you work through the practice tests in this book, so they'll be second nature to you by exam day.

Combating Test Anxiety

The first thing you need to know is that a little test anxiety is a good thing. Everyone gets nervous before a big exam—and if that nervousness motivates you to prepare thoroughly, so much the better. It's said that Sir Laurence Olivier, one of the foremost British actors of last century, was ill before every performance. His stage fright didn't impair his performance; in fact, it probably gave him a little extra edge—just the kind of edge you need to do well, whether on a stage or in an exam room.

On page 11 is the Test Stress Test. Stop here and answer the questions on that page to find out whether your level of test anxiety is something you should worry about.

Stress Management before the Test

If you feel your level of anxiety getting the best of you in the weeks before the test, here is what you need to do to bring the level down again:

- **Get prepared.** There's nothing like knowing what to expect. Being prepared will put you in control of test anxiety. That's why you're reading this book. Use it faithfully, and remind yourself that you're better prepared than most of the people taking the test.
- **Practice self-confidence.** A positive attitude is a great way to combat test anxiety. This is no time to be humble or shy. Stand in front of the mirror and say to your reflection, "I'm prepared. I'm full of self-confidence. I'm going to ace this test. I

know I can do it." Say it into a recorder and play it back once a day. If you hear it often enough, you'll believe it.

- **Fight negative messages.** Every time someone starts telling you how hard the exam is or how it's almost impossible to get a high score, start telling them your self-confidence messages. If the someone with the negative messages is you, telling yourself you don't do well on exams and you just can't do this, don't listen. Listen to your self-confidence messages instead.

- **Visualize.** Imagine yourself reporting for your first day on the job. Visualizing success can help make it happen—and it reminds you why you're preparing for the exam so diligently.

- **Exercise.** Physical activity helps calm down your body and focus your mind. Besides, being in good physical shape can actually help you do well on the exam. Go for a run, lift weights, go swimming—and do it regularly.

Stress Management on Test Day

There are several ways you can bring down your level of test anxiety on test day. To find a comfort level, experiment with the following exercises in the weeks before the test, and use the ones that work best for you.

- **Deep breathing.** Take a deep breath while you count to five. Hold it for a count of one, then let it out on a count of five. Repeat several times.

- **Move your body.** Try rolling your head in a circle. Rotate your shoulders. Shake your hands from the wrist. Many people find these movements very relaxing.

- **Visualize again.** Think of the place where you are most relaxed: lying on the beach in the sun, walking through the park, or sipping a cup of hot tea.

Now close your eyes and imagine you're actually there. If you practice in advance, you'll find that you need only a few seconds of this exercise to experience a significant increase in your sense of well-being.

When anxiety threatens to overwhelm you right there during the exam, there are still things you can do to manage your stress level:

- **Repeat your self-confidence messages.** You should have them memorized by now. Say them silently to yourself, and believe them!

- **Visualize one more time.** This time, visualize yourself moving smoothly and quickly through the test answering every question right and finishing just before time is up. Like most visualization techniques, this one works best if you've practiced it ahead of time.

- **Find an easy question.** Skim over the test until you find an easy question, and then answer it. Filling in even one circle gets you into the test-taking groove.

- **Take a mental break.** Everyone loses concentration once in a while during a long test. It's normal, so you shouldn't worry about it. Instead, accept what has happened. Say to yourself, "Hey, I lost it there for a minute. My brain is taking a break." Put down your pencil, close your eyes, and do some deep breathing for a few seconds. Then you're ready to go back to work.

Try these techniques ahead of time, and see if they work for you!

Test Stress Test

You only need to worry about test anxiety if it is extreme enough to impair your performance. The following questionnaire will provide a diagnosis of your level of test anxiety. In the blank before each statement, write the number that most accurately describes your experience.

0 = never
1 = once or twice
2 = sometimes
3 = often

_____ I have gotten so nervous before an exam that I simply put down the books and didn't study for it.

_____ I have experienced disabling physical symptoms such as vomiting and severe headaches because I was nervous about an exam.

_____ I have simply not showed up for an exam because I was scared to take it.

_____ I have experienced dizziness and disorientation while taking an exam.

_____ I have had trouble filling in the little circles because my hands were shaking too hard.

_____ I have failed an exam because I was too nervous to complete it.

_____ Total: Add up the numbers in the blanks.

Your Test Stress Score

Here are the steps you should take, depending on your score. If you scored:

- Below 3, your level of test anxiety is nothing to worry about; it's probably just enough to give you the motivation to excel.

- Between 3 and 6, your test anxiety may be enough to impair your performance, and you should practice the stress management techniques listed in this chapter to try to bring your test anxiety down to manageable levels.

- Above 6, your level of test anxiety is a serious concern. In addition to practicing the stress management techniques listed in this chapter, you may want to seek additional, personal help. Call your local high school or community college and ask for the academic counselor. Tell the counselor that you have a level of test anxiety that sometimes keeps you from being able to take an exam. The counselor may be willing to help you or may suggest someone else you should talk to.

▶ Step 3: Make a Plan

Time to complete: 50 minutes

Activity: Construct a study plan

Maybe the most important thing you can do to get control of yourself and your exam is to make a study plan. Too many people fail to prepare simply because they fail to plan. Spending hours on the day before the exam poring over sample test questions not only raises your level of test anxiety, it is also no substitute for careful preparation and practice.

Don't fall into the cram trap. Take control of your preparation time by mapping out a study schedule. If you're the kind of person who needs deadlines and assignments to motivate you for a project, here they are. If you're the kind of person who doesn't like to follow other people's plans, you can use the suggested schedules here to construct your own.

Even more important than making a plan is making a commitment. You can't review everything you need to know for a civil service exam in one night. You have to set aside some time every day for study and practice. Try for at least 20 minutes a day. Twenty minutes daily will do you much more good than two hours on Saturday.

Don't put off your study until the day before the exam. Start now. A few minutes a day, with half an hour or more on weekends can make a big difference in your score.

If you have months before the exam, you're lucky. Don't put off your studying until the week before the exam! Start now. Even ten minutes a day, with half an hour or more on weekends, can make a big difference in your score—and in your chances of making the grade you want!

Schedule A: The 30-Day Plan

If you have at least one month before you take your test, you have plenty of time to prepare—as long as you don't procrastinate! If you have less than a month, turn to Schedule B.

TIME	PREPARATION
Day 1	Read Section 1 of this book. Also, skim over any written materials you may have about the civil service exam.
Day 2	Read Chapter 3, "Arithmetic, Powers, and Roots." Work through practice questions 1–50. Score yourself.
Day 3	Review any Chapter 3 concepts you feel are necessary for you to brush up on.
Day 4	Read Chapter 4, "Fractions and Decimals." Work through practice questions 1–50. Score yourself.
Day 5	Read Chapter 5, "Percents." Work through practice questions 1–49. Score yourself.
Day 6	Review any Chapter 4 or Chapter 5 concepts you feel are necessary for you to brush up on.
Day 7	Read Chapter 6, "Number Series and Analogies." Work through practice questions 1–50. Score yourself.
Day 8	Review any Chapter 6 concepts you feel are necessary for you to brush up on.
Day 9	Read Chapter 7, "Word Problems." Work through practice questions 1–50. Score yourself.

TIME	PREPARATION
Day 10	Review any Chapter 7 concepts you feel are necessary for you to brush up on.
Day 11	Read Chapter 8, "Charts, Tables, and Graphs." Work through practice questions 1–50. Score yourself.
Day 12	Review any Chapter 8 concepts you feel are necessary for you to brush up on.
Day 13	Read Chapter 9, "Measurement and Geometry." Work through practice questions 1–50. Score yourself.
Day 14	Review any Chapter 9 concepts you feel are necessary for you to brush up on. Turn to "Section 5: Helpful Resources" and read through the Glossary of Math Terms and the Math Formula Sheet. If you choose, make index cards for unfamiliar items.
Day 15	Read Chapter 10, "Vocabulary in Context." Work through the practice exercises and questions. Score yourself.
Day 16	Review any Chapter 10 concepts you feel are necessary for you to brush up on.
Day 17	Read Chapter 11, "Synonyms and Antonyms." Work through practice questions 1–50. Score yourself.
Day 18	Review any Chapter 11 concepts you feel are necessary for you to brush up on.
Day 19	Read Chapter 12, "Reading Comprehension." Work through practice questions 1–50. Score yourself.
Day 20	Review any Chapter 12 concepts you feel are necessary for you to brush up on.
Day 21	Read Chapter 13, "Grammar." Work through practice questions 1–50. Score yourself.
Day 22	Review any Chapter 13 concepts you feel are necessary for you to brush up on.
Day 23	Read Chapter 14, "Spelling." Work through practice questions 1–50. Score yourself.
Day 24	Review any Chapter 14 concepts you feel are necessary for you to brush up on. Turn to "Section 5: Helpful Resources" and read through the Commonly Tested Vocabulary Words and Prefixes, Suffixes, and Word Roots appendices. If you choose, make index cards for unfamiliar terms or concepts.
Day 25	In Chapter 15, take Practice Test 1. Score yourself and review any incorrect questions.
Day 26	Review any concepts you feel are necessary for you to brush up on. Work through similar questions in the appropriate chapters.
Day 27	In Chapter 16, take Practice Test 2. Score yourself and review any incorrect questions.
Day 28	Review any concepts you feel are necessary for you to brush up on. Work through similar questions in the appropriate chapters.
Day 29	Review the chapters that contain the topics you were weak on during the Practice Exams.
Day before the exam	Relax. Do something unrelated to the exam and go to bed at a reasonable hour.

Schedule B: The 14-Day Plan

If you have two weeks or less before the exam, you may have your work cut out for you. Use this 14-day schedule to help you make the most of your time.

TIME	PREPARATION
Day 1	Read Chapters 1 and 2.
Day 2	Complete Chapters 3, 4, and 5, including the practice questions.
Day 3	Complete Chapters 6 and 7, including the practice questions.
Day 4	Complete Chapters 8 and 9, including the practice questions.
Day 5	Review the math chapters that contained the topics in which you were weak, in addition to the helpful resources geared for math review.
Day 6	Complete Chapter 10, including the practice questions.
Day 7	Complete Chapters 11 and 12, including the practice questions.
Day 8	Complete Chapters 13 and 14, including the practice questions.
Day 9	Review the vocabulary chapters that contained the topics in which you were weak, in addition to the helpful resources geared for vocabulary review.
Day 10	Complete Practice Test 1 (Chapter 15) and score yourself. Review all of the questions that you missed.
Day 11	Review any concepts you feel are necessary for you to brush up on. Work through similar questions in the appropriate chapters.
Day 12	Complete Practice Test 2 (Chapter 16) and score yourself. Review all of the questions that you missed.
Day 13	Review any topics as indicated by the questions you missed on the practice tests. Then, look at the questions you missed again and make sure you understand them.
Day before the exam	Relax. Do something unrelated to the exam and go to bed at a reasonable hour.

▶ Step 4: Learn to Manage Your Time

Time to complete: 10 minutes to read, many hours of practice!

Activities: Use these strategies as you take the practice tests in this book

Steps 4, 5, and 6 of the LearningExpress Test Preparation System put you in charge of your exam by showing you test-taking strategies that work. Practice these strategies as you take the sample tests in this book, and then you'll be ready to use them on test day.

First, take control of your time on the exam. Civil service exams have a time limit, which may give you more than enough time to complete all the questions—or not enough time. It's a terrible feeling to hear the examiner say, "Five minutes left, " when you're only three-quarters of the way through the test. Here are some tips to keep that from happening to you.

- **Follow directions.** If the directions are given orally, listen closely. If they're written on the exam booklet, read them carefully. Ask questions before the exam begins if there is anything you don't understand. If you're allowed to write in your exam booklet, write down the beginning time and ending time of the exam.

- **Pace yourself.** Glance at your watch every few minutes, and compare the time to how far you've gotten in the test. When one-quarter of the time has elapsed, you should be a quarter of the way through the section, and so on. If you're falling behind, pick up the pace a bit.

- **Keep moving.** Don't waste time on one question. If you don't know the answer, skip the question and move on. Circle the number of the question in your test booklet in case you have time to come back to it later.

- **Keep track of your place on the answer sheet.** If you skip a question, make sure you skip on the answer sheet too. Check yourself every 5–10 questions to make sure the question number and the answer sheet number are still the same.

- **Don't rush.** Although you should keep moving, rushing won't help. Try to keep calm and work methodically and quickly.

▶ Step 5: Learn to Use the Process of Elimination

Time to complete: 20 minutes
Activity: Complete worksheet on Using the Process of Elimination

After time management, your most important tool for taking control of your exam is using the process of elimination wisely. It's standard test-taking wisdom that you should always read all the answer choices before choosing your answer. This helps you find the right answer by eliminating wrong answer choices. And, sure enough, that standard wisdom applies to your exam, too.

Choosing the Right Answer by Process of Elimination

As you read a question, you may find it helpful to underline important information or make some notes about what you're reading. When you get to the heart of the question, circle it and make sure you understand what it is asking. If you're not sure of what's being asked, you'll never know whether you've chosen the right answer. What you do next depends on the type of question you're answering.

- If it's math, take a quick look at the answer choices for some clues. Sometimes this helps to put the question in a new perspective and makes it easier to answer. Then make a plan of attack to solve the problem.

- Otherwise, follow this simple process-of-elimination plan to manage your testing time as efficiently as possible: Read each answer choice and make a quick decision about what to do with it, marking your test book accordingly:

  - The answer seems reasonable; keep it. Put a ✔ next to the answer.

  - The answer is awful. Get rid of it. Put an **X** next to the answer.

  - You can't make up your mind about the answer, or you don't understand it. Keep it for now. Put a **?** next to it.

Whatever you do, don't waste time with any one answer choice. If you can't figure out what an answer choice means, don't worry about it. If it's the right answer, you'll probably be able to eliminate all the others, and, if it's the wrong answer, another answer will probably strike you more obviously as the right answer.

- If you haven't eliminated any answers at all, skip the question temporarily, but don't forget to mark the question so you can come back to it later if you have time. If the test has no penalty for wrong answers, and you're certain you could never answer this question in a million years, pick an answer and move on!

- If you've eliminated all but one answer, just reread the circled part of the question to make sure you're answering exactly what's asked. Mark your answer sheet and move on to the next question.

- Here's what to do when you've eliminated some, but not all of the answer choices. Compare the remaining answers looking for similarities and differences, reasoning your way through these choices. Try to eliminate those choices that don't seem as strong to you. But *don't* eliminate an answer just because you don't understand it. You may even be able to use relevant information from other parts of the test. If you've narrowed it down to a single answer, check it against the circled question to be sure you've answered it. Then mark your answer sheet and move on. If you're down to only two or three answer choices, you've improved your odds of getting the question right. Make an educated guess and move on. However, if you think you can do better with more time, mark the question as one to return to later.

If You're Penalized for Wrong Answers

You must know whether you'll be penalized for wrong answers before you begin the civil service exam. If you don't, ask the proctor before the test begins. Whether you make a guess or not depends upon the penalty. Some standardized tests are scored in such a way that every wrong answer reduces your score by a fraction of a point, and these can really add up against you! Whatever the penalty, if you can eliminate enough choices to make the odds of answering the question better than the penalty for getting it wrong, make a guess. This is called educated guessing.

Let's imagine you are taking a test in which each answer has five choices and you are penalized one-fourth of a point for each wrong answer. If you cannot eliminate any of the answer choices, you're better off leaving the answer blank because the odds of guessing correctly are one in five. However, if you can eliminate two of the choices as definitely wrong, the odds are now in your favor. You have a one in three chance of answering the question correctly. Fortunately, few tests are scored using such elaborate means, but if your test is one of them, know the penalties and calculate your odds before you take a guess on a question.

If You Finish Early

Use any time you have left to do the following:

- Go back to questions you marked to return to later and try them again.
- Check your work on all the other questions. If you have a good reason for thinking a response is wrong, change it.
- Review your answer sheet. Make sure you've put the answers in the right places and you've marked only one answer for each question. (Most tests are scored in such a way that questions with more than one answer are marked wrong.)
- If you've erased an answer, make sure you've done a good job of it.
- Check for stray marks on your answer sheet that could distort your score.

Whatever you do, don't waste time when you've finished a test section. Make every second count by checking your work over and over again until time is called.

Try using your powers of elimination on the questions in the worksheet on page 17 called "Using the Process of Elimination." The answer explanations that follow show one possible way you might use the process to arrive at the right answer.

The process of elimination is your tool for the next step, which is knowing when to guess.

Using the Process of Elimination

Use the process of elimination to answer the following questions.

1. Ilsa is as old as Meghan will be in five years. The difference between Ed's age and Meghan's age is twice the difference between Ilsa's age and Meghan's age. Ed is 29. How old is Ilsa?
   a. 4
   b. 10
   c. 19
   d. 24

2. "All drivers of commercial vehicles must carry a valid commercial driver's license whenever operating a commercial vehicle." According to this sentence, which of the following people need NOT carry a commercial driver's license?
   a. a truck driver idling his engine while waiting to be directed to a loading dock
   b. a bus operator backing her bus out of the way of another bus in the bus lot
   c. a taxi driver driving his personal car to the grocery store
   d. a limousine driver taking the limousine to her home after dropping off her last passenger of the evening

3. Smoking tobacco has been linked to
   a. an increased risk of stroke and heart attack.
   b. all forms of respiratory disease.
   c. increasing mortality rates over the past ten years.
   d. juvenile delinquency.

4. Which of the following words is spelled correctly?
   a. incorrigible
   b. outragous
   c. domestickated
   d. understandible

Answers

Here are the answers, as well as some suggestions as to how you might have used the process of elimination to find them.

1. d. You should have eliminated choice **a** immediately. Ilsa can't be four years old if Meghan is going to be Ilsa's age in five years. The best way to eliminate other answer choices is to try plugging them in to the information given in the problem. For instance, for choice **b**, if Ilsa is 10, then Meghan must be 5. The difference in their ages is 5. The difference between Ed's age, 29, and Meghan's age, 5, is 24. Is 24 two times 5? No. Then choice **b** is wrong. You could have eliminated choice **c** in the same way and be left with choice **d**.

2. c. Note the word *not* in the question, and go through the answers one by one. Is the truck driver in choice **a** "operating a commercial vehicle"? Yes, idling counts as "operating," so he needs to have a commercial driver's license. Likewise, the bus operator in choice **b** is operating a commercial vehicle; the question doesn't say the operator has to be on the street. The limo driver in choice **d** is operating a commercial vehicle, even if it doesn't have a passenger in it. However, the taxi driver in choice **c** is not operating a commercial vehicle, but his own private car.

3. a. You could eliminate choice **b** simply because of the presence of the word *all*. Such absolutes hardly ever appear in correct answer choices. Choice **c** looks attractive until you think a little about what you know—aren't fewer people smoking these days, rather than more? So how could smoking be responsible for a higher mortality rate? (If you didn't know that mortality rate means the rate at which people die, you might keep this choice as a possibility, but you'd still be able to eliminate two answers and have only two to choose from.) Choice **d** can't be proven, so you could eliminate that one, too. Now you're left with the correct choice, **a**.

4. a. How you used the process of elimination here depends on which words you recognized as being spelled incorrectly. If you knew that the correct spellings were *outrageous*, *domesticated*, and *understandable*, then you were home free. Surely you knew that at least one of those words was wrong.

▶ Step 6: Know When to Guess

Time to complete: 20 minutes

Activity: Complete worksheet on Your Guessing Ability

Armed with the process of elimination, you're ready to take control of one of the big questions in test-taking: Should I guess? The first and main answer is, it depends on the scoring rules of the test and if you're able to eliminate any answers. Some exams have what's called a "guessing penalty," in which a fraction of your wrong answers is subtracted from your right answers. Check with the administrators of your particular exam to see if this is the case. In many instances, the number of questions you answer correctly yields your raw score. So you have nothing to lose and everything to gain by guessing.

The more complicated answer to the question, "Should I guess?" depends on you, your personality, and your "guessing intuition." There are two things you need to know about yourself before you go into the exam:

1. Are you a risk-taker?
2. Are you a good guesser?

You'll have to decide about your risk-taking quotient on your own. To find out if you're a good guesser, complete the worksheet called "Your Guessing Ability" that begins on page 20. Frankly, even if you're a play-it-safe person with terrible intuition, you're still safe in guessing every time, as long as your exam has no guessing penalty. The best thing would be if you could overcome your anxieties and go ahead and mark an answer. But you may want to have a sense of how good your intuition is before you go into the exam.

The following are ten really hard questions. You're not supposed to know the answers. Rather, this is an assessment of your ability to guess when you don't have a clue. Read each question carefully, just as if you did expect to answer it. If you have any knowledge at all of the subject of the question, use that knowledge to help you eliminate wrong answer choices. Use this answer grid to fill in your answers to the questions.

1.	ⓐ	ⓑ	ⓒ	ⓓ
2.	ⓐ	ⓑ	ⓒ	ⓓ
3.	ⓐ	ⓑ	ⓒ	ⓓ
4.	ⓐ	ⓑ	ⓒ	ⓓ
5.	ⓐ	ⓑ	ⓒ	ⓓ
6.	ⓐ	ⓑ	ⓒ	ⓓ
7.	ⓐ	ⓑ	ⓒ	ⓓ
8.	ⓐ	ⓑ	ⓒ	ⓓ
9.	ⓐ	ⓑ	ⓒ	ⓓ
10.	ⓐ	ⓑ	ⓒ	ⓓ

1. September 7 is Independence Day in
   a. India.
   b. Costa Rica.
   c. Brazil.
   d. Australia.

2. Which of the following is the formula for determining the momentum of an object?
   a. $p = mv$
   b. $F = ma$
   c. $P = IV$
   d. $E = mc^2$

3. Because of the expansion of the universe, the stars and other celestial bodies are all moving away from each other. This phenomenon is known as
   a. Newton's first law.
   b. the big bang.
   c. gravitational collapse.
   d. Hubble flow.

4. American author Gertrude Stein was born in
   a. 1713.
   b. 1830.
   c. 1874.
   d. 1901.

5. Which of the following is NOT one of the Five Classics attributed to Confucius?
   a. the *I Ching*
   b. the *Book of Holiness*
   c. the *Spring and Autumn Annals*
   d. the *Book of History*

6. The religious and philosophical doctrine that holds that the universe is constantly in a struggle between good and evil is known as
   a. pelagianism.
   b. manichaeanism.
   c. neo-Hegelianism.
   d. epicureanism.

7. The third chief justice of the U.S. Supreme Court was
   a. John Blair.
   b. William Cushing.
   c. James Wilson.
   d. John Jay.

8. Which of the following is the poisonous portion of a daffodil?
   a. the bulb
   b. the leaves
   c. the stem
   d. the flowers

9. The winner of the Masters golf tournament in 1953 was

    a. Sam Snead.

    b. Cary Middlecoff.

    c. Arnold Palmer.

    d. Ben Hogan.

10. The state with the highest per capita personal income in 1980 was

    a. Alaska.

    b. Connecticut.

    c. New York.

    d. Texas.

Answers

Check your answers against the correct answers.

1. c.

2. a.

3. d.

4. c.

5. b.

6. b.

7. b.

8. a.

9. d.

10. a.

How Did You Do?

You may have simply gotten lucky and actually known the answer to one or two questions. In addition, your guessing was more successful if you were able to use the process of elimination on any of the questions. Maybe you didn't know who the third chief justice was (question 7), but you knew that John Jay was the first. In that case, you would have eliminated choice **d** and therefore improved your odds of guessing right from one in four to one in three.

According to probability, you should get two and a half answers correct, so getting either two or three right would be average. If you got four or more right, you may be a really terrific guesser. If you got one or none right, you may decide not to guess.

Keep in mind, though, that this is only a small sample. You should continue to keep track of your guessing ability as you work through the sample questions in this book. Circle the numbers of questions you guess; or, if you don't have time during the practice tests, go back afterward and try to remember which questions you guessed. Remember, on a test with four answer choices, your chances of getting a right answer is one in four. So keep a separate "guessing" score for each exam. How many questions did you guess? How many did you get right? If the number you got right is at least one-fourth of the number of questions you guessed, you are at least an average guesser, maybe better—and you should always go ahead and guess on the real exam. If the number you got right is significantly lower than one-fourth of the number you guessed on, you should not guess on exams where there is a guessing penalty unless you can eliminate a wrong answer. If there's no guessing penalty, you would be safe in guessing anyway, but maybe you'd feel more comfortable if you guessed only selectively, when you can eliminate a wrong answer or at least have a good feeling about one of the answer choices.

▶ Step 7: Reach Your Peak Performance Zone

Time to complete: 10 minutes to read; weeks to complete!
Activity: Complete the Physical Preparation Checklist
To get ready for a challenge like a big exam, you have to take control of your physical, as well as your mental state. Exercise, proper diet, and rest will ensure that your body works with, rather than against, your mind on test day, as well as during your preparation.

Exercise

If you don't already have a regular exercise program going, the time during which you're preparing for an exam is actually an excellent time to start one. If you're already keeping fit—or trying to get that way—don't let the pressure of preparing for an exam fool you into quitting now. Exercise helps reduce stress by pumping wonderful good-feeling hormones called endorphins into your system. It also increases the oxygen supply throughout your body and your brain, so you'll be at peak performance on test day.

A half hour of vigorous activity—enough to break a sweat—every day should be your aim. If you're really pressed for time, every other day is OK. Choose an activity you like and get out there and do it. Jogging with a friend always makes the time go faster as does listening to music.

But don't overdo it. You don't want to exhaust yourself. Moderation is the key.

Diet

First of all, cut out the junk. Go easy on caffeine and nicotine, and eliminate alcohol and any other drugs from your system at least two weeks before the exam. Promise yourself a special treat the night after the exam, if need be.

What your body needs for peak performance is simply a balanced diet. Eat plenty of fruits and vegetables, along with protein and complex carbohydrates. Foods that are high in lecithin (an amino acid), such as fish and beans, are especially good "brain foods."

Rest

You probably know how much sleep you need every night to be at your best, even if you don't always get it. Make sure you do get that much sleep, though, for at least a week before the exam. Moderation is important here, too. Extra sleep will just make you groggy.

If you're not a morning person and your exam will be given in the morning, you should reset your internal clock so that your body doesn't think you're taking an exam at 3 A.M. You have to start this process well before the exam. The way it works is to get up half an hour earlier each morning, and then go to bed half an hour earlier that night. Don't try it the other way around; you'll just toss and turn if you go to bed early without getting up early. The next morning, get up another half an hour earlier, and so on. How long you will have to do this depends on how late you're used to getting up. Use the "Physical Preparation Checklist" on pages 23–24 to make sure you're in tip-top form.

▶ Step 8: Get Your Act Together

Time to complete: 10 minutes to read; time to complete will vary
Activity: Complete Final Preparations worksheet
Once you feel in control of your mind and body, you're in charge of test anxiety, test preparation, and test-taking strategies. Now it's time to make charts and gather the materials you need to take to the exam.

Physical Preparation Checklist

For the week before the test, write down what physical exercise you engaged in and for how long and what you ate for each meal. Remember, you're trying for at least half an hour of exercise every other day (preferably every day) and a balanced diet that's light on junk food.

Exam minus 7 days

Exercise: _____ for _____ minutes

Breakfast: _____

Lunch: _____

Dinner: _____

Snacks: _____

Exam minus 6 days

Exercise: _____ for _____ minutes

Breakfast: _____

Lunch: _____

Dinner: _____

Snacks: _____

Exam minus 5 days

Exercise: _____ for _____ minutes

Breakfast: _____

Lunch: _____

Dinner: _____

Snacks: _____

Gather Your Materials

The night before the exam, lay out the clothes you will wear and the materials you have to bring with you to the exam. Plan on dressing in layers because you won't have any control over the temperature of the exam room. Have a sweater or jacket you can take off if it's warm. Use the checklist on the worksheet entitled "Final Preparations" on page 25 to help you pull together what you'll need.

Don't Skip Breakfast

Even if you don't usually eat breakfast, do so on exam morning. A cup of coffee doesn't count. Don't eat doughnuts or other sweet foods, either. A sugar high will leave you with a sugar low in the middle of the exam. A mix of protein and carbohydrates is best: Cereal with milk or eggs with toast will do your body a world of good.

Physical Preparation Checklist

Exam minus 4 days

Exercise: _____ for _____ minutes

Breakfast: _____

Lunch: _____

Dinner: _____

Snacks: _____

Exam minus 3 days

Exercise: _____ for _____ minutes

Breakfast: _____

Lunch: _____

Dinner: _____

Snacks: _____

Exam minus 2 days

Exercise: _____ for _____ minutes

Breakfast: _____

Lunch: _____

Dinner: _____

Snacks: _____

Exam minus 1 day

Exercise: _____ for _____ minutes

Breakfast: _____

Lunch: _____

Dinner: _____

Snacks: _____

▶ Step 9: Do It!

Time to complete: 10 minutes, plus test-taking time
Activity: Ace Your Test!

Fast-forward to exam day. You're ready. You made a study plan and followed through. You practiced your test-taking strategies while working through this book. You're in control of your physical, mental, and emotional state. You know when and where to show up and what to bring with you. In other words, you're better prepared than most of the other people taking the test with you. You're psyched!

Just one more thing. When you're done with the exam, you will have earned a reward. Plan a night out. Call your friends and plan a party, or have a nice dinner for two—whatever your heart desires. Give yourself something to look forward to.

Final Preparations

Getting to the Exam Site

Location of exam: _____

Date of exam: _____

Time of exam: _____

Do I know how to get to the exam site? Yes _____ No _____

If no, make a trial run.

Time it will take to get to the exam site: _____

Things to lay out the night before

Clothes I will wear _____

Sweater/jacket _____

Watch _____

Photo ID _____

Admission card _____

4 no. 2 pencils _____

_____   _____

_____   _____

And then do it. Go into the exam, full of confidence, armed with test-taking strategies you've practiced until they're second nature. You're in control of yourself, your environment, and your performance on exam day. You're ready to succeed. So do it. Go in there and ace the civil service exam! And, then, look forward to your new career.

2 ▶ Math Prep for Civil Service Exams

Not all civil service exams test your math knowledge, but many do. The math portion of the civil service exam covers subjects you probably studied in grade school and high school. Knowledge of basic arithmetic, as well as the complex reasoning necessary for algebra, are important qualifications for almost any profession. You have to be able to add up dollar figures, evaluate budgets, compute percentages, and perform similar math tasks in many civil service positions. Many jobs require someone able to understand and interpret data presented in the form of tables and graphs. So even if your exam doesn't include math, you'll probably need to review the material in this section to be successful on the job.

Before you begin working your way through Section 2, take a look at the following math strategies. These suggestions are tried and true, and will help you as you maneuver through this book. You may use one or all of them. Or, you may decide to pick and choose the combination that works best for you.

- It's best not to work in your head! Use your test book or scratch paper to take notes, draw pictures, and calculate. Although you might think that you can solve math questions more quickly in your head, that's a good way to make mistakes. Instead, write out each step.

- Before you begin to make your calculations, read a math question in chunks rather than straight through from beginning to end. As you read each chunk, stop to think about what it means. Then make notes or draw a picture to represent that chunk.

- When you get to the actual question, circle it. This will keep you more focused as you solve the problem.

- Glance at the answer choices for clues. If they're fractions, you should do your work in fractions; if they're decimals, you should work in decimals, and so on.

- Make a plan of attack to help you solve the problem.

- When you get your answer, reread the circled question to make sure you've answered it. This helps avoid the careless mistake of answering the wrong question.

- Check your work after you get an answer. Test takers get a false sense of security when they get an answer that matches one of the multiple-choice answers. It could be right, but you should always check your work. Remember to:
  - Ask yourself if your answer is reasonable, if it makes sense.
  - Plug your answer back into the problem to make sure the problem holds together.
  - Do the question a second time, but use a different method.
  - Approximate when appropriate. For example: $5.98 + $8.97 is a little less than $15 (Add $6 + $9).
    0.9876×5.0342 is close to 5 (Multiply 1×5).

- Skip hard questions and come back to them later. Mark them in your test book so you can find them quickly.

CHAPTER

Arithmetic, Powers, and Roots

You may have forgotten what the term **arithmetic** encompasses, but you most likely use it every day. Arithmetic consists of the following four familiar operations:

- addition
- subtraction
- multiplication
- division

When solving arithmetic problems, it's helpful to keep in mind the following definitions regarding the operations:

- A **sum** is obtained by adding.
- A **difference** is obtained by subtracting.
- A **product** is obtained by multiplying.
- A **quotient** is obtained by dividing.

Basic arithmetic problems require you to add, subtract, multiply, or divide. You may be asked to find the sum, difference, product, or quotient. More advanced arithmetic questions deal with **combined operations**. This simply means that two or more of the basic operations are combined into an equation or expression. For example, a question that has you find the product of two sums would be considered a combined operations question.

When dealing with basic arithmetic and combined operations, it is helpful to understand three basic number laws: the commutative law, the associative law, and the distributive law. Sometimes these three laws are referred to as properties (such as the commutative property).

- The **commutative law** applies to addition and multiplication and can be represented as $a + b = b + a$ or $a \times b = b \times a$. For example, $2 + 3 = 3 + 2$ and $4 \times 2 = 2 \times 4$ exhibit the commutative law.
- The **associative law** applies to grouping of addition or multiplication equations and expressions. It can be represented as $a + (b + c) = (a + b) + c$ or $a \times (b \times c) = (a \times b) \times c$. For example, $10 + (12 + 14) = (10 + 12) + 14$.
- The **distributive law** applies to multiplication *over* addition and can be represented as $a(b + c) = ab + ac$. For example, $3(5 + 7) = 3 \times 5 + 3 \times 7$.

It is also especially important to understand the **order of operations**. When dealing with a combination of operations, you must perform the operations in a particular order. An easy way to remember the order of operations is to use the mnemonic **PEMDAS**, where each letter stands for an operation:

- **Parentheses:** Always calculate the values inside the parentheses first.
- **Exponents:** Exponents (or powers) are calculated second.
- **Multiplication/Division:** Third, multiply or divide in order from left to right.
- **Addition/Subtraction:** Last, add or subtract in order from left to right.

▶ Powers

When you raise a number (the base) to an exponent, this is sometimes called raising the number to a **power**.

$$\text{Base}^{\text{power}} \text{ or Base}^{\text{exponent}}$$

If the terms have different bases, you cannot combine them. When you have the same base, it is easy to combine the exponents according to the following rules:

- When multiplying like bases, such as $a^x \times a^y$, simply add the exponents: $a^x \times a^y = a^{x+y}$
- When dividing, such as $a^x \div a^y$, simply subtract the exponents: $a^x \div a^y = a^{x-y}$
- When raising a power to a power, such as $(a^x)^y$, simply multiply the exponents: $(a^x)^y = a^{xy}$
- If one of the bases doesn't have an exponent written, that means its exponent is 1: $a = a^1$

Note that if more than one base is included in the parentheses, you must raise all of the bases to the power outside the parentheses, so $(a^x b^y)^z = a^{xz} b^{yz}$. $(ab^x)^y$ equals $a^y b^{xy}$ because a is equal to a^1.

Two common powers have special names. When raising a number to the second power, it is called **squaring** the number. When raising a number to the third power, it is called **cubing** the number.

Let's take a look at $(6^2)^5$. Remember, when raising a power to a power, you can just multiply the exponents. Here you should multiply 2×5, so $(6^2)^5 = 6^{2 \times 5} = 6^{10}$. You can check your work by writing out the solution: $(6^2)^5 = (6 \times 6)^5 = (6 \times 6)(6 \times 6)(6 \times 6)(6 \times 6)(6 \times 6)$. This is 6 to the tenth power, or 6^{10}.

▶ Roots

On the civil service exam, you may be asked to take the square root of a number. This is denoted by a radical sign, which looks like this: $\sqrt{}$. In order to find the square root of a number, try to figure out what number when squared will equal the number under the radical sign. For example, you know that $2^2 = 4$, so $\sqrt{4} = 2$.

Square roots are easy to calculate for **perfect squares**. For example $\sqrt{4} = 2$, $\sqrt{9} = 3$, $\sqrt{16} = 4$, $\sqrt{25} = 5$, and so forth. Other times you can approximate the value of a radical by pinpointing it between two perfect squares. For example, because $\sqrt{4} = 2$ and $\sqrt{9} = 3$, $\sqrt{7}$ must be a number between 2 and 3.

In other cases, it is helpful to find equivalents of the radical by applying the rules governing the manipulation of radicals. These rules can be summarized as:

- $\sqrt{ab} = \sqrt{a} \times \sqrt{b}$
  This rule is helpful when simplifying $\sqrt{12}$, for example. $\sqrt{12} = \sqrt{4 \times 3} = \sqrt{4} \times \sqrt{3} = 2\sqrt{3}$
- $\sqrt{\frac{a}{b}} = \sqrt{a} \div \sqrt{b}$
  This rule is helpful when finding the equivalent of a radical like $\sqrt{\frac{1}{25}}$. First take the radical of the top and bottom: $\sqrt{\frac{1}{25}} = \frac{\sqrt{1}}{\sqrt{25}}$. Because $\sqrt{1} = 1$ and $\sqrt{25} = 5$, you have $\sqrt{1} \div \sqrt{25} = 1 \div 5$.

Once you are able to convert the radicals into equivalents that have the same number under the radical, you can combine them effectively through addition and subtraction. For example, $2\sqrt{2} + 3\sqrt{2} = 5\sqrt{2}$ and $5\sqrt{3} - 4\sqrt{3} = 1\sqrt{3}$.

▶ Practice Questions

1. Find the sum of 7,805 and 987.
   a. 17,675
   b. 8,972
   c. 8,987
   d. 8,792

2. Lawrence gave $281 to Joel. If he originally had $1,375, how much money does he have left?
   a. $1,656
   b. $1,294
   c. $1,094
   d. $984

3. Peter had $10,573 in his savings account. He then deposited $2,900 and $317. How much is in the account now?
   a. $13,156
   b. $13,790
   c. $7,356
   d. $6,006

4. What is the positive difference between 10,752 and 675?
   a. 11,427
   b. 10,077
   c. 3,822
   d. −10,077

5. 287,500 − 52,988 + 6,808 =
   a. 347,396
   b. 46,467
   c. 333,680
   d. 241,320

6. What is the product of 450 and 122?
   a. 54,900
   b. 6588
   c. 572
   d. 328

7. Find the quotient of 12,440 and 40.
   a. 497,600
   b. 12,480
   c. 12,400
   d. 311

8. What is the product of 523 and 13 when rounded to the nearest hundred?
   a. 6,799
   b. 536
   c. 6,800
   d. 500

9. When the sum of 1,352 and 731 is subtracted from 5,000, the result is
   a. 7,083
   b. 2,917
   c. 2,083
   d. 4,379

10. What is the quotient of 90 divided by 18?
   a. 5
   b. 6
   c. 72
   d. 1,620

11. What is the product of 52 and 22?
   a. 30
   b. 74
   c. 104
   d. 1,144

12. What is the sum of the product of 3 and 2 and the product of 4 and 5?

a. 14

b. 26

c. 45

d. 90

13. Find the difference of 582 and 73.

a. 42,486

b. 655

c. 509

d. 408

14. How much greater is the sum of 523 and 65 than the product of 25 and 18?

a. 138

b. 545

c. 588

d. 33,545

15. Solve the following:

589 + 7,995 ÷ 15

a. 572 with a remainder of 4

b. 1,122

c. 8,569

d. 8,599

16. 540 ÷ 6 + 3 × 24 =

a. 2,232

b. 1,440

c. 1,260

d. 162

17. 78 × (32 + 12) =

a. 2,508

b. 3,432

c. 6,852

d. 29,953

18. Which of the following demonstrates the commutative property?

a. $2 + 3 = 4 + 1$

b. $2 + (3 + 4) = (2 + 3) + 4$

c. $2 \times 3 = 3 \times 2$

d. $2 \times (3 \times 4) = (2 \times 3) \times 4$

19. Which of the following demonstrates the associative property?

a. $4 + 5 = 5 + 4$

b. $2 \times (3 + 4) = (2 \times 3) + 4$

c. $4 \times 5 = 5 \times 4$

d. $2 \times (3 \times 4) = (2 \times 3) \times 4$

20. Which of the following demonstrates the distributive property?

a. $(4 \times 5) + 1 = 4 \times (5 + 1)$

b. $4 \times (5 + 1) = 4 \times 5 + 4 \times 1$

c. $4 \times 5 \times 1 = 1 \times 5 \times 4$

d. $(4 + 5) + 1 = 4 + (5 + 1)$

21. $4 \times 4 \times 4 \times 4$ is equivalent to

a. 4×4^2

b. $4^2 \times 4^3$

c. $(4^2)^2$

d. $4^3 + 4^2$

22. What is the square root of 81?

a. 8

b. 9

c. 10

d. 11

23. $11^3 =$

a. 121

b. 1,331

c. 14,641

d. 15,551

24. $(8^3)^5 =$
   a. 8^{15}
   b. 8^8
   c. 8^4
   d. 8^2

25. $\sqrt{72} =$
   a. 12
   b. $6\sqrt{3}$
   c. $6\sqrt{2}$
   d. $36\sqrt{2}$

26. $7^3 =$
   a. 343
   b. 49
   c. 38
   d. 21

27. $2\sqrt{128} =$
   a. $8\sqrt{2}$
   b. $16\sqrt{2}$
   c. $32\sqrt{2}$
   d. $64\sqrt{2}$

28. $\sqrt{50} + \sqrt{162} =$
   a. $106\sqrt{2}$
   b. $14\sqrt{2}$
   c. $9\sqrt{2}$
   d. $5\sqrt{2}$

29. $75 - 3(9 - 7)^4 =$
   a. 3^3
   b. 1,444
   c. 694
   d. 54

30. $\sqrt{1,225} =$
   a. 30
   b. 35
   c. 40
   d. 45

31. $3 \times 3 \times 3 \times 3 \times 3 \times 3 =$
   a. $(3^3)^3$
   b. $3^2 \times 3^2 \times 3^2$
   c. $3^2 \times 3^3$
   d. $(3^4)^2$

32. $2\sqrt{3} + 2\sqrt{2} + 5\sqrt{3} =$
   a. $4\sqrt{3} + 2\sqrt{2}$
   b. $4\sqrt{2} + 5\sqrt{3}$
   c. $8\sqrt{2} + 2\sqrt{3}$
   d. $7\sqrt{3} + 2\sqrt{2}$

33. $\sqrt{\frac{1}{81}} =$
   a. $1 \div 9$
   b. $1 \div 81$
   c. $1 \div \sqrt{3}$
   d. $1 \div \sqrt{9}$

34. $(-3)^3 + (3)^3 =$
   a. 54
   b. 27
   c. 0
   d. -27

35. $\sqrt{70}$ is between which of the following two numbers?
   a. 5 and 6
   b. 6 and 7
   c. 7 and 8
   d. 8 and 9

36. 18^3 is how much greater than 16^2?

   a. 6,088

   b. 5,576

   c. 265

   d. 68

37. 42^2 is how much greater than 24^2?

   a. 1,188

   b. 1,764

   c. 576

   d. 2,340

38. $\sqrt{(-3)^2(4)^2} =$

   a. $12\sqrt{2}$

   b. $-\sqrt{122}$

   c. 12

   d. −12

39. $(-12)^2 =$

   a. −144

   b. −121

   c. 121

   d. 144

40. $(-3)^3 =$

   a. 9

   b. −9

   c. 27

   d. −27

41. The square root of 48 is between which two numbers?

   a. 6 and 7

   b. 5 and 6

   c. 4 and 5

   d. 3 and 4

42. $2^4 + 2^7 =$

   a. 2^{28}

   b. 2^{11}

   c. 2^5

   d. 2^3

43. $3^2 + 3^3 =$

   a. 18

   b. 27

   c. 6^2

   d. 6^5

44. $7^{11} \div 7^9 =$

   a. 7^{20}

   b. 7^{-20}

   c. 49

   d. $1 \div 49$

45. $3^5 \times 3^2 \times 5^3 \times 5^9 =$

   a. $3^7 \times 5^{12}$

   b. $3^{12} \times 5^7$

   c. $3^3 \times 5^6$

   d. $3^6 \times 5^3$

46. $(6^9 \times 2^5) \div (6^8 \times 2^2) =$

   a. 64

   b. 48

   c. 32

   d. 16

47. $\frac{10 \times 10^{10}}{5 \times 10^2} =$

   a. 10×10^8

   b. 5×10^{-8}

   c. 2×10^8

   d. 5×10^8

48. Find the sum of (3×10^2) and (2×10^5).

    a. 200,300

    b. 23,000

    c. 2,300

    d. 230

49. What is the product of 2×10^6 and 6×10^7?

    a. 12×10^{42}

    b. 12×10^{13}

    c. 12×10^5

    d. 12×10^3

50. A rod that is 8×10^6 mm is how much longer than a rod that is 4×10^4 mm?

    a. twice as long

    b. four times as long

    c. 20 times as long

    d. 200 times as long

▶ Answers

1. d. *Sum* means addition, so 7,805 + 987 = 8,792.

2. c. To find the *difference,* subtract: 1,375 − 281 = 1,094. He now has $1,094.

3. b. Add all three values together: 10,573 + 2,900 + 317 = $13,790.

4. b. To find a *difference,* just subtract. The term *positive difference* means you are solving for a positive answer. This means you should subtract the smaller number from the larger number: 10,752 − 675 = 10,077.

5. d. 287,500 − 52,988 = 234,512. Next, add: 234,512 + 6,808 = 241,320.

6. a. *Product* means multiply. 450 × 122 = 54,900.

7. d. A quotient results from division. 12,440 ÷ 40 = 311.

8. c. To find the product, just multiply: 523 × 13 = 6,799. Rounding to the nearest hundred yields 6,800.

9. b. The sum of 1,352 and 731 is obtained by adding: 1,352 + 731 = 2,083. Next you subtract this value from 5,000: 5,000 − 2,083 = 2,917.

10. a. 90 divided by 18 equals 5. Thus, the quotient is 5.

11. d. The product is obtained by multiplying: 52 × 22 = 1,144.

12. b. First, find the two products:
3 × 2 = 6 and 4 × 5 = 20.
Next, add these two products together: 6 + 20 = 26.

13. c. To find a difference, you subtract: 582 − 73 = 509.

14. a. First, calculate the two equations:
The sum of 523 and 65: 523 + 65 = 588
The product of 25 and 18: 25 × 18 = 450
Next, find the difference:
588 − 450 = 138

15. b. The rules for the order of operations state that division should be done before addition. Recall **PEMDAS:** *parentheses, exponents, multiplication, division, addition, subtraction.* 7,995 ÷ 15 = 533. Next, add: 589 + 533 = 1,122.

16. d. Consider **PEMDAS:** *parentheses, exponents, multiplication, division, addition, subtraction.* Here you must solve the division first: 540 ÷ 6 = 90. The equation becomes 90 + 3 × 24. Again, considering PEMDAS, you know you should calculate the multiplication first. 3 × 24 = 72, so the equation reduces to 90 + 72 = 162.

17. b. Remember **PEMDAS:** *parentheses, exponents, multiplication, division, addition, subtraction.* Here you must solve the part inside the parentheses first: 32 + 12 = 44. The equation becomes 78 × 44. Multiplying, you get 3,432.

18. c. Note that this question is not looking for a true equation. It is asking which equation represents the commutative property. The commutative property applies for addition and multiplication and can be represented as $a + b = b + a$ or $a \times b = b \times a$. Choice **c** shows this relationship: 2 × 3 = 3 × 2. In other words, the order in which you multiply two numbers does not matter.

19. d. The associative property applies to grouping of addition or multiplication problems. It can be represented as $a + (b + c) = (a + b) + c$, or $a \times (b \times c) = (a \times b) \times c$. Note that you CANNOT combine addition and multiplication as in choice **b.** 2 × (3 + 4) ≠ (2 × 3) + 4. Only choice **d** correctly shows this property: 2 × (3 × 4) = (2 × 3) × 4.

20. b. The distributive property applies to multiplication over addition such as in choice **b**: $4 \times (5 + 1) = 4 \times 5 + 4 \times 1$. Notice that multiplying the sum of the two terms by 4 is equivalent to multiplying each term by 4 and then adding these values.

21. c. $4 \times 4 \times 4 \times 4$ is the same as 4^4. Choice **c** also equals 4^4 because when you raise a power to another power, you simply multiply the exponents. Thus, $(4^2)^2 = 4^{2+2}$. Choice **a** equals 4^3, choice **b** equals 4^5, and choice **d** equals $64 + 16$, or 80.

22. c. The square root of 81 simply means $\sqrt{81}$. To solve, just ask yourself "What number squared equals 81?" $9^2 = 81$, so $\sqrt{81} = 9$.

23. b. $11^3 = 11 \times 11 \times 11 = 121 \times 11 = 1,331$.

24. a. When raising a power of a base to another power, you just multiply the exponents. Here $(8^3)^5 = 8^{3 \times 5} = 8^{15}$.

25. c. $\sqrt{72} = \sqrt{36 \times 2}$. Because $36 = 6^2$, you can pull a 6 out from under the radical. Thus, you have $6\sqrt{2}$.

26. a. $7^3 = 7 \times 7 \times 7$, which equals $49 \times 7 = 343$.

27. b. $2\sqrt{128}$ is equal to $\sqrt{64 \times 2}$, or $2 \times \sqrt{64} \times \sqrt{2}$. Since $\sqrt{64} = 8$, you have $2 \times 8 \times \sqrt{2} = 16\sqrt{2}$.

28. b. Each radical can be rewritten. First, $\sqrt{50} = \sqrt{2 \times 25} = \sqrt{2} \times \sqrt{25} = \sqrt{2} \times 5 = 5\sqrt{2}$. Next, $\sqrt{162} = \sqrt{81 \times 2} = \sqrt{81} \times \sqrt{2} = 9\sqrt{2}$. Finally, add the two radicals: $5\sqrt{2} + 9\sqrt{2} = 14\sqrt{2}$.

29. a. To solve, use PEMDAS: *parentheses, exponents, multiplication, division, addition, subtraction*. First, calculate the value inside the parentheses: $75 - 3(9 - 7)^4 = 75 - 3(2)^4$. Second, calculate the exponent $75 - 3(2)^4 = 75 - 3(16)$. Third, calculate the multiplication: $75 - 3(16) = 75 - 48$. Finally, subtract: $75 - 48 = 27$. Because 27

is not listed as an answer choice, figure out which choice equals 27. Here, choice **a**, $3^3 = 3 \times 3 \times 3 = 27$.

30. b. In this case, it is easiest to see which answer choice when squared equals 1,225. Choice **a**, 30, would yield $30 \times 30 = 900$, and is thus too small. Choice **b**, 35, yields $35 \times 35 = 1,225$. Thus, $\sqrt{1,225} = 35$ and choice **b** is correct.

31. b. $3 \times 3 \times 3 \times 3 \times 3 \times 3$ is equivalent to 3^6. Choice **b** is equivalent to 3^6 because $3^2 \times 3^2 \times 3^2$ equals 3^{2+2+2}. Remember to add the powers when multiplying numbers with the same base. Choice **a** equals 3^9, choice **c** equals 3^5, and choice **d** equals 3^8.

32. d. You can combine the two terms with the $\sqrt{3}$. $2\sqrt{3} + 5\sqrt{3} = 7\sqrt{3}$, so the entire expression equals $7\sqrt{3} + 2\sqrt{2}$.

33. a. $\sqrt{\frac{1}{81}} = \sqrt{1} \div \sqrt{81} = 1 \div 9$, choice **a**.

34. c. Cubing a negative number (or taking any odd power of a negative number, for that matter) results in a negative value. Here, $-3^3 = -3 \times -3 \times -3 = -27$. $3^3 = 27$. Thus, the sum $(-3)^3 + (3)^3 = -27 + 27 = 0$.

35. d. 8^2 is 64 and 9^2 is 81. Thus, the square root of 70 (which is between 64 and 81) must be between 8 and 9.

36. b. First, calculate both quantities: $18^3 = 18 \times 18 \times 18 = 5,832$ and $16^2 = 16 \times 16 = 256$. Next, in order to find out how much greater the first quantity is, you find the *difference* (by subtracting): $5,832 - 256 = 5,576$.

37. a. Calculate both of the given quantities: $42^2 = 1,764$ and $24^2 = 576$. Next, subtract to obtain the difference: $1,764 - 576 = 1,188$.

38. c. To solve $\sqrt{(-3)^2(4)^2}$ you will first simplify the value under the radical. $-3^2 = 9$ and $4^2 = 16$, so $\sqrt{(-3)^2(4)^2} = \sqrt{9 \times 16}$. This can be rewritten as $\sqrt{9} \times \sqrt{16}$ and simplified to 3×4, which equals 12.

39. d. When you square a negative number (or raise a negative number to any even power), the result is a positive number. So, $(-12)^2 = 144$.

40. d. When you raise a negative number to any odd power, the result is a negative number. So, $(-3)^3 = -3 \times -3 \times -3 = -27$.

41. a. $6^2 = 36$ and $7^2 = 49$. So $\sqrt{48}$ (which is between 36 and 49) will equal a number that is between 6 and 7.

42. b. Since the base (2) is the same, you can simply add the exponents. $2^4 \times 2^7 = 2^{4+7} = 2^{11}$.

43. c. $3^2 = 9$ and $3^3 = 27$; $9 + 27 = 36$. Because 36 is not listed as an answer choice, calculate which choice equals 36. Here, choice **c**, $6^2 = 6 \times 6 = 36$, and is correct.

44. c. Because the base (7) is the same, you can simply subtract the exponents. $7^{11} \div 7^9 = 7^{11-9} = 7^2 = 49$.

45. a. You can apply the rules of exponents to the terms that have the same bases. Thus, $3^5 \times 3^2 \times 5^3 \times 5^9 = 3^{5+2} \times 5^{3+9} = 3^7 \times 5^{12}$.

46. b. You can apply the rules of exponents to the terms that have the same bases. Thus, $(6^9 \times 2^5) \div (6^8 \times 2^2)$ is equivalent to $6^{9-8} \times 2^{5-2} = 6^1 \times 2^3 = 6 \times 8 = 48$.

47. c. $\frac{10 \times 10^{10}}{5 \times 10^2} = \frac{10}{5} \times \frac{10^{10}}{10^2} = 2 \times 10^{10-2} = 2 \times 10^8$. Remember that according to the rules of exponents, when dividing, you can simply subtract the exponents of the two powers of 10.

48. a. $3 \times 10^2 = 3 \times 100 = 300$ and $2 \times 10^5 = 2 \times 100,000 = 200,000$. Adding these 2 values yields $200,000 + 300 = 200,300$.

49. b. The product of 2×10^6 and 6×10^7 would be $2 \times 10^6 \times 6 \times 10^7 = 2 \times 6 \times 10^6 \times 10^7$. Applying the rules of exponents, you can simply add the exponents of the 2 powers of 10. Thus, $2 \times 6 \times 10^6 \times 10^7 = 2 \times 6 \times 10^{6+7} = 2 \times 6 \times 10^{13}$. Multiplying the first 2 terms yields 12×10^{13}.

50. d. 8×10^6 mm $= 8 \times 1,000,000 = 8,000,000$ mm. 4×10^4 mm $= 4 \times 10,000 = 40,000$. How many times larger is 8,000,000 than 40,000? $8,000,000 \div 40,000 = 200$. Thus, the first rod is 200 times longer than the second.

Fractions and Decimals

On the civil service exam, the problems involving fractions you'll encounter may be straightforward calculation questions, or they may be word problems. Typically, they ask you to add, subtract, multiply, divide, or compare fractions.

A **fraction** is a part of something (a whole). Fractions are written as $\frac{part}{whole}$, or more technically as $\frac{numerator}{denominator}$. Look at three kinds of fractions:

Proper fraction:

$\frac{1}{2}, \frac{2}{3}, \frac{4}{9}, \frac{8}{13}$

The numerator is less than the denominator. The value of a proper fraction is less than 1.

Improper fraction:

$\frac{3}{2}, \frac{5}{3}, \frac{14}{9}, \frac{12}{12}$

The numerator is greater than or equal to the denominator. The value of an improper fraction is 1 or more.

Mixed number:

$3\frac{1}{2}$; $4\frac{2}{3}$; $12\frac{3}{4}$; $24\frac{3}{4}$

A fraction is written to the right of a whole number. The value of a mixed number is more than 1; it is the sum of the whole number plus the fraction.

▶ Changing Improper Fractions into Mixed or Whole Numbers

To change an improper fraction, say $\frac{13}{2}$, into a mixed number, follow these steps:

1. Divide the denominator (2) into the numerator (13) to get the whole number portion (6) of the mixed number:
   $13 \div 2 = 6\ \text{r}1.$
2. Write the remainder of the division (1) over the old denominator (2):
   $6\frac{1}{2}$
3. Check: Change the mixed number back into an improper fraction (see steps in the next section).

▶ Changing Mixed Numbers into Improper Fractions

It's easier to multiply and divide fractions when you're working with improper fractions rather than mixed numbers. To change a mixed number, say $2\frac{3}{4}$, into an improper fraction, follow these steps:

1. Multiply the whole number (2) by the denominator (4):
   $2 \times 4 = 8$
2. Add the result (8) to the numerator (3):
   $8 + 3 = 11$
3. Put the total (11) over the denominator (4):
   $\frac{11}{4}$
4. Check: Reverse the process by changing the improper fraction into a mixed number. If you get back the number you started with, your answer is right.

▶ Reducing Fractions

Reducing a fraction means writing it in lowest terms, that is, with smaller numbers. For instance, 50¢ is $\frac{50}{100}$ of a dollar, or $\frac{1}{2}$ of a dollar. In fact, if you have a 50¢ piece in your pocket, you say that you have a half dollar. Reducing a fraction does not change its value. Follow these steps to reduce a fraction:

When the numerator and denominator both end in zeros, cross out the same number of zeros in both numbers to begin the reducing process. For example, $\frac{300}{4,000}$ reduces to $\frac{3}{40}$ when you cross out two zeros in both numbers.

1. Find a whole number that divides evenly into both the numerator and the denomination.
2. Divide that number into the numerator, and replace the numerator with the quotient (the answer you got when you divided).
3. Do the same thing to the denominator.
4. Repeat the first three steps until you can't find a number that divides evenly into both the numerator and the denominator.

For example, let's reduce $\frac{8}{24}$. You could do it in two steps: $\frac{8 \div 4}{24 \div 4} = \frac{2}{6}$; then $\frac{2 \div 2}{6 \div 2} = \frac{1}{3}$. Or you could do it in a single step: $\frac{8 \div 8}{24 \div 8} = \frac{1}{3}$.

Whenever you do arithmetic with fractions, reduce your answer. On a multiple-choice test, don't panic if your answer isn't listed. Try to reduce it and then compare it to the choices.

▶ Raising Fractions to Higher Terms

Before you can add and subtract fractions, you have to know how to raise a fraction to higher terms. This is actually the opposite of reducing a fraction.

Follow these steps to raise $\frac{2}{3}$ to 24ths:

1. Divide the old bottom number (3) into the new one (24): $3\overline{)24} = 8$
2. Multiply the answer (8) by the old top number (2): $2 \times 8 = 16$
3. Put the answer (16) over the new bottom number (24): $\frac{16}{24}$
4. Check your answer by reducing the new fraction to see if you get back the original one: $\frac{16 \div 8}{24 \div 8} = \frac{2}{3}$

▶ Adding Fractions

It's important to remember that when adding or subtracting fractions, you always need them to have the same denominator. Then, whenever you subtract or add, you only need to perform the operation on the numerators, and keep the same denominator.

If the fractions have the same denominators, add the numerators together and write the total over the denominator.

Examples: $\frac{2}{9} + \frac{4}{9} = \frac{2+4}{9} = \frac{6}{9}$

Reduce the fraction: $\frac{2}{3}$

$\frac{5}{8} + \frac{7}{8} = \frac{12}{8}$

Change the sum to a mixed number: $1\frac{4}{8}$; then reduce: $1\frac{1}{2}$

There are a few extra steps to add mixed numbers with the same denominators, say $2\frac{3}{5} + 1\frac{4}{5}$:

1. Add the fractions: $\qquad\qquad\qquad\qquad\qquad\qquad\qquad$ $\frac{3}{5} + \frac{4}{5} = \frac{7}{5}$

2. Change the improper fraction into a mixed number: $\qquad$ $\frac{7}{5} = 1\frac{2}{5}$

3. Add the whole numbers: $\qquad\qquad\qquad\qquad\qquad\qquad$ $2 + 1 = 3$

4. Add the results of steps 2 and 3: $\qquad\qquad\qquad\qquad$ $1\frac{2}{5} + 3 = 4\frac{2}{5}$

▶ Finding a Common Denominator

If the fractions you want to add don't have the same denominator, you'll have to raise some or all of the fractions to higher terms so that they all have the same denominator, the **common denominator**.

See if all the denominators divide evenly into the biggest denominator. If this fails, check out the multiplication table of the largest denominator until you find a number into which all the other denominators evenly divide. **When all else fails, multiply all the denominators together.**

Example: $\frac{2}{3} + \frac{4}{5}$

1. Find the common denominator. Multiply the denominators: $\qquad$ $3 \times 5 = 15$

2. Raise each fraction to 15ths: $\qquad\qquad\qquad\qquad\qquad$ $\frac{2}{3} = \frac{10}{15}$

$\qquad\qquad\qquad\qquad\qquad\qquad\qquad\qquad\qquad\qquad\qquad$ $\frac{4}{5} = \frac{12}{15}$

3. Add as usual: $\qquad\qquad\qquad\qquad\qquad\qquad\qquad\qquad$ $\frac{22}{15}$

▶ Finding the Least Common Denominator

If you are asked to find the **least common denominator** (LCD), you will need to find the smallest number that is a multiple of the original denominators present. Sometimes you can figure this out mentally, or you will stumble onto the LCD by following the previous steps.

However, to be sure that you have the *least* common denominator, you can use one of two methods:

1. Find the least common multiple. This can be done by checking out the multiplication table of the largest denominator until you find a number that all the other denominators evenly divide into, as described previously.
2. Determine the prime factorization of each of the denominators. The least common denominator will encompass every denominator's prime factorization.

Prime numbers are numbers that have only two factors, the number 1 and itself. For example, 3 is prime because its only factors are 1 and 3. 1 is not a prime number. Also, 2 is the only even prime number. Numbers that are not prime can be expressed in terms of prime factors. For example, let's determine the prime factorization of 12.

$12 = 3 \times 4 = 3 \times 2 \times 2$

The prime factorization of 12 is $3 \times 2 \times 2$.

In order to find the LCD of $\frac{3}{4}$ and $\frac{5}{6}$, you can use the prime factorization method as follows:

1. Find the prime factorization of both denominators:

$4 = 2 \times 2$
$6 = 2 \times 3$

2. The LCD will contain the prime factorization of both denominators:

$4 = 2 \times 2$ (the LCD must have two 2s.)
$6 = 2 \times 3$ (the LCD must have a 2 and a 3.)

The LCD will be $2 \times 2 \times 3$. Note that this LCD contains the prime factorization of 4 and 6.

► Subtracting Fractions

If the fractions have the same denominators, subtract the numerators and write the difference over the denominator.

Example: $\frac{4}{9} - \frac{3}{9} = \frac{4-3}{9} = \frac{1}{9}$

If the fractions you want to subtract don't have the same denominator, you'll have to raise some or all of the fractions to higher terms so that they all have the same denominator, or LCD. If you forgot how to find the LCD, just read the section on adding fractions with different denominators.

Example: $\frac{5}{6} - \frac{3}{4}$

1. Raise each fraction to 12ths because 12 is the LCD, the smallest number that both 6 and 4 divide into evenly:

$\frac{5}{6} = \frac{10}{12} \qquad \frac{3}{4} = \frac{9}{12}$

2. Subtract as usual:

$\frac{1}{12}$

Subtracting mixed numbers with the same denominator is similar to adding mixed numbers.

Example: $4\frac{3}{5} - 1\frac{2}{5}$

1. Subtract the fractions:	$\frac{3}{5} - \frac{2}{5} = \frac{1}{5}$
2. Subtract the whole numbers:	$4 - 1 = 3$
3. Add the results of steps 1 and 2:	$\frac{1}{5} + 3 = 3\frac{1}{5}$

Sometimes there is an extra "borrowing" step when you subtract mixed numbers with the same denominators, say $7\frac{3}{5} - 2\frac{4}{5}$:

1. You can't subtract the fractions the way they are because $\frac{4}{5}$ is bigger than $\frac{3}{5}$.

So you borrow 1 from the 7, making it 6, and change that 1 to $\frac{5}{5}$ because

5 is the bottom number: $\qquad\qquad\qquad\qquad\qquad 7\frac{3}{5} = 6\frac{5}{5} + \frac{3}{5}$

2. Add the numbers from step 1: $\qquad\qquad\qquad\quad 6\frac{5}{5} + \frac{3}{5} = 6\frac{8}{5}$

3. Now you have a different version of the original problem: $\quad 6\frac{8}{5} - 2\frac{4}{5}$

4. Subtract the fractional parts of the two mixed numbers: $\quad \frac{8}{5} - \frac{4}{5} = \frac{4}{5}$

5. Subtract the whole number parts of the two mixed numbers: $\quad 6 - 2 = 4$

6. Add the results of the last two steps together: $\qquad\quad 4 + \frac{4}{5} = 4\frac{4}{5}$

▶ Multiplying Fractions

Multiplying fractions is actually easier than adding them. All you do is multiply the numerators and then multiply the denominators.

For example, $\frac{2}{3} \times \frac{5}{7} = \frac{2 \times 5}{3 \times 7} = \frac{10}{21}$

Sometimes you can cancel before multiplying. Cancelling is a shortcut that makes the multiplication go faster because you're multiplying with smaller numbers. It's very similar to reducing: if there is a number that divides evenly into a numerator and denominator, do that division before multiplying. If you forget to cancel, you'll still get the right answer, but you'll have to reduce it.

Example: $\frac{5}{6} \times \frac{9}{20}$

1. Cancel the 6 and the 9 by dividing 3 into both of them: $6 \div 3 = 2$ and $9 \div 3 = 3$.

Cross out the 6 and the 9:

$\frac{5}{\cancel{6}_2} \times \frac{\cancel{9}^3}{20}$

When you find a fraction *of* a number, you just find the product of the two numbers. For example, $\frac{1}{2}$ of 10 could be written $\frac{1}{2} \times \frac{10}{1}$. This becomes $\frac{10}{2}$, or 5.

2. Cancel the 5 and the 20 by dividing 5 into both of them: $5 \div 5 = 1$ and $20 \div 5 = 4$.
   Cross out the 5 and the 20:

   $$\frac{\overset{1}{\cancel{5}}}{2} \times \frac{3}{\underset{4}{\cancel{20}}}$$

3. Multiply across the new numerators and the new denominators:

   $$\frac{1 \times 3}{2 \times 4} = \frac{3}{8}$$

To multiply a fraction by a whole number, first rewrite the whole number as a fraction with a denominator of 1:

Example: $5 \times \frac{2}{3} = \frac{5}{1} \times \frac{2}{3} = \frac{10}{3}$ (Optional: convert $\frac{10}{3}$ to a mixed number: $3\frac{1}{3}$)

To multiply with mixed numbers, it's easier to change them to improper fractions before multiplying.

Example: $4\frac{2}{3} \times 5\frac{1}{2}$

1. Convert $4\frac{2}{3}$ to an improper fraction: $4\frac{2}{3} = \frac{4 \times 3 + 2}{3} = \frac{14}{3}$
2. Convert $5\frac{1}{2}$ to an improper fraction: $5\frac{1}{2} = \frac{5 \times 2 + 1}{2} = \frac{11}{2}$
3. Cancel and multiply the fractions: $\frac{14}{3} \times \frac{11}{2} = \frac{77}{3}$
4. Optional: convert the improper fraction to a mixed number: $\frac{77}{3} = 25\frac{2}{3}$

▶ Dividing Fractions

To divide one fraction by a second fraction, invert the second fraction (that is, flip the numerator and denominator) and then multiply. That's all there is to it!

Example: $\frac{1}{2} \div \frac{3}{5}$

1. Invert the second fraction $(\frac{3}{5}): \frac{5}{3}$
2. Change the division sign (÷) to a multiplication sign (× or •)
3. Multiply the first fraction by the new second fraction: $\frac{1}{2} \times \frac{5}{3} = \frac{1 \times 5}{2 \times 3} = \frac{5}{6}$

To divide a fraction by a whole number, first change the whole number to a fraction by putting it over 1. Then, follow the division steps given.

Example: $\frac{3}{5} \div 2 = \frac{3}{5} \div \frac{2}{1} = \frac{3}{5} \times \frac{1}{2} = \frac{3 \times 1}{5 \times 2} = \frac{3}{10}$

When the division problem has a mixed number, convert it to an improper fraction and then divide as usual.

Example: $2\frac{3}{4} \div \frac{1}{6}$

1. Convert $2\frac{3}{4}$ to an improper fraction:

2. Divide $\frac{11}{4}$ by $\frac{1}{6}$:

3. Flip $\frac{1}{6}$ to $\frac{6}{1}$, change $\div$ to $\times$, cancel and multiply:

$$2\frac{3}{4} = \frac{2 \times 4 + 3}{4} = \frac{11}{4}$$

$$\frac{11}{4} \div \frac{1}{6} = \frac{11}{4} \times \frac{6}{1}$$

$$\frac{11}{\underset{2}{4}} \times \frac{\overset{3}{6}}{1} = \frac{33}{2}$$

▶ What's a Decimal?

A decimal is a special kind of fraction. You use decimals every day when you deal with money—for example, $10.35 is a decimal that represents ten dollars and 35 cents. The decimal point separates the dollars from the cents. Because there are 100 cents in one dollar, 1¢ is $\frac{1}{100}$ of a dollar, or $0.01.

Each decimal digit to the right of the decimal point has a name:

.1 = 1 tenth = $\frac{1}{10}$

.02 = 2 hundredths = $\frac{2}{100}$

.003 = 3 thousandths = $\frac{3}{1,000}$

.0004 = 4 ten-thousandths = $\frac{4}{10,000}$

When you add zeros after the rightmost number, you don't change the value of the decimal. For example, 6.17 is the same as all of these:

6.170

6.1700

6.17000000000000000

If there are digits on both sides of the decimal point (like 10.35), the number is called a mixed decimal. If there are digits only to the right of the decimal point (like .53), the number is called a decimal. A whole number (like 15) is understood to have a decimal point at its right. Thus, 15 is the same as 15.0, 15.00, 15.000, and so on.

▶ Changing Fractions to Decimals

To change a fraction to a decimal, divide the denominator into the numerator. You will need to put a decimal point and a few zeros on the right side of the numerator. When you divide, bring the decimal point up into your answer.

Example: Change $\frac{3}{4}$ to a decimal.

1. Add a decimal point and two zeros to the top number (3): 3.00
2. Divide the bottom number (4) into 3.00: 0.75 (Be sure to bring the decimal point up into the answer.)
   The quotient (result of the division) is the answer: 0.75.

Some fractions may require you to add many decimal zeros in order for the division to come out evenly. In fact, when you convert a fraction like $\frac{2}{3}$ to a decimal, you can keep adding decimal zeros to the numerator forever because the division will never come out evenly. As you divide 3 into 2, you'll keep getting 6's:

$2 \div 3 = 0.6666666666 \ldots$

This is called a repeating decimal and it can be written as $.66\overline{6}$. You can approximate it as .67, .667, .6667, and so on.

▶ Changing Decimals to Fractions

To change a decimal to a fraction, write the digits of the decimal as the numerator of a fraction, and write the decimal's name as the denominator of the fraction. Then, reduce the fraction, if possible.

Example: 0.018

1. Write 18 as the top of the fraction: $\underline{18}$
2. Three places to the right of the decimal means thousandths, so write 1,000 as the bottom number: $\frac{18}{1,000}$
3. Reduce the numerator and denominator by dividing by 2: $\frac{18 \div 2}{1,000 \div 2} = \frac{9}{500}$

▶ Comparing Decimals

Because decimals are easier to compare when they have the same number of digits after the decimal point, tack zeros onto the end of the shorter decimals. Then all you have to do is compare the numbers as if the decimal points weren't there:

Example: Compare 0.08 and 0.1

1. Tack one zero at the end of .01 to get 0.10.
2. To compare 0.10 to 0.08, just compare 10 to 8.
3. Since 10 is larger than 8, 0.1 is larger than 0.08.

▶ Adding and Subtracting Decimals

To add or subtract decimals, line them up so their decimal points are even. You may want to tack on zeros at the end of shorter decimals so you can keep all your digits lined up evenly. Remember, if a number doesn't have a decimal point, then put one at the right end of the number.

Examples: 1.23 + 57 + 0.038 =

1. Line up the numbers like this:

$$
\begin{array}{r}
1.230 \\
57.000 \\
+\ .038 \\
\hline
\end{array}
$$

2. Add the columns: 58.268

1.23 − .038 =

1. Line up the numbers by decimal point:

$$
\begin{array}{r}
1.230 \\
-\ 0.038 \\
\hline
\end{array}
$$

2. Subtract the bottom number in each column from the top: 1.192

▶ Multiplying Decimals

To multiply decimals, ignore the decimal points and multiply the numbers. Then count the total number of decimal digits (the digits to the right of the decimal point) in the numbers you're multiplying. Count off that number of digits in your answer beginning at the right side and put the decimal point to the left of those digits.

Example: 215.7 × 2.4 =

1. Multiply 2,157 times 24:

$$
\begin{array}{r}
2,157 \\
\times\ 24 \\
\hline
51,768 \\
\end{array}
$$

2. Because there are a total of 2 decimal digits in 215.7 and 2.4, count off two places from the right in 51,768, placing the decimal point to the left of the last two digits: 517.68

If your answer doesn't have enough digits, tack zeros on to the left of the answer.

Example: 0.03 × 0.006 =

1. Multiply 3 times 6: 3 × 6 = 18
2. You need five decimal digits in your answer, so tack on three zeros: 00018
3. Put the decimal point at the front of the number (which is five digits in from the right): 0.00018

▶ Dividing Decimals

To divide a decimal (.256) by a whole number (8), set up the division (8)‾.256) and immediately bring the decimal point straight up into the answer (8). Then divide as you would normally divide whole numbers:

$$
\begin{array}{r}
0.032 \\
8\overline{)\,.256} \\
\underline{-24} \\
16
\end{array}
$$

Example:

To divide any decimal by a decimal, there is an extra step to perform before you can divide. Move the decimal point to the very right of the number you're dividing by, counting the number of places you're moving it. Then, inside the long division sign, move the decimal point the same number of places to the right in the number you're dividing into. In other words, first change the problem to one in which you're dividing by a whole number.

Example: $0.06\overline{)1.218}$

1. Because there are two decimal digits in 0.06, move the decimal point two places to the right in both numbers and move the decimal point straight up into the answer: $06.\overline{)121.8}$
2. Divide using the new numbers:

$$
\begin{array}{r}
20.3 \\
06.\overline{)121.8} \\
\underline{-12} \\
01 \\
\underline{-0} \\
18 \\
\underline{-18} \\
0
\end{array}
$$

Under the following conditions, you have to tack on zeros to the right of the last decimal digit in the number you're dividing into:

- if there aren't enough digits for you to move the decimal point to the right
- if the answer doesn't come out evenly when you do the division
- if you're dividing a whole number by a decimal

▶ Practice Questions

1. Which of the following choices has a 6 in the tenths place?
   a. 60.17
   b. 76.01
   c. 1.67
   d. 7.061

2. Which of the following choices has a 3 in the hundredths place?
   a. 354.01
   b. 0.54031
   c. 0.54301
   d. 0.03514

3. 234.816 when rounded to the nearest hundredth is
   a. 200
   b. 234.8
   c. 234.81
   d. 234.82

4. Which of these decimals has the greatest value?
   a. 0.03
   b. 0.003
   c. 0.031
   d. 0.0031

5. 25.682 rounded to the nearest tenth is
   a. 26
   b. 25
   c. 25.68
   d. 25.7

6. What is 3.133 when rounded to the nearest tenth?
   a. 3
   b. 3.1
   c. 3.2
   d. 3.13

7. $\frac{3}{20}$ is equivalent to which of the following decimals?
   a. 0.03
   b. 0.06
   c. 0.60
   d. 0.15

8. Which number sentence is true?
   a. $0.23 \geq 2.3$
   b. $0.023 \leq 0.23$
   c. $0.023 \leq 0.0023$
   d. $0.023 \geq 2.3$

9. Which decimal is the smallest?
   a. 0.00782
   b. 0.00278
   c. 0.2780
   d. 0.000782

10. Which decimal is equivalent to the fraction $\frac{7}{25}$?
   a. 0.07
   b. 0.35
   c. 0.28
   d. 0.725

11. What is the sum of 8.514 and 4.821?
   a. 12.335
   b. 13.335
   c. 12.235
   d. 13.235

12. What is the sum of 2.523 and 6.76014?
 a. 9.3
 b. 92.8314
 c. 9.28314
 d. 928.314

13. 67.104 + 51.406 =
 a. 11.851
 b. 1,185.1
 c. 118.51
 d. 118.61

14. What is the sum of 3.75, 12.05, and 4.2?
 a. 20
 b. 19.95
 c. 19.00
 d. 19.75

15. 14.02 + 0.987 + 0.145 =
 a. 14.152
 b. 15.152
 c. 14.142
 d. 15.142

16. 5.25 + 15.007 + 0.87436 =
 a. 211.3136
 b. 20.13136
 c. 201.3136
 d. 21.13136

17. $\frac{1}{5}$ + 0.25 + $\frac{1}{8}$ + 0.409 =
 a. $\frac{1}{13}$ + 0.659
 b. 0.659 + $\frac{1}{40}$
 c. 0.984
 d. 1.084

18. What is the sum of 12.05, 252.11, 7.626, 240, and 8.003?
 a. 5,197.86
 b. 519.789
 c. 518.685
 d. 518.786

19. What is the sum of −8.3 and 9?
 a. 17.3
 b. 0.7
 c. 1.73
 d. −17.3

20. The following is a list of the thickness of four boards: 0.52 inches, 0.81 inches, 0.72 inches, and 2.03 inches. If all four boards are stacked on top of one another, what will the total thickness be?
 a. 40.8 inches
 b. 0.408 inches
 c. 4.008 inches
 d. 4.08 inches

21. 324.0073 − 87.663 =
 a. 411.6703
 b. 236.3443
 c. 236.3443
 d. 23.634443

22. 8.3 − 1.725 =
 a. 6.575
 b. 6.775
 c. 7.575
 d. 10.025

23. 12.125 − 3.44 =
 a. 9.685
 b. 8.785
 c. 8.685
 d. 8.585

24. $89.037 - 27.0002 - 4.02 =$
a. 62.0368
b. 59.0168
c. 58. 168
d. 58.0168

25. $0.89735 - 0.20002 - 0.11733 =$
a. 0.69733
b. 0.59733
c. 0.58033
d. 0.58

26. What is $287.78 - 0.782$ when rounded to the nearest hundred?
a. 286.998
b. 286.90
c. 286.99
d. 300

27. $0.0325 - (-0.0235) =$
a. 0
b. 0.0560
c. 0.0650
d. 0.560

28. $0.667 - (-0.02) - 0.069 =$
a. 0.618
b. 0.669
c. 0.596
d. 0.06

29. $-12.3 - (-4.2) =$
a. −8.1
b. −16.5
c. 16.5
d. 8.1

30. $-6.5 - 8.32 =$
a. 14.82
b. 1.82
c. −0.82
d. −14.82

31. $0.205 \times 0.11 =$
a. 0.02255
b. 0.2255
c. 2.255
d. 22.55

32. $0.88 \times 0.22 =$
a. 0.01936
b. 0.1936
c. 0.1616
d. 1.616

33. $8.03 \times 3.2 =$
a. 24.06
b. 24.6
c. 25.696
d. 156.96

34. $0.56 \times 0.03 =$
a. 168
b. 16.8
c. 0.168
d. 0.0168

35. $0.32 \times 0.04 =$
a. 0.128
b. 0.0128
c. 128
d. 12.8

36. What is the product of 5.49 and 0.02?
  a. 0.1098
  b. 5.51
  c. 5.47
  d. 274.5

37. $0.125 \times 0.8 \times 0.32 =$
  a. 0.32
  b. $\frac{1}{10}$
  c. $\frac{8}{250}$
  d. $\frac{32}{100}$

38. $0.15 \times \frac{1}{5} =$
  a. 0.2
  b. 0.3
  c. 0.02
  d. 0.03

39. If each capsule contains 0.03 grams of active ingredients, how many grams of active ingredients are in 380 capsules?
  a. $126\frac{2}{3}$ grams
  b. 11.4 grams
  c. 12.6 grams
  d. 1.14 grams

40. If a piece of foil is 0.032 centimeters thick, how thick would a stack of 200 pieces of foil be?
  a. 64 centimeters
  b. 16 centimeters
  c. 6.4 centimeters
  d. 1.6 centimeters

41. $3.26 \div 0.02 =$
  a. 163
  b. 65.2
  c. 16.3
  d. 652

42. $512 \div 0.256 =$
  a. 20
  b. 2,000
  c. 200
  d. 2

43. $3.4 \div 0.17 =$
  a. 3
  b. 2
  c. 30
  d. 20

44. What is the quotient of $83.4 \div 2.1$ when rounded to the nearest tenth?
  a. 40
  b. 39.71
  c. 39.7
  d. 39.8

45. $0.895 \div 0.005 =$
  a. 0.0079
  b. 0.179
  c. 179
  d. 1,790

46. What is the quotient of $0.962 \div 0.023$ when rounded to the nearest hundredth?
  a. 41.83
  b. 41.826
  c. 40
  d. 41.82

47. $\frac{8.4}{.09} =$
a. $93\frac{1}{3}$
b. 0.0107
c. 0.756
d. 75.6

48. $\frac{375}{.125} =$
a. 5,625
b. 3,000
c. 56.25
d. 30

49. A 70-pound bag of cement can be divided into how many smaller bags, each weighing 3.5 pounds?
a. 20
b. 16
c. 10
d. 5

50. Markers will be placed along a roadway at 0.31 kilometer intervals. If the entire roadway is 1.55 kilometers, how many markers will be used?
a. 480.5
b. 50
c. 48.05
d. 5

▶ Answers

1. c. The places to the right of the decimal point are (in order): the *tenths place*, the *hundredths place*, *thousandths place*, and so on. You are looking for a 6 in the tenths place, which is the first spot to the right of the decimal point. Only choice **c** has a 6 in this place:

units (ones)	tenths	hundredths
1.	6	7

Note that choice **a** has a 6 in the *tens* place and NOT the *tenths* place.

2. d. The places to the right of the decimal point are (in order): the *tenths place*, *hundredths place*, *thousandths place*, and so on. You are looking for a 3 in the hundredths place, which is the second spot to the right of the decimal point. Only choice **d** has a 3 in this place:

units (ones)	tenths	hundredths	thousandths	ten thousandths	hundred thousandths
0.	0	3	5	1	4

Note that choice **a** has a 6 in the *hundreds* place and NOT the *hundredths* place.

3. d. When rounding to the nearest hundredth, you need to truncate (cut short) the number, leaving the last digit in the hundredths place. If the number after the hundredths place is a 5 or higher, you would round up.

hundreds	tens	units (ones)	tenths	hundredths	thousandths
2	3	4.	8	1	6

6 is higher than 5, so you round the 1 in the hundredths place up to 2. Thus, the answer is 234.82, choice **d.**

4. c. Choice **c** has the greatest value, $\frac{31}{1,000}$. Here is a comparison of the four choices:

a. .03	$\frac{3}{100} = \frac{30}{1,000}$
b. .003	$\frac{3}{1,000}$
c. .031	$\frac{31}{1,000}$
d. .0031	$\frac{31}{10,000}$

5. d. 25.682 has a 6 in the tenths place. Because the number in the hundredths place (8) is greater than 5, you will round up to 25.7.

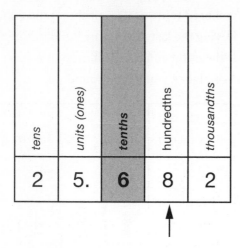

You round up because 8 ≥ 5.

6. b. In order to round to the nearest tenth, you need to cut the number short, leaving the last digit in the tenths place. Here you cut the number short without rounding up because the number in the hundredths place is not ≥ 5.

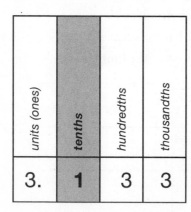

You don't round up because 3 is less than 5. Thus, the answer is 3.1, choice **b.**

7. d. $\frac{3}{20}$ can quickly be converted to hundredths by multiplying by $\frac{5}{5}$: $\frac{3}{20} \times \frac{5}{5} = \frac{15}{100}$; $\frac{15}{100}$ is the same as 15 *hundredths*, or 0.15, choice **d.**

8. b. 0.023 equals $\frac{23}{1,000}$, which is less than 0.23, which equals $\frac{23}{100}$. Thus $0.023 \le 0.23$. The symbol "≤" means *less than or equal to*.

9. d. Each answer choice is equivalent to the following values:

a. $0.00782 = \frac{782}{100,000} = \frac{7,820}{1,000,000}$

b. $0.00278 = \frac{278}{100,000} = \frac{2,780}{1,000,000}$

c. $0.2780 = \frac{2,780}{10,000} = \frac{287,000}{1,000,000}$

d. $0.000782 = \frac{782}{1,000,000}$

Thus, choice **d** is the smallest number listed.

10. c. $\frac{7}{25}$ can be translated into *hundredths* by multiplying by $\frac{4}{4}$. Thus, $\frac{7}{25} \times \frac{4}{4} = \frac{28}{100}$. 28 *hundredths* can be rewritten as 0.28, choice **c.**

11. b. *Sum* means *add*. Make sure you line up the decimal points and then add:

$$8.514$$
$$+\,4.821$$
$$13.335$$

12. c. *Sum* means *add*. Line up the decimal points and add:

$$2.523$$
$$+\,6.76014$$
$$9.28314$$

13. c. Line up the decimal points and add:

$$67.104$$
$$+\,51.406$$
$$118.51$$

14. a. 4.2 is equivalent to 4.20. Line up all the decimal points and add:

$$3.75$$
$$12.05$$
$$+\,4.20$$
$$20.00$$

15. b. 14.02 is equivalent to 14.020. Line up all the decimal points and add:

$$14.020$$
$$.987$$
$$+\,.145$$
$$15.152$$

16. d. Add zeros as space holders to the numbers 5.25 and 15.007. Then, line all the numbers up by their decimal points and add:

5.25000

15.00700

+ .87436

2,1.13136

17. c. First convert the fractions to decimals: $\frac{1}{5}$ = .2 and $\frac{1}{8}$ = .125. Next, line up all the numbers by their decimal points and add (note that zeros are added as place holders):

0.200

0.250

0.125

+ .409

.984

18. b. *Sum* signifies addition. Line up the decimal points and add. Note that zeros can be added as place holders:

12.050

252.110

7.626

240.000

+ 8.003

519.7890

19. b. 9 plus −8.3 is the same as 9 minus 8.3. Rewrite 9 as 9.0 and subtract:

9.0

− 8.3

.7

20. d. Line up the decimal points and add:

0.52

0.81

0.72

+ 2.03

4.08

21. b. Line up the decimal points and subtract:

324.0073

− 87.663

236.3443

22. a. Rewrite 8.3 as its equivalent 8.300. Line up the decimal points and subtract:

8.300

−1.725

6.575

23. c. Line up the decimal points and subtract:

12.125

− 3.44

8.685

24. d. First, rewrite 89.037 as its equivalent 89.0370. Next, subtract 27.0002:

89.0370

− 27.0002

6,2.0368

Now you must subtract 4.02 from the 62.0386. (If you selected choice **a**, you forgot the next step.)

62.0368

− 4.02

58.0168

25. d. Perform the indicated operations (subtractions) in two steps:

0.89735

− 0.20002

0.69733

Next, subtract 0.11733 from 0.69733 to get 0.58.

26. d. The question asks you to round to the hundred (not *hundredth!*). 287.78 − 0.782 = 286.998. When this value is rounded to the nearest hundred, you get 300.

27. b. Subtracting a negative is the same as adding a positive. Thus, 0.0325 − (− 0.0235) is the same as 0.0325 + 0.0235. Adding, you get 0.0560.

28. a. Subtracting a negative is the same as adding a positive. Thus, 0.667 − (−0.02) − 0.069 = 0.667 + 0.02 − 0.069. This equals 0.687 − 0.069 = 0.618.

29. a. Subtracting a negative number is the same as adding a positive number. Thus, −12.3 − (−4.2) = −12.3 + 4.2; −12.3 and 4.2 will yield a negative value because you are starting 12.3 units away from zero in the *negative* direction. Adding 4.2 will bring you closer to 0, but you will still have a negative answer. To figure out what the answer is, subtract 4.2 from 12.3 and add a minus sign. Thus, you get −8.1.

30. d. −6.5 − 8.32 is the same as −6.5 + −8.32. When adding two negative numbers, first ignore the negative signs and add in the normal fashion. 6.5 + 8.32 = 14.82. Next, insert the negative sign to get −14.82, choice **d.**

31. a. First, multiply in the usual fashion (ignoring the decimal points): 0.205 × 0.11 = 2,255. Next, you need to insert the decimal point in the correct position, so take note of the position of each decimal point in the two factors:

0.532	The decimal point is **3** places to the left.
0.89	The decimal point is **2** places to the left.
In the answer . . .	The decimal point should be **3 + 2**, or **5** places to the left.

2,255 becomes .02255, choice **a.**

32. b. First, multiply in the usual fashion (ignoring the decimal points): 0.88 × 0.22 = 1,936. Next, you need to insert the decimal point in the correct position, so take note of the position of each decimal point in the two factors:

0.88	The decimal point is **2** places to the left.
0.22	The decimal point is **2** places to the left.
In the answer . . .	The decimal point should be **2 + 2**, or **4** places to the left.

1,936 becomes 0.1936, choice **b.**

33. c. First, multiply in the usual fashion (ignoring the decimal points): 8.03 × 3.2 = 25,696. Next, you need to insert the decimal point in the correct position, so take note of the position of each decimal point in the two factors:

8.03	The decimal point is **2** places to the left.
3.2	The decimal point is **1** place to the left.
In the answer . . .	The decimal point should **3** places to the left.

25,696 becomes 25.696, choice **c.**

34. d. Multiply in the usual fashion, and insert the decimal point 4 places to the left:

0.56	The decimal point is **2** places to the left.
0.03	The decimal point is **2** places to the left.
In the answer . . .	The decimal point should **4** places to the left.

0.56 × 0.03 = 168 (when ignoring decimal) and becomes .0168 when you insert the decimal point four places to the left. Thus, the answer is choice **d.**

35. b. Multiply in the usual fashion, and insert the decimal point 4 places to the left: $0.32 \times 0.04 = 0.0128$.

36. a. The term *product* signifies multiplication. Multiply 5.49 by 0.02 in the usual fashion, and insert the decimal point 4 places to the left: $5.49 \times 0.02 = 0.1098$.

37. c. First multiply 0.125 by 0.8 to get 0.1. Next multiply 0.1 by 0.32 to get 0.032. This answer is equivalent to 32 thousandths, or $\frac{32}{100}$. This reduces to $\frac{8}{250}$, choice **c.**

38. d. First convert $\frac{1}{5}$ to a decimal: $\frac{1}{5} = 1 \div 5 = 0.2$. Next multiply: $0.15 \times 0.2 = 0.03$

39. b. Multiply the amount of active ingredients in one capsule (0.03) by the number of capsules (380): $380 \times 0.03 = 11.4$ grams.

40. c. To solve, simply multiply the thickness of each piece by the total number of pieces. $200 \times 0.032 = 6.4$ centimeters.

41. a. The problem $3.26 \div .02$ can be solved with long division. First, move the decimal point two places to the right in each number:

$$0{,}2\,\overline{)\,3{.}2{,}6{,}}$$

Next, divide as usual to get 163, choice **a.**

42. b. The problem $512 \div 0.256$ can be solved with long division. Move the decimal point three places to the right in each number:

$$2{,}5{,}6{,}\overline{)\,5\,1\,2{.}0{,}0{,}0{,}}$$

Next, divide as usual to get 2,000, choice **b.**

43. d. The problem $3.4 \div 0.17$ can be solved with long division. First, move the decimal point two places to the right in each number:

$$.1{,}7{,}\overline{)\,3{.}4{,}0{,}}$$

Next, divide as usual to get 20, choice **d.**

44. c. The problem $83.4 \div 2.1$ can be solved with long division, moving the decimal point in each number one place to the right:

$$2{.}1{,}\overline{)\,8\,3{.}4{,}}$$

Next, divide as usual to get 39.714286. Finally, round to the nearest tenth: 39.7, choice **c.**

45. c. The problem $895 \div 0.005$ can be solved with long division, moving the decimal point in each number three places to the right:

$$.0{,}0{,}5{,}\overline{)\,.8{.}9{,}5{,}}$$

Next, divide to get the answer: 179, choice c.

46. a. The problem $0.962 \div 0.023$ can be solved with long division, moving the decimal point in each number three places to the right:

$$.0{,}2{,}3{,}\overline{)\,.9\,6{,}2{,}}$$

Next, divide to get 41.826087. Rounding this number to the nearest hundredth yields 41.83, choice **a.**

47. a. The problem $8.4 \div 0.09$ can be solved with long division, moving the decimal point in each number two places to the right:

$$.0{,}2{,}3{,}\overline{)\,.9\,6{,}2{,}}$$

Dividing yields an answer of 93.333333 . . . or $93\frac{1}{3}$, choice **a.**

48. **b.** The problem 375 ÷ 0.125 can be solved with long division, moving the decimal point in each number three places to the right:

$$1{,}2{,}5{,}\overline{)3\ 7\ 5{.}0{,}0{,}0{,}}$$

Dividing yields 3,000, choice **b.**

49. **a.** To solve, divide 70 by 3.5. This can be solved with long division, moving the decimal point in each number one place to the right:

$$3{.}5{,}\overline{)7\ 0{.}0{,}}$$

Next, divide as usual to get 20, choice **a.**

50. **d.** To solve, divide the 1.55 kilometer distance by the interval, 0.31 kilometers. 1.55 ÷ 0.31 can be solved with long division. The decimal point in each number is moved two places to the right:

$$.3{,}1{,}\overline{)1{.}5{,}5{,}}$$

Next, divide to get 5, choice **d.**

5 ▶ Percents

Percents are a way of expressing values out of 100. For example, 30% (30 percent) is equivalent to 30 out of 100 or $\frac{30}{100}$. Thus, you can express a percent as a fraction by placing the value before the percent symbol over 100. You can express a percent as a decimal by moving the current decimal point two places to the left. For example, 30% is also equivalent to 0.30.

You can convert a decimal value into an equivalent percent by moving the current decimal point two places to the right. For example, 0.30 = 30%. This makes sense because percents are just *hundredths,* so 0.30 is 30 *hundredths,* or $\frac{30}{100}$, otherwise known as 30%.

Fractions can be converted to percentages by converting to a denominator of 100. This can be done by setting up a simple proportion. For example, to convert $\frac{2}{5}$ into an equivalent percentage, you set up this proportion:

$$\frac{2}{5} = \frac{?}{100}$$

Cross multiply to get $2 \times 100 = 5 \times ?$, or $200 = 5 \times ?$. Divide both sides by 5 to get $? = 40$. Thus, $\frac{2}{5}$ is equivalent to 40%.

▶ Taking the Percent of a Number

When you are calculating the percent of a number, just remember that *of* means multiply. For instance, 50% of 40 is 50% × 40. You can convert 50% to 0.50 and multiply $0.50 \times 40 = 20$.

To save time, you should be familiar with the following equivalencies:

FRACTION	PERCENT
$\frac{1}{5}$	20%
$\frac{1}{4}$	25%
$\frac{1}{3}$	approximately 33%
$\frac{1}{2}$	50%
$\frac{2}{3}$	approximately 66%
$\frac{3}{4}$	75%

▶ Unknown Percents

When you do not know the percent of a value, you can express this percent as $\frac{?}{100}$. This means that when you see the phrase *what percent*, you can express this mathematically as $\frac{?}{100}$.

▶ Percent Change, Percent Error, and Percent Profit or Loss

When calculating a **percent change** (such as a **percent increase** or **decrease**) you simply express the ratio of the change to the initial as a value over 100. The general proportion to use is:

$$\frac{\text{Change}}{\text{Initial}} = \frac{?}{100}$$

Similarly, when calculating the **percent error**, you set a proportion that equates the difference between the calculated value and the actual value to the actual value with an unknown out of 100:

$$\frac{\text{Difference in values}}{\text{Actual value}} = \frac{?}{100}$$

When setting up a proportion to calculate percent profit or loss, you create a ratio of the net profit (or loss) to the initial cost and set this ratio equal to an unknown out of 100:

$$\frac{\text{net profit}}{\text{initial}} = \frac{?}{100} \qquad \frac{\text{net loss}}{\text{initial}} = \frac{?}{100}$$

▶ Simple and Compound Interest

The formula for simple interest is $I = PRT$. The amount of money deposited is called the principal, P. The interest rate per year is represented by R, and T represents the time in years.

When calculating compound interest, it is easiest to sequentially calculate the interest earned using $I = PRT$. You should be familiar with the following ways of compounding interest:

- **compounded annually:** interest is paid each year
- **compounded semiannually:** interest is paid two times per year
- **compounded quarterly:** interest is paid four times a year
- **compounded monthly:** interest is paid every month
- **compounded daily:** interest is paid every day

▶ Practice Questions

1. 15% is equivalent to which fraction?

   a. $\frac{3}{20}$

   b. $\frac{15}{1,000}$

   c. $\frac{1}{5}$

   d. $\frac{1}{15}$

2. 20% is equivalent to which decimal value?

   a. 0.020

   b. 2.0

   c. 0.2

   d. 0.002

3. When converted to a decimal, 45% is equivalent to

   a. 0.045

   b. 0.45

   c. 4.5

   d. 45

4. 73% can be expressed as which of the following fractions?

   a. $\frac{0.73}{100}$

   b. $\frac{73}{100}$

   c. $\frac{73}{1,000}$

   d. $\frac{0.73}{0.10}$

5. 1.5% is equivalent to which decimal value?

   a. 0.15

   b. 1.5

   c. 0.0015

   d. 0.015

6. When expressed as a percent, $\frac{31}{50}$ is equivalent to

   a. 62%

   b. $\frac{31}{50}$%

   c. $\frac{3}{5}$%

   d. 31%

7. Another way to write 26.5% is

   a. $\frac{0.265}{100}$

   b. $\frac{26}{80}$

   c. $\frac{53}{200}$

   d. $\frac{26.5}{1,000}$

8. 0.0037% is equivalent to which of the following fractions?

   a. $\frac{37}{1,000}$

   b. $\frac{37}{10,000}$

   c. $\frac{37}{1,000,000}$

   d. $\frac{37}{10,000,000}$

9. Which of the following is 17% of 6,800?

   a. 115,600

   b. 340

   c. 578

   d. 1,156

10. Which number sentence is false?

   a. 20% $\leq \frac{1}{5}$

   b. 25% $= \frac{2}{8}$

   c. 35% $> \frac{24}{50}$

   d. $\frac{3}{4} \leq$ 80%

11. Express 12 out of 52 to the nearest percent.

    a. 23%

    b. 24%

    c. 25%

    d. 26%

12. $\frac{4}{5}$% is equal to

    a. 80

    b. 8

    c. 0.08

    d. 0.008

13. 50% of what number equals 20% of 2,000?

    a. 200

    b. 400

    c. 600

    d. 800

14. 300% of 54.2 equals

    a. 16.26

    b. 162.6

    c. 1,626

    d. none of the above

15. What percent of $\frac{1}{2}$ is $\frac{1}{8}$?

    a. 25%

    b. 50%

    c. 80%

    d. none of the above

16. To calculate 75% of a dollar amount, you can

    a. multiply the amount by 75.

    b. divide the amount by 75.

    c. multiply the amount by $\frac{3}{4}$.

    d. divide the amount by $\frac{3}{4}$.

17. 40% of what number is equal to 460?

    a. 575

    b. 640

    c. 860

    d. 1,150

18. Larry makes a 12% commission on every car he sells. If he sold $40,000 worth of cars over the course of three months, what was his commission on these sales?

    a. $44,800

    b. $35,200

    c. $8,000

    d. $4,800

19. USB drives cost $100 each. When more than 50 are purchased, an 8% discount is applied. At a store that charges 8% tax, how much money will 62 USB drives cost? (Round to the nearest cent.)

    a. $6,200.00

    b. $6,160.32

    c. $5,704.00

    d. $456.32

20. Aesha made $64,000 in 2007, but she had to pay 26% tax on that amount. How much did she make after taxes?

    a. $16,640

    b. $67,640

    c. $47,360

    d. $42,360

21. What percent of $\frac{8}{9}$ is $\frac{2}{3}$?

    a. 33%

    b. 66%

    c. 75%

    d. 133%

22. 400 books went on sale this week. So far, 120 have been sold. What percent of the books remain?

a. 15%

b. 30%

c. 70%

d. 80%

23. What percent of the circle is shaded?

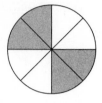

a. 25%

b. 50%

c. 75%

d. 100%

24. What percent of the square is shaded?

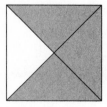

a. 25%

b. 50%

c. 75%

d. 100%

25. What percent of the square is shaded?

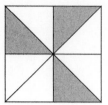

a. 20%

b. 37.5%

c. 40%

d. 80%

26. What percent of the square is shaded?

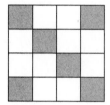

a. 20%

b. 37.5%

c. 40%

d. 80%

27. A dealer buys a car from the manufacturer for $13,000. If the dealer wants to earn a profit of 20% based on the cost, at what price should he sell the car?

a. $16,250

b. $15,600

c. $15,200

d. $10,833

28. 33 is 12% of which of the following?

a. 3,960

b. 396

c. 275

d. 2,750

29. Of the numbers listed, which choice is NOT equivalent to the others?

a. 52%

b. $\frac{13}{25}$

c. 52×10^{-2}

d. 0.052

30. Emily made $8,000 and put half that amount into an account that earned interest at a rate of 6%. After 2 years, what is the dollar amount of the interest earned? (Use the formula $I = PRT$.)

a. $4,800

b. $960

c. $660

d. $480

31. If Kamil puts $10,000 in the bank at a 6% rate of interest, how much interest will he make in 8 months? (Use the formula $I = PRT$.)

a. $400

b. $350

c. $300

d. $250

32. If Veronica deposits $5,000 in an account with a yearly interest rate of 9%, and leaves the money in the account for 8 years, how much interest will her money earn?

a. $360,000

b. 45,000

c. 3,600

d. 450

33. At the city park, 32% of the trees are oaks. If there are 400 trees in the park, how many trees are NOT oaks?

a. 128

b. 272

c. 278

d. 312

34. Which ratio best expresses the following: five hours is what percent of a day?

a. $\frac{5}{100} = \frac{x}{24}$

b. $\frac{5}{24} = \frac{24}{x}$

c. $\frac{5}{24} = \frac{x}{100}$

d. $\frac{x}{100} = \frac{24}{5}$

35. If 10% of a number is 45, what would 20% of that number be?

a. 9

b. 90

c. 450

d. 900

36. A dozen staplers cost $10.00, and they will then be sold for $2.50 each. What is the rate of profit?

a. 75%

b. 100%

c. 150%

d. 200%

37. A statue was bought at a price of $50 and sold for $38. What is the percent loss?

a. 12%

b. 15%

c. 24%

d. 30%

38. The price of a $130 jacket was reduced by 10% and again by 15%. What is the new cost of the jacket?
- **a.** $97.50
- **b.** $99.45
- **c.** $117
- **d.** $105

39. At an electronics store, all items are sold at 15% above cost. If the store purchased a printer for $85, how much will they sell it for?
- **a.** $90
- **b.** $98.50
- **c.** $97.75
- **d.** $95.50

40. Marla paid $14,105 for her new car. This price included 8.5% for tax. What was the price of the car excluding tax?
- **a.** $13,000.00
- **b.** $13,850.00
- **c.** $11,989.25
- **d.** $1,198.93

41. Steven's income was $34,000 last year. He must pay $2,380 for income taxes. What is the rate of taxation?
- **a.** 70%
- **b.** 7%
- **c.** 0.7%
- **d.** 0.007%

42. $8,000 is deposited into an account. If interest is compounded semiannually at 5% for 1 year, how much money is in the account at the end of the year?
- **a.** $8,175
- **b.** $8,200
- **c.** $8,400
- **d.** $8,405

43. $14,000 is deposited into an account. If interest is compounded quarterly at 8% for 9 months, how much money will be in the account at the end of this period?
- **a.** $14,280.00
- **b.** $14,565.60
- **c.** $14,856.91
- **d.** $15,154.05

44. Suki has $1,000 to invest. She would like to invest $\frac{3}{5}$ of it at 6% simple interest. The remainder would be invested at 8% simple interest. How much interest would she have earned after one year?
- **a.** $32
- **b.** $36
- **c.** $68
- **d.** $70

45. How many twelfths are there in $33\frac{1}{3}$%?
- **a.** 1
- **b.** 4
- **c.** 33
- **d** 100

46. What is the percent increase from 150 to 200?
- **a.** 25%
- **b.** $33\frac{1}{3}$%
- **c.** 75%
- **d.** $66\frac{2}{3}$%

47. What is the percent decrease from 200 to 150?

    a. 25%

    b. $33\frac{1}{3}$%

    c. 75%

    d. $66\frac{2}{3}$%

48. If a crate weighing 600 pounds weighs 540 pounds on a broken scale, what is the percent error?

    a. 10%

    b. 11%

    c. 15%

    d. 25%

49. A five-gallon tank is completely filled with a solution of 50% water and 50% alcohol. Half of the tank is drained and 2 gallons of water are added. How much water is in the resulting mixture?

    a. 2.5 gallons

    b. 3.25 gallons

    c. 3.5 gallons

    d. 4.5 gallons

► Answers

1. a. 15 percent equals $\frac{15}{100}$. $\frac{15}{100}$ reduces to $\frac{3}{20}$.

2. c. To change 20% to its equivalent decimal form, move the decimal point two places to the left. Thus, 20% = .20. Choice **c**, 0.2, is equivalent to 0.20.

3. b. When you see a percent symbol (%), you move the decimal point two places to the left. Thus, 45% is equivalent to 0.45.

4. b. When you see a percent symbol (%), you can rewrite the percent as a fraction by placing the value over 100. Thus, 73% is equivalent to $\frac{73}{100}$.

5. d. 1.5% can be converted to its equivalent decimal form by moving its decimal point two places to the left. Thus, 1.5% is equivalent to 0.015, choice **d**.

6. a. When written as fractions, percents have a denominator of 100. You can convert $\frac{31}{50}$ to a fraction with a denominator of 100 by multiplying by $\frac{2}{2}$; $\frac{31}{50} \times \frac{2}{2} = \frac{62}{100} = 62\%$, choice **a**.

7. c. First, put 26.5 over $100 = \frac{26.5}{100}$. This is not an answer choice, so you need to reduce. Multiply $\frac{26.5}{100}$ by $\frac{10}{10}$ before reducing: $\frac{26.5}{100} \times \frac{10}{10} = \frac{265}{1,000}$. Now you reduce $\frac{265}{1,000} = \frac{53}{200}$.

8. c. To change a percent to a fraction, first put the percent over 100. Thus, 0.0037% = $\frac{0.0037}{100}$. In order to get a whole number in the numerator, multiply the fraction by $\frac{10,000}{10,000}$. Thus, $\frac{0.0037}{100} \times \frac{10,000}{10,000} = \frac{37}{1,000,000}$.

9. d. You need to find 17%, or 0.17 of 6800. Remember that *of* means multiply: $0.17 \times 6,800 = 1,156$.

10. c. 20% = $\frac{20}{100}$, or $\frac{1}{5}$, so choice **a** represents a true statement. 25% = $\frac{25}{100} = \frac{1}{4}$, and $\frac{2}{8} = \frac{1}{4}$, so choice **b** is also true. In choice **c**, 35% = $\frac{35}{100}$ and $\frac{24}{50} = \frac{48}{100}$. Thus, the statement 35% > $\frac{24}{50}$ is not true. Choice **c** is therefore the correct

answer. In choice **d**, $\frac{3}{4}$ = 75%, which is in fact less than 80%.

11. a. "12 out of 52" is written as $\frac{12}{52}$. Set up a proportion to see how many hundredths $\frac{12}{52}$ is equivalent to: $\frac{12}{52} = \frac{?}{100}$. Cross multiplying yields $100 \times 12 = 52 \times ?$, or $1,200 = 52 \times ?$. Dividing both sides by 52 yields ? = 23.07623. When expressed to the nearest percent, this rounds to 23%.

12. d. It is easier to change $\frac{4}{5}$ into 0.8 before dealing with the percent symbol. $\frac{4}{5}\% = 0.8\% = 0.008$.

13. d. "50% of what number equals 20% of 2,000?" can be written mathematically as $0.50 \times ? = 0.20 \times 2,000$. Dividing both sides by 0.5 will yield ? $= \frac{(.2)(2,000)}{.5} = 800$.

14. b. 300% equals $\frac{300}{100}$, or 3. To find 300% of 54.2, multiply 3 times 54.2: $3 \times 54.2 = 162.6$.

15. a. "What percent" can be expressed as $\frac{?}{100}$. The question "What percent of $\frac{1}{2}$ is $\frac{1}{8}$?" can be expressed as: $\frac{?}{100} \times \frac{1}{2} = \frac{1}{8}$. This simplifies to $\frac{?}{200} = \frac{1}{8}$. Cross multiplying yields $8 \times ? = 200$. Dividing both sides by 8 yields 25.

16. c. 75% = $\frac{75}{100}$. This reduces to $\frac{3}{4}$. Taking $\frac{3}{4}$ of a dollar amount means you multiply the dollar amount by $\frac{3}{4}$.

17. d. The question: "40% of what number is equal to 460?" can be written mathematically as: $0.40 \times ? = 460$. Next, divide both sides by 0.40 to yield ? = 1,150.

18. d. He gets 12% of $40,000, or $0.12 \times \$40,000 = \$4,800$.

19. b. Since more than 50 drives are being purchased, use the discounted price. Take 8% ($8) off the cost of each drive. So, instead of costing $100 each, the drives will be $92 each.

Next, multiply 62 drives by the price of each drive: $62 \times 92 = \$5,704$. Next, calculate the tax. $\$5,704 \times 0.08 = \$456.32$. Add the tax to the $5,704 to get $6,160.32.

20. c. The tax on the $64,000 will equal $0.26 \times 64,000 = \$16,640$. Subtract the tax from her earnings: $64,000 - 16,640 = 47,360$.

21. c. The question "What percent of $\frac{8}{9}$ is $\frac{2}{3}$?" can be expressed mathematically as $\frac{?}{100} \times \frac{8}{9} = \frac{2}{3}$. Divide both sides by $\frac{8}{9}$ to get $\frac{?}{100} = \frac{2}{3} \div \frac{8}{9}$ or $\frac{?}{100} = \frac{2}{3} \times \frac{9}{8}$. This simplifies to $\frac{?}{100} = \frac{18}{24}$, or $\frac{?}{100} = \frac{3}{4}$. Multiply both sides by 100 to get $? = \frac{300}{4}$, so $? = 75$.

22. c. 120 out of a total of 400 were sold. Set up a proportion to see what this would be equivalent to when expressed out of 100. $\frac{120}{400} = \frac{?}{100}$ Cross multiplying, you get $120 \times 100 = 400 \times ?$, which is the same as $12,000 = 400 \times ?$, and dividing both sides by 400 yields $? = 30$. Thus 30% were sold, so 70% remain.

23. b. $\frac{1}{2}$ of the circle is shaded. $\frac{1}{2} = \frac{50}{100} = 50\%$.

24. c. $\frac{3}{4}$ of the square is shaded. $\frac{3}{4} = \frac{75}{100} = 75\%$.

25. b. $\frac{3}{8}$ of the square is shaded. $3 \div 8 = 0.375$. To express this as a percent, move the decimal two places to the right: 37.5%.

26. b. $\frac{6}{16}$ of the square is shaded. $\frac{6}{16}$ reduces to $\frac{3}{8}$. $3 \div 8 = 0.375$. To express this as a percent, move the decimal two places to the right: 37.5%.

27. b. A 20% markup yields a new price that is 120% of the original price. $\$13,000 \times 1.20 = \$15,600$.

28. c. "33 is 12% of what number" can be expressed mathematically as $33 = 0.12 \times ?$. Divide 33 by 0.12 (12%) to get 275.

29. d. 52% is the same as 0.52 (drop the % sign and move the decimal point two places to the left). $\frac{13}{25} = \frac{26}{50} = \frac{52}{100}$; $52 \div 100 = 0.52$. And $52 \times$

$10^{-2} = 52 \times 0.01 = 0.52$. Obviously, 0.052 does not equal 0.52, so your answer is **d**.

30. d. $I = PRT$ means $Interest = principal \times rate\ of\ interest \times time$. Principal = your original amount of money (in dollars), and time is in years. Be careful; the original amount of money (P) is \$4,000 because Emily put $\frac{1}{2}$ of the \$8,000 into the account. $I = 0.06$ and $T = 2$ years. Substituting into $I = PRT$, you get $I = (4,000)(0.06)(2) = \$480$.

31. a. Use the formula $I = PRT$ to solve this problem. Here, you were given the timeframe of 8 months, so you need to convert to years. 8 months $\times \frac{1\ yr}{12\ months} = \frac{8}{12}$ yr $= \frac{2}{3}$ yr. You are given $P = \$10,000$ and $R = 6\%$ or 0.06. Next, you substitute these values into the equation:
$I = PRT$
$I = (\$10,000)(0.06)(\frac{2}{3})$
$= 600 \times \frac{2}{3}$
$= \frac{1,200}{3}$
$= \$400$

32. c. In the formula $I = PRT$, the amount of money deposited is called the principal, P. The interest rate per year is represented by R, and T represents the number of years. The interest rate must be written as a decimal. Here $P = 5,000$, $R = 9\% = 0.09$, and $T = 8$. Substitute these numbers for the respective variables and multiply: $I = 5,000 \times 0.09 \times 8 = \$3,600$.

33. b. First, determine what percent of the trees are not oaks by subtracting. $100\% - 32\% = 68\%$. Change 68% to a decimal (0.68) and multiply: $0.68 \times 400 = 272$.

34. c. The problem can be restated as: 5 hours is to 24 hours as $x\%$ is to 100%. This is the same as $\frac{5}{24} = \frac{x}{100}$.

35. b. First figure out what the number is. If 10% of a number is 45, you can call the number "?" and write $0.10 \times ? = 45$. Divide both sides by

0.10 to get ? = 450. Next, take 20% of 450: $0.20 \times 450 = 90$.

36. d. When all of the staplers sold, the amount collected is $\$2.50 \times 12 = \$30$. Since a dozen staplers cost $10, the profit is $20. Next, set up a proportion:
$$\frac{\$20\ \text{profit}}{\text{initial}\ \$10} = \frac{?}{100}$$
Cross multiply to get $(100)(20) = (10)(?)$, or $2,000 = (10)(?)$. Divide both sides by 10 to get $? = 200$. Thus, the rate of profit is 200%.

37. c. Find the net loss: $\$50 - \$38 = \$12$. Next, set up a proportion:
$$\frac{\$12\ \text{loss}}{\text{initial}\ \$50} = \frac{?}{100}$$
Cross multiply to get $12 \times 100 = 50 \times ?$, or $1,200 = 50 \times ?$. Divide both sides by 50 to get $? = 24$. Thus, there is a 24% loss.

38. b. $\$130 - 10\%$ of $130 = 130 - 13 = \$117$. Next take 15% of $117 = 0.15 \times 117 = 17.55$. Deduct this amount: $117 - 17.55 = \$99.45$. Choice **a**, 97.5 is incorrect because this represents a 25% reduction in price. You cannot add 10% and 15% and deduct 25%.

39. c. The printer will sell for 115% of the cost. $115\% \times \$85 = 1.15 \times 85 = 97.75$. This question can also be solved in two steps: 15% of $85 = \$12.75$ markup. Add $12.75 to $85 (the cost) to get $97.75.

40. a. If the price of the car is p, then you know that the price of the car plus 8.5% of that price added up to $14,105; 8.5% equals 0.085. Thus, $p + .085p = 14,105$; $1.085p = 14,105$. Dividing both sides by 1.085 yields $p = \$13,000$.

41. b. You can solve this problem by asking yourself: "2,380 is what percent of 34,000?" and then expressing this question mathematically: $2,380 = \frac{?}{100} \times 34,000$. Divide both sides by 34,000 to get $\frac{2,380}{34,000} = \frac{?}{100}$. Cross multiply to get $238,000 = (34,000)(?)$. Divide both sides by 34,000 to get 7. Thus, the answer is 7%.

42. d. Because the interest is compounded semiannually (twice a year), after $\frac{1}{2}$ a year the amount of interest earned $I = PRT = 8,000 \times 0.05 \times \frac{1}{2} = \$200$. Now the account has $8,200 in it. Next, calculate the interest for the second half of the year with $I = PRT = 8,200 \times 0.05 \times \frac{1}{2} = 205$. Thus, the answer is $8,405.

43. c. Note that 9 months $= \frac{3}{4}$ of a year. Because interest is compounded quarterly (4 times a year), after $\frac{1}{4}$ of a year, the amount of interest earned will be $I = PRT = 14,000 \times 0.08 \times \frac{1}{4} = \$280$. The amount in the account after this time will be $14,280. After another $\frac{1}{4}$ of a year, you add $I = PRT = 14,280 \times .08 \times \frac{1}{4} = \$285.60$. The new total is $14,565.60. After the next $\frac{1}{4}$ of a year, the amount of interest earned is $I = PRT = 14565.60 \times 0.08 \times \frac{1}{4} = \$291.312$. The amount in the account after $\frac{3}{4}$ of a year is $14,856.91.

44. c. Because Suki is making 2 investments, first find $\frac{3}{5}$ of $1,000. Divide $1,000 into 5 equal parts ($\$\frac{1,000}{5} = \$200$) and take 3 parts ($600). $600 is invested at 6% simple interest, which yields:
$\$600(6\%) = \$600(0.06) = \$36$
The remaining $400 is invested at 8% simple interest, which yields:
$\$400(8\%) = \$400(0.08) = \$32$
The total interest earned is $\$36 + \$32 = \$68$.

45. b. Convert $33\frac{1}{3}\%$ into a fraction, remembering that the percent sign is equivalent to $\frac{1}{100}$. $33\frac{1}{3}\% = \frac{100}{3} \times \frac{1}{100} = \frac{1}{3}$. Now, $\frac{1}{3} = \frac{4}{12}$. Therefore, there are 4 twelfths in $33\frac{1}{3}\%$

46. b. Use the proportion:
$$\frac{\text{Change}}{\text{Initial}} = \frac{?}{100}$$
where the change $= 200 - 150 = 50$, and the initial value is 150. Thus, you have:
$$\frac{50}{150} = \frac{?}{100}$$
Cross multiply to get $50 \times 100 = 150 \times ?$, or

5,000 = 150 × ?. Divide both sides by 150 to get ? = $33\frac{1}{3}$. Thus, there was a $33\frac{1}{3}$% increase.

47. a. Use the proportion:

$$\frac{\text{Change}}{\text{Initial}} = \frac{?}{100}$$

where the change = 200 − 150 = 50, and the initial value is 200. Thus, you have:

$$\frac{50}{200} = \frac{?}{100}$$

Cross multiply to get 50 × 100 = 200 × ?, or 5,000 = 200 × ?. Divide both sides by 200 to get ? = 25. Thus, there was a 25% decrease.

48. a. Use the proportion:

$$\frac{\text{Difference in values}}{\text{Actual value}} = \frac{?}{100}$$

Here the difference in values is 600 pounds − 540 pounds = 60 pounds. The actual value is 600 pounds. Thus, you get:

$$\frac{60}{600} = \frac{?}{100}$$

Cross multiplying yields 60 × 100 = 600 × ?, or 6,000 = 600 × ?. Divide both sides by 600 to get ? = 10. Thus, there is a 10% error, choice **a**.

49. b. Draining half the 5-gallon tank leaves 2.5 gallons inside. Because you know the solution is a 50-50 mixture, there must be 1.25 gallons of water present at this point. After adding 2 gallons of water, there will be 1.25 + 2, or 3.25 gallons of water in the final mixture.

6 ▶ Number Series

Some number series can be categorized as **arithmetic** or **geometric**. Other number series are neither arithmetic or geometric and thus must be analyzed in search of a pattern. Let's review the two general types of number series you may see on the civil service exam.

▶ Arithmetic Series

This type of number series progresses by adding (or subtracting) a constant number to each term. For example, look at the series:

   4, 7, 10, 13, 16, . . .

Notice that each term is 3 more than the term that comes before it. Therefore, this is an arithmetic series with a *common difference* of 3.

▶ Geometric Series

Geometric series progress by multiplying (or dividing) each term by a constant number to get the next term. For example, look at the series:

$\frac{1}{2}$, 1, 2, 4, 8, 16, 32, . . .

Notice that each term is two times the prior term. Therefore, this is a geometric series with a *common ratio* of 2.

▶ Letter Series

Instead of containing numbers, letter series use the relationships of the letters in the alphabet to generate patterns. Study the series and try to figure out what the relationship is. For example, look at the series:

ABC, CBA, DEF, FED, GHI, ____

Which answer choice will correctly fill in the blank—IJK, JKL, LKJ, or IHG?

Notice that the first *triplet* of the series is ABC. The next triplet contains the same 3 letters listed in reverse order: CBA. The third triplet is DEF, followed by its inverse FED. Next comes GHI, so the missing 3 letters will be GHI in reverse order, or IHG.

▶ Symbol Series

Symbol series are visual series based on the relationship between images. Carefully analyze this visual series to find the pattern.

For example, look at the following symbol series:

↑ ↗ → ↘ ↓ ↙ ____

What symbol comes next—↖, ←, ↑, or ↔?

Notice that the position of each arrow can be found by rotating the previous arrow 45° clockwise. Thus, the next arrow will be ←.

▶ Practice Questions

1. What number is missing from the following series?

18, 14, _____, 6, 2
a. 12
b. 10
c. 8
d. 4

2. What number is missing from the following series?

5, 15, 45, _____, 405
a. 50
b. 60
c. 75
d. 135

3. What number is missing from the following series?

72, 67, _____, 57, 52
a. 62
b. 63
c. 59
d. 58

4. What number is missing from the following series?

8.2, _____, 7.6, 7.3, 7.0
a. 8.1
b. 8
c. 7.9
d. 7.8

5. What number is missing from the following series?

1, 4, 6, 1, _____, 6, 1
a. 6
b. 4
c. 1
d. 2

6. What number is missing from the following series?

9.7, 10.1, _____, 10.9, 11.3
a. 9.7
b. 9.9
c. 10.5
d. 11.3

7. What number is missing from the following series?

0, 1, 8, 27, _____
a. 34
b. 54
c. 64
d. 76

8. Look at this series:

567, 542, 517, 492, ...
What number should come next?
a. 499
b. 483
c. 477
d. 467

9. What number is missing from the following series?

90, 45, _____, 11.25, 5.625
a. 0
b. 12.5
c. 16
d. 22.5

10. What number is missing from the following series?

_____, 0.34, 0.068, 0.0136

a. 1.7

b. .408

c. 4.08

d. 17

11. Look at this series:

$2, 1, \frac{1}{2}, \frac{1}{4}, \ldots.$

What number should come next?

a. $\frac{1}{3}$

b. $\frac{1}{8}$

c. $\frac{2}{8}$

d. $\frac{1}{16}$

12. What number is missing from the following series?

$0, 1,$ _____, $6, 10, 15$

a. 2

b. 3

c. 4

d. 5

13. What number is missing from the following series?

$4, 1, 5, 4, 1, 7, 4, 1, 9, 4, 1,$ _____

a. 1

b. 4

c. 9

d. 11

14. What number is missing from the following series?

$\frac{2}{5}, \frac{1}{15},$ _____, $\frac{1}{540}, \frac{1}{3,240}$

a. $\frac{2}{30}$

b. $\frac{1}{45}$

c. $\frac{1}{90}$

d. $\frac{1}{270}$

15. What number is missing from the following series?

$30,$ _____, $27, 25, \frac{1}{2}, 24$

a. $29\frac{1}{2}$

b. 29

c. $28\frac{1}{2}$

d. 28

16. What number is missing from the following series?

$10, 12, 16, 22, 30, 40,$ _____

a. 33

b. 34

c. 40

d. 52

17. What number is missing from the following series?

$-12, 6, 4, -13, 7, 3, -14,$ _____, 2

a. 8

b. 10

c. 12

d. 13

18. What number is missing from the following series?

$5,423; 5,548; 5,673; 5,798;$ _____

a. 5,823

b. 5,848

c. 5,923

d. 5,948

19. What number is missing from the following series?

6, 11, 16, 16, 21, 26, 26, _____

a. 16
b. 26
c. 30
d. 31

20. What number is missing from the following series?

10, 14, 84, 88, 264, _____

a. 18
b. 188
c. 268
d. 334

21. What number is missing from the following series?

38, 20, 5, −7, −16, _____

a. −25
b. −22
c. −20
d. −19

22. What number is missing from the following series?

9, 8, 16, 15, _____, 29, 58

a. 30
b. 14
c. 9
d. 8

23. Look at this series:

53, 53, _____, 40, 27, 27, ...

What number should fill the blank?

a. 14
b. 38
c. 40
d. 51

24. Look at this series:

0.2, $\frac{1}{5}$, 0.4, $\frac{2}{5}$, 0.8, $\frac{4}{5}$, ...

What number should come next?

a. $\frac{8}{10}$
b. 0.7
c. 1.6
d. 0.16

25. Look at this series:

1.5, 2.3, 3.1, 3.9, ...

What number should come next?

a. 4.2
b. 4.4
c. 4.7
d. 5.1

26. Look at this series:

29, 27, 28, 26, 27, 25, ...

What number should come next?

a. 23
b. 24
c. 26
d. 27

27. Look at this series:

31, 29, 24, 22, 17, ...

What number should come next?

a. 15
b. 14
c. 13
d. 12

28. Look at this series:

10, 34, 12, 31, _____, 28, 16, ...

What number should fill the blank?

a. 14
b. 18
c. 30
d. 34

29. What is the missing term in the following number pattern?

240, 120, 60, 30, 15, _____, $3\frac{3}{4}$

a. $7\frac{1}{2}$

b. $9\frac{1}{4}$

c. 10

d. $11\frac{1}{4}$

30. Look at this series:

3, 4, 7, 8, 11, 12, ...

What number should come next?

a. 7

b. 10

c. 14

d. 15

31. Look at this series:

1, 4, 9, 5, 17, ...

What number should come next?

a. 6

b. 8

c. 22

d. 25

32. Look at this series:

1, $\frac{7}{8}$, $\frac{3}{4}$, $\frac{5}{8}$, ...

What number should come next?

a. $\frac{2}{3}$

b. $\frac{1}{2}$

c. $\frac{3}{8}$

d. $\frac{1}{4}$

33. Look at this series:

8, 22, 12, 16, 22, 20, 24, ...

What two numbers should come next?

a. 28, 32

b. 28, 22

c. 22, 28

d. 22, 26

34. If the pattern $\frac{1}{2}$, $\frac{1}{4}$, $\frac{1}{8}$, $\frac{1}{16}$, . . . is continued, what is the denominator of the tenth term?

a. 64

b. 212

c. 512

d. 1,024

35. Look at this series:

14, 28, 20, 40, 32, 64, ...

What number should come next?

a. 52

b. 56

c. 96

d. 128

36. Look at this series:

9, 12, 11, 14, 13, 16, 15, ...

What two numbers should come next?

a. 14, 13

b. 8, 21

c. 14, 17

d. 18, 17

37. Look at this series:

21, 24, 30, 21, 36, 42, ...

What number should come next?

a. 21

b. 27

c. 42

d. 46

38. Look at this series:

XX, XVI, XII, VIII, ...

What number should come next?

a. IV

b. V

c. VI

d. III

39. Look at this series:

J14, L11, N8, P5, ...

What number should come next?

a. Q2

b. Q3

c. R2

d. S2

40. Look at this series:

VI, 10, V, 11, IV, 12, ...

What number should come next?

a. VII

b. III

c. IX

d. 13

41. Select the answer choice that best completes the following sequence.

JAK, KBL, LCM, MDN, _____

a. OEP

b. NEO

c. MEN

d. PFQ

42. Select the letters that best complete the following sequence.

QPO, NML, KJI, _____, EDC

a. HGF

b. CAB

c. JKL

d. GHI

43. Select the letters that best complete the following sequence.

ELFA, GLHA, ILJA, _____, MLNA

a. OLPA

b. KLMA

c. LLMA

d. KLLA

44. Select the pattern that best completes the following sequence.

a. ▢▫

b. ▢◼

c. △▲

d. ◻▢

45. Select the pattern that best completes the following sequence.

△▢△|▢◯▢|◯◇◯|◇▢ __

a. ◇

b. ▢

c. ◯

d. △

46. Select the pattern that best completes the following sequence.

⇨⇨|⇧⇩|⇨⇨|⇧⇩| __

a. ⇩⇩

b. ⇨⇨

c. ⇧⇩

d. ⇦⇦

47. What best completes the following sequence?

∫⌐|⌐₹|∫⌐|__

a. ₹⌐

b. ⇌

c. ∫₹

d. ⌐₹

48. What best completes the following sequence?

⊞⊞⊟|⊟⊞⊞__⊟

a. ⊞⊞

b. ⊞⊞

c. ⊞⊞

d. ⊞⊟

49. What best completes the following sequence?

ⰀmE|mmm|EⱲE|Ⱳ__Ⱳ

a. Ⰰ

b. E

c. Ⱳ

d. ⱻ

50. What best completes the following sequence?

⬭△|⌂8|⬭△|8__

a. 8

b. 8

c. 8

d. 8

▶ Answers

1. b. This is an arithmetic series that decreases by four as the series progresses. Thus, the missing number is $14 - 4 = 10$. You can check that this is correct by applying the rule to the 10: $10 - 4 = 6$, which is in fact the next term.

2. d. This is a geometric series. You multiply each term by 3 to get the next term. The missing term is $45 \times 3 = 135$. You can check that this rule works by multiplying 135 by 3. This yields 405, which is the next term.

3. a. This is an arithmetic series. Each term is 5 less than the prior term. To find the missing term, subtract 5 from 67 to get 62. Next, check that the rule is correct by verifying $62 - 5 = 57$, the next term.

4. c. This is an arithmetic series with a common difference of 0.3. This simply means that each term is 0.3 less than the term before it. $8.2 - 0.3 = 7.9$, so the missing term is 7.9. To check that you found the right rule, subtract 0.3 from 7.9 to get 7.6, the next term.

5. b. This series is neither arithmetic or geometric. It is simply three numbers repeating over and over in order. The numbers 1, 4, and 6 repeat. Thus, the missing number is 4.

6. c. This is an arithmetic series. Each term is 0.4 greater than the previous term. $10.1 + 0.4 = 10.5$. Using this rule, the term following 10.5 should be $10.5 + 0.4 = 10.9$, and it is. Thus, you know you used the correct rule.

7. c. This series is neither arithmetic or geometric. If you look carefully at the numbers, you should notice that each is a cube of a number. In other words, 0, 1, 8, 27 corresponds to 0^3, 1^3, 2^3, 3^3, so the next term should equal 4^3, or 64.

8. d. This is an arithmetic series; each number is 25 less than the previous number. Thus, the answer is $492 - 25 = 467$.

9. d. This is a geometric series with a common ratio of $\frac{1}{2}$. In other words, each term is $\frac{1}{2}$ of the term that precedes it. Thus, the missing term is $\frac{1}{2}$ of 45; $\frac{1}{2} \times 45 = 22.5$. To check that you used the correct rule, take $\frac{1}{2}$ of 22.5: $22.5 \times \frac{1}{2} = 11.25$. This is the next term in the series so you know you are right.

10. a. This is a geometric series with a common ratio of 0.2. In other words, each term is 0.2 times the term that precedes it. You can divide 0.34 by 0.2 to figure out what the first term is. $0.34 \div 0.2 = 1.7$. You can check that you have the correct answer by applying the rule: $0.34 \times 0.2 = 0.068$.

11. b. This is a geometric series; each number is one-half of the previous number. Thus, the next number should be $\frac{1}{2} \times \frac{1}{4} = \frac{1}{8}$.

12. b. Here the numbers are increasing, but the amount by which they are increasing is increasing as well. $0 (+1)\ 1 (+2)\ 3 (+3)\ 6 (+4)\ 10 (+5)\ 15$. Thus, the missing number is 3.

13. d. Consider this series as a triplet. The first 2 terms of the triplet are always 4 followed by 1. Notice that every third term gets 2 added to it: 4, 1, 5, 4, 1, 7, 4, 1, 9, 4, 1, ___. Thus, the missing number is $9 + 2 = 11$.

14. c. This is a geometric series with a common ratio of $\frac{1}{6}$. This means that each term is the prior term multiplied by $\frac{1}{6}$. This is more evident when looking at the last two terms of the series: $\frac{2}{5} (\times \frac{1}{6})\ \frac{1}{15} (\times \frac{1}{6})$ ___ $(\times \frac{1}{6})\ \frac{1}{540} (\times \frac{1}{6})\ \frac{1}{3,240}$. Thus, the missing term is $\frac{1}{15} \times \frac{1}{6} = \frac{1}{90}$.

15. c. This is an arithmetic series with a common difference of $1\frac{1}{2}$. The missing term is $30 - 1\frac{1}{2} = 28\frac{1}{2}$. You can check your work by applying the rule to $28\frac{1}{2}$; $28\frac{1}{2} - 1\frac{1}{2} = 27$, which is the next term.

16. d. Here the numbers are increasing. Notice that it is not a steady common difference (arithmetic), nor a steady common ratio (geometric). The amount of increase corresponds more to an addition, and each term is increasing by having a larger number added to it. The pattern here is 10 (+2) 12 (+4) 16 (+6) 22 (+8) 30 (+10) 40 (+12) ___. Thus, the missing number is 40 + 12, or 52.

17. a. Here the series can be considered as triplets. The first number of each triplet is decreased by 1: –12, 6, 4 –13, 7, 3 –14, ___, 2. The second number of each triplet is increased by 1: –12, 6, 4 –13, 7, 3 –14, ___, 2. Thus, the missing number is 7 + 1 = 8. (Notice also that the third number in each triplet is decreased by 1: –12, 6, 4 –13, 7, 3 –14, ___, 2.)

18. c. This is an arithmetic series in which each number is increased by 125. The missing number will be 5,798 + 125, or 5,923.

19. d. The pattern here is +5, +5, repeat, +5, +5, repeat.
6 (+5) 11 (+5) 16 (repeat ➔) 16 (+5) 21 (+5) 26 (repeat ➔) 26 (+5) ___
Thus, the missing number is 26 + 5 = 31.

20. c. The pattern here is +4, × 6, +4, × 6, and so forth.
10 (+ 4) 14 (× 6) 84 (+ 4) 88 (× 6) 264 (+ 4) ___
Thus, the missing number is 264 + 4 = 268.

21. b. Here the numbers are decreasing, though not by a steady amount or by a common ratio. The pattern of decrease is:
38 (minus 3 × 6) 20 (minus 3 × 5) 5 (minus 3 × 4) –7 (minus 3 × 3) –16 (minus 3 × 2) ___
Thus, the missing number is –16 minus 3 × 2, or –16 – 6 = –22.

22. a. Here the pattern is – 1, × 2, – 1, × 2, and so forth:
9 (– 1) 8 (× 2) 16 (–1) 15 (× 2) ___ (– 1) 29 (× 2) 58
Thus, the missing number is $15 \times 2 = 30$. You can check that you are right by subtracting 1; 30 – 1 = 29, which is the next number in the series.

23. c. In this series, each number is repeated, then 13 is subtracted to arrive at the next number. Thus, the missing number is 53 – 13 = 40.

24. c. This is a multiplication series with repetition. The decimals (0.2, 0.4, 0.8) are repeated by a fraction with the same value ($\frac{1}{5}, \frac{2}{5}, \frac{4}{5}$) and are then multiplied by 2. Thus, the next number will be 0.8×2, or 1.6.

25. c. In this arithmetic series, each number increases by 0.8. Thus, the next number should be 3.9 + 0.8 = 4.7, choice **c**.

26. c. In this simple alternating addition and subtraction series, 2 is subtracted, then 1 is added, and so on. Thus, the next number should be 25 + 1, or 26.

27. a. This is an alternating subtraction series, which subtracts 2, then 5. Thus, the next number will be 17 – 2 = 15.

28. a. This is an alternating addition and subtraction series. The first series begins with 10 and adds 2 (10, 12, <u>14</u>, 16); the second begins with 34 and subtracts 3 (34, 31, 28). Thus, the number that belongs in the blank is 14.

29. a. Each number in the pattern is one-half of the previous number. Half of 15 is $7\frac{1}{2}$. You can check the pattern by taking half of $7\frac{1}{2}$, which is $3\frac{3}{4}$, the next term.

30. d. This alternating addition series begins with 3. 1 is added to give 4; then 3 is added to give 7; then 1 is added, and so on. Thus, the next number will be 12 + 3 = 15.

31. a. This is an alternating series. In the first pattern, 8 is added (1, 9, 17); in the second pattern, 1 is added (4, 5, 6). Thus, the next number will be 6.

32. b. This is a subtraction series. Each number decreases by $\frac{1}{8}$. The next number is $\frac{5}{8} - \frac{1}{8}$, which is $\frac{4}{8}$, or $\frac{1}{2}$.

33. c. This is an alternating repetition series, with a random number, 22, introduced as every third number into an otherwise simple addition series. In the addition series, 4 is added to each number to arrive at the next number. Thus, the next two numbers will be 22 (the random number) followed 24 + 4, or 28.

34. d. Given the pattern $\frac{1}{2}, \frac{1}{4}, \frac{1}{8}, \frac{1}{16} \ldots$ notice that the denominators double as the pattern advances. There are 4 terms so far. The fifth term will have a denominator of 32, the sixth term will be 64, the seventh term will be 128, the eighth term will be 256, the ninth term will be 512, and the tenth term will be 1,024. So the tenth term is $\frac{1}{1,024}$.

35. b. This is an alternating multiplication and subtraction series: First, multiply by 2, and then subtract 8. The next term will be 64 − 8 = 56.

36. d. This is an alternating addition and subtraction series. First, 3 is added, then 1 is subtracted; then 3 is added, 1 subtracted, and so on. Thus the next term will be 15 + 3 = 18. The term after that will be 18 − 1 = 17.

37. a. This is an addition series with a random number, 21, introduced as every third number. In the series, 6 is added to each number except 21, to arrive at the next number. The next number is the *random number, 21.*

38. a. This is a subtraction series; each number (represented in Roman numerals) is 4 less than the previous number. XX = 20, XVI = 16, XII = 12, VIII = 8, so the next number

should be 4. In Roman numerals, 4 is written as IV, choice **a.**

39. c. In this series, the letters progress by 2 (J, L, N, P), while the numbers decrease by 3 (14, 11, 8, 5). Thus, the next term will be R2, choice **c.**

40. b. This is an alternating addition and subtraction series. Roman numerals alternate with standard numbers. In the Roman numeral pattern, each number decreases by 1 (VI, V, IV, III, corresponding to 6, 5, 4, 3). In the standard numeral pattern, each number increases by 1 (10, 11, 12, 13). Thus, the next number should be the Roman numeral for 3, which is III.

41. b. If you consider each triplet of letters, the first letter in each triplet progresses from J ➔ K ➔ L ➔ M ➔ ___. The second letter in each triplet progresses from A ➔ B ➔ C ➔ D ➔ ___, and the third letter in each triplet progresses from K ➔ L ➔ M ➔ N ➔ ___. Therefore, the last triplet should be NEO.

42. a. If you look carefully at this sequence, you will notice that the *entire* sequence is the alphabet (starting at C) written *backward.* Therefore, the missing three letters are HGF.

43. d. If you look at the first letter in each quadruplet, you can see that one letter is skipped: ELFA, GLHA, ILJA, ___, MLNA, so the first missing letter is K. Looking at the second letter in each quadruplet, you see that the letter L is constant: ELFA, GLHA, ILJA, ___, MLNA, so the second missing letter must be L. Next, look at the third letter in each quadruplet: ELFA, GLHA, ILJA, ___, MLNA. Again, one letter is skipped, so the missing letter is L. Finally, look at the last letter in each quadruplet: ELFA, GLHA, ILJA, ___, MLNA. The letter A is a constant, so the last missing letter is A. Thus, the entire missing piece is KLLA.

44. b. Notice that each group of symbols has three versions of the same shape, the middle version being the largest: ○ ◯ ● | ▲ △ △ | □ __ . Also, a black and a white version of the shape border this large middle shape. Notice that the circle is on the right and the black triangle is on the left. The missing shapes will be squares (thus choice **c** is incorrect). The next two shapes will be a large square with the black square on the right: ☐ ■ .

45. a. The first group contains a *square* between two triangles. Next, there is a circle between 2 *squares*. Third, there is a *diamond* between two circles. The last set has a rectangle in the middle. It should be between two *diamonds*.

46. b. This is an alternating pattern. First, the two arrows point right, then one points up and one points down. Thus, the next part of the sequence should contain the two arrows pointing right.

47. d. The first image is reflected (flipped), generating the second image. Then the second is flipped to form the third. Thus, the fourth image will be the reflection of ⌐↪ which will look like this: ↪⌐ .

48. a. Look at the number of dots on each domino in each triplet: ⊞ ⊞ ⊟ | ⊟ ⊟ ⊞ | __ ⊡ . The first triplet has 5 dots, 3 dots, 1 dot. The next triplet has 1 dot, 3 dots, 5 dots. The last triplet ends with 1 dot. It is safe to assume that the pattern here is 5-3-1; 1-3-5; and 5-3-1. The missing 2 dominos are ⊞ ⊟ , the 5 and the 3.

49. c. Notice that the first and the third segments are upside-down versions of each other. The second and the fourth should also be upside-down versions of each other. Thus, the missing piece of the last segment looks like this: ⊔ .

50. c. The first and the third figures swap the inner shape for the outer shape. The second and fourth would then be expected to swap the top and bottom shapes. Thus, you would expect the missing shape to be a square on top of a circle, choice **c**.

Word Problems

In addition to dealing with basic operations, fractions, decimals, and percents, the civil service exam may use word problems to test your math and logic skils. This chapter will introduce a few common types of word problems.

▶ Ratios and Proportions

A **ratio** is a way of comparing two or more numbers. There are several different ways to write ratios. Here are some examples.

- with the word *to:* 1 to 2
- using a colon (:) to separate the numbers: 1 : 2
- using the term *for every:* 1 for every 2
- separated by a division sign or fraction bar: $\frac{1}{2}$

Usually, a fraction represents a part over a whole:

$\frac{part}{whole}$

Often, a ratio represents a part over a part:

$\frac{part}{part}$

But ratios can also represent a part over a whole:

$\frac{part}{whole}$

When a ratio represents a part over a part, you can often find the whole if you know all the parts. A **proportion** is a way of relating two ratios to one another. If you equate a given ratio to the part that you know, you can find an unknown part. Once you know the unknown parts, you can calculate the whole.

Many word problems require you to use ratios and proportions to find unknown values.

Example: If the ratio of union workers to nonunion workers is 2:3 and there are 360 nonunion workers, how many workers are there in all?

Here, you are given a 2:3 ratio. You know one part: that there are 360 nonunion workers. You can set up a proportion in order to calculate the unknown part:

$\frac{2}{3} = \frac{?}{360}$

Cross multiply to get $360 \times 2 = 3 \times ?$, or $720 = 3 \times ?$. Now, divide both sides by 3 to get ? = 240. This is the missing part: the number of union workers. Finally, add the number of union workers to nonunion workers to get the whole: $360 + 240 = 600$.

▶ Work and Salaries in Word Problems

Some word problems deal with salaries. You should be familiar with the following salary schedules:

- **per hour:** amount earned each hour
- **daily:** amount earned each day
- **weekly:** amount earned each week
- **semiweekly:** amount earned twice a week
- **semimonthly:** amount earned twice a month
- **monthly:** amount earned each month
- **annually:** amount earned each year

Other problems involving work need to be dissected logically. For example, consider the following.

Example: If 14 workers can complete a job in 2 days, how long will it take 4 workers to complete the same job? Assume all workers work at the same rate.

Most people try to set up the following proportion when confronted with this scenario:

$$\frac{14 \text{ workers}}{2 \text{ days}} = \frac{4 \text{ workers}}{? \text{ days}}$$

Notice that the ? in the denominator of the second ratio will be smaller than the 2 days in the denominator of the first ratio. Does it make sense that 4 workers will be able to finish the job of 14 workers in less than 2 days? No.

This sort of question needs to be broken apart logically. If 14 workers can complete the job in 2 days, it will take one person 14 times as long to complete the same job: 28 days. It will take 4 people $\frac{1}{4}$ as long to complete this amount of work, or 7 days.

▶ Tank and Pipe Word Problems

Tank and pipe word problems must also be solved logically. Tank and pipe questions involve the filling and draining of tanks through various pipes. Once you see what the net (overall) effect is, you are able to solve the question posed to you.

Example: A tank is partly filled with water. Pipe X leads into the tank and can fill the entire tank in 4 minutes. Pipe Y drains the tank and can drain the entire tank in 3 minutes. At a certain point in time, the tank is halfway full, and the valves leading to pipes X and Y are closed. When these valves are opened simultaneously, how long will it take for the tank to drain?

First, consider Pipe X. It can fill the tank in 4 minutes. This means that for every minute that goes by, $\frac{1}{4}$ of the tank would get filled. Next, consider Pipe Y. This pipe can empty the tank in 3 minutes. This means that for every minute that goes by, $\frac{1}{3}$ of the tank would get drained. When you consider these fractions as twelfths, you see that Pipe X fills $\frac{3}{12}$ per minute and Pipe Y drains $\frac{4}{12}$ per minute. The net effect is a draining of $\frac{1}{12}$ of the tank every minute. Since the tank starts out $\frac{1}{2}$ full (or $\frac{6}{12}$ full), it will take 6 minutes to drain the $\frac{6}{12}$ of water (at the rate of $\frac{1}{12}$ out per minute).

▶ Distance Word Problems

Distance questions can be solved with the formula $D = RT$, where D = distance, R = rate, and T = time, assuming that a constant rate is maintained. Here you have the flexibility to use many different combinations of rates, distances, and times, so long as the units you use in the equation match each other. For example, rates can be measured in meters per second, kilometers per hour, feet per second, miles per hour, and so forth. Just be sure that if you use, for example, a rate in miles per hour as your R in the equation, that your D is in miles, and your T is in hours.

Example: Train A leaves its station and travels at a constant rate of 65 miles per hour in an eastward direction. At the same time, Train B leaves a western station heading east at a constant rate of 70 miles per hour. If the 2 trains pass each other after 3 hours, how far apart were they initially?

The 2 trains' initial distance apart equals the sum of the distance each travels in 3 hours. Using $D = RT$, you know Train A travels a distance of $(65)(3) = 195$ miles, and Train B travels $(70)(3) = 210$ miles. This means that they were $195 + 210 = 405$ miles apart initially. It is helpful to draw a diagram to understand this better:

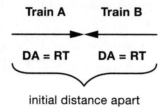

initial distance apart

► Practice Questions

1. Pete made $4,000 in January, $3,500 in February, and $4,500 in March. If he put 30% of his total earnings into his checking account and the rest into his saving account, how much money does he have in his checking account?
   a. $3,600
   b. $4,200
   c. $6,300
   d. $8,400

2. Denise had $120. She gave $\frac{1}{8}$ of this amount to Suzanne. She then gave $\frac{1}{4}$ of the remainder to Darlene. How much money does Denise have left?
   a. $26.25
   b. $30.00
   c. $78.75
   d. $80.00

3. Greg had $12,000 in his savings account. Of this amount, he transferred $\frac{1}{3}$ into checking, $\frac{1}{4}$ into a certificate of deposit, and spent $\frac{1}{8}$ on a computer system. How much money remains in his savings account?
   a. $3,500
   b. $5,000
   c. $5,600
   d. $6,000

4. If two pieces of wood measuring $2\frac{1}{2}$ feet and $3\frac{1}{3}$ feet are laid end to end, how long will their combined length be?
   a. 5 feet 5 inches
   b. 5 feet 10 inches
   c. 6 feet
   d. 6 feet 5 inches

5. A shipment of cable weighs 3.2 lbs. per foot. If the total weight of 3 identical reels of cable is 6,720 lbs, how many feet of cable are in each reel?
   a. 64,512 feet
   b. 21,504 feet
   c. 2,000 feet
   d. 700 feet

6. A school is purchasing 5 monitors at $175 each, 3 printers at $120 each, and 8 surge suppressors at $18 each. If the school receives a 12% discount, what is the final cost (excluding tax)?

   a. $1,379.00
   b. $1,313.52
   c. $1,213.52
   d. $1,200.00

7. The Huntington Golf Club has a ratio of two women to every three men. A 2:3 ratio is equivalent to which of the following ratios?

   a. 3:2
   b. 4:8
   c. 8:12
   d. 4:12

8. A map drawn to scale shows that the distance between 2 towns is 3 inches. If the scale is such that 1 inch equals 1 kilometer, how far away are the two towns in kilometers?

   a. 3 miles
   b. 3 kilometers
   c. 30 miles
   d. 30 kilometers

9. If it takes 27 nails to build 3 boxes, how many nails will it take to build 7 boxes?

   a. 64
   b. 72
   c. 56
   d. 63

10. Mia can hike 1.3 miles in 45 minutes. Which equation could be used to find d, the distance in miles that Mia can hike in 3 hours?

   a. $\frac{d}{3} = \frac{0.75}{1.3}$
   b. $\frac{1.3}{0.75} = \frac{d}{3}$
   c. $\frac{0.75}{d} = \frac{3}{1.3}$
   d. $\frac{0.75}{3} = \frac{d}{1.3}$

11. If Jack always spends $18 on gaming equipment in a week, how much does he spend in 6 weeks?

   a. $60
   b. $48
   c. $108
   d. $180

12. If it takes a machine 5 minutes to build 3 components, how long would it take the same machine to build 18 components?

   a. 90 minutes
   b. 18 minutes
   c. 15 minutes
   d. 30 minutes

13. Dr. Martin sees an average of 2.5 patients per hour. If she takes an hour lunch break, about how many patients does she see during the typical 9-to-5 work day?

   a. 16
   b. 18
   c. 20
   d. 22

14. A diagram drawn to scale shows a diagonal of 12 centimeters. If the scale is 1.5 centimeters = 1 foot, how long is the actual diagonal?

a. 8 feet

b. 7.5 feet

c. 6.8 feet

d. 6 feet

15. The height of the Statue of Liberty from foundation to torch is 305 feet 1 inch. Webster's American Mini-Golf has a 1:60 scale model of the statue. Approximately how tall is the scale model?

a. 5 inches

b. 5 feet 1 inch

c. 6 feet 5 inches

d. 18,305 feet

16. Scott can pot 100 plants in 30 minutes. Henri can do the same job in 60 minutes. If they worked together, how many minutes would it take them to pot 200 plants?

a. 20

b. 30

c. 40

d. 60

17. Francine and Lydia are in the same book club, and both are reading the same 350-page novel. Francine has read $\frac{4}{5}$ of the novel. Lydia has read half as much as Francine. What is the ratio of the number of pages Lydia has read to the number of pages in the novel?

a. 1:2

b. 2:5

c. 2:3

d. 1:4

18. A construction job calls for $2\frac{5}{6}$ tons of sand. Four trucks, each filled with $\frac{3}{4}$ tons of sand, arrive on the job. Is there enough sand, or is there too much sand for the job?

a. There is not enough sand; $\frac{1}{6}$ ton more is needed.

b. There is not enough sand; $\frac{1}{3}$ ton more is needed.

c. There is $\frac{1}{3}$ ton more sand than is needed.

d. There is $\frac{1}{6}$ ton more sand than is needed.

19. Jessica earns a semimonthly salary of $1,200. What is her yearly salary?

a. $144,000

b. $48,000

c. $28,800

d. $14,400

20. During a normal 40-hour workweek, Mitch earns $800. His boss wants him to work this weekend, and Mitch will get paid time and a half for these overtime hours. How much will Mitch make for 10 weekend hours?

a. $200

b. $240

c. $300

d. $340

21. Gary earns $22 an hour as a lab technician. Monday he worked 5 hours, Tuesday he worked 8 hours, and Wednesday he worked $4\frac{1}{2}$ hours. How much did he earn during those three days?

a. $363.00

b. $374.00

c. $385.00

d. $407.00

22. This month Louise earned $2,300 as her gross pay. Of this amount, $160.45 was deducted for FICA tax, $82.50 was deducted for state tax, $73.25 was deducted for city tax, and $100 was diverted to her 401(k). How much was her net paycheck?
  a. $1,883.80
  b. $1,888.30
  c. $1,983.80
  d. $1,988.33

23. Two men can load a truck in 4 hours. How many trucks can they load in 6 hours?
  a. 1
  b. $1\frac{1}{2}$
  c. 2
  d. $2\frac{1}{2}$

24. A machine can assemble 400 parts in half an hour. Of the 400 parts, 5% will be defective. If two machines are working, how many non-defective parts will be assembled in 5 hours?
  a. 800
  b. 1,600
  c. 3,800
  d. 7,600

25. Kate's daily salary is $120. If she worked 24 days this month, how much did she earn?
  a. $3,600
  b. $3,200
  c. $3,000
  d. $2,880

26. John earns $1,600 a month plus 8% commission on all sales. He sold $825 worth of merchandise during November, $980 worth of merchandise during December, and $600 worth of merchandise during January. What were his total earnings for these three months?
  a. $1,792.40
  b. $2,597.40
  c. $1,924.00
  d. $4,992.40

27. Four machines can complete a job in 6 hours. How long will it take 3 machines to complete the same job?
  a. 4 hours
  b. 8 hours
  c. 10 hours
  d. 12 hours

28. One construction job can be completed by 16 workers in 10 days. How many days would it take 8 workers to complete the job?
  a. 12 days
  b. 16 days
  c. 18 days
  d. 20 days

29. A job can be completed by 6 workers in 18 days. How many days would it take 9 workers to complete the job?
  a. 12 days
  b. 16 days
  c. 18 days
  d. 20 days

30. Nine workers working at the same pace can complete a job in 12 days. If this job must be completed in 3 days, how many workers should be assigned?
a. 27
b. 30
c. 36
d. 48

31. When Anthony and Elise work together they can complete a task in 3 hours. When Anthony works alone he can complete the same task in 8 hours. How long would it take Elise to complete the task alone?
a. $6\frac{1}{2}$ hours
b. 6 hours
c. $4\frac{4}{5}$ hours
d. 4 hours

32. Rose and Marie worked on a project together. Rose put in 40 hours of work and Marie put in 60 hours of work. The contract for the entire project paid $2,000. The women decide to split the money up according to the ratio of the amount of time each put into the project. How much did Marie get?
a. $400
b. $600
c. $1,000
d. $1,200

33. Alison and Artie worked on a project together. Alison put in 18 hours of work and Artie put in 24 hours of work. The contract for the entire project was $7,000. If the two decide to split the money up according to the ratio of the amount of time each put into the project, how much will Artie get?
a. $3,000
b. $3,500
c. $4,000
d. $4,500

34. Tina's semiweekly salary is $400. Jim's semi-monthly salary is $1,800. If both of them work a standard 40-hour workweek, who earns more for the month of February? (Assume that this is NOT a leap year.)
a. Tina by $1,400
b. Jim by $400
c. Tina by $400
d. Jim by $1,400

35. Kayla can type 60 reports in 3 hours. Ethan can type 110 reports in 6 hours. Working together, how long will it take them to type 375 reports?
a. 13 hours
b. 12 hours
c. 10 hours
d. 9 hours

36. For an employee who works a 30-hour workweek, a $28,000 yearly salary translates into which of the following hourly wages?
a. $13.46
b. $14.50
c. $17.95
d. $19.46

37. A tank containing fluid is half full. A pipe that can fill $\frac{1}{16}$ of the tank per minute begins letting more fluid in. At the same time, a drain that can empty $\frac{1}{8}$ of the tank in one minute is opened. How long will it take to empty the tank?

a. 8 minutes

b. 16 minutes

c. 18 minutes

d. 32 minutes

38. Pipe T leads into a tank and Pipe V drains the tank. Pipe T can fill the entire tank in 6 minutes. Pipe V can drain the entire tank in 4 minutes. At a certain point in time, the valves leading to both pipes are shut and the tank is $\frac{1}{4}$ full. If both valves are opened simultaneously, how long will it take for the pipe to drain?

a. 2 minutes

b. 3 minutes

c. 4 minutes

d. 6 minutes

39. For every 10,000 liters of water that pass through a filtering system, 0.7 gram of a pollutant is removed. How many grams of the pollutant are removed when 106 liters have been filtered?

a. 7

b. 70

c. 700

d. 7,000

40. Rudy forgot to replace his gas cap the last time he filled up his car with gas. The gas is evaporating out of his 14-gallon tank at a constant rate of $\frac{1}{3}$ gallon per day. How much gas does Rudy lose in 1 week?

a. 2 gallons

b. $2\frac{1}{3}$ gallons

c. $3\frac{1}{3}$ gallons

d. $4\frac{2}{3}$ gallons

41. Pipe A leads into a tank and Pipe B drains the tank. Pipe A can fill the entire tank in 10 minutes. Pipe B can drain the entire tank in 8 minutes. At a certain point in time, the valves leading to both pipes are shut and the tank is $\frac{1}{2}$ full. If both valves are opened simultaneously, how long will it take for the pipe to drain?

a. 18 minutes

b. 20 minutes

c. 22 minutes

d. 24 minutes

42. A car travels at a constant rate of 60 kilometers per hour for 3 hours. How far did the car travel?

a. 180 kilometers

b. 180 miles

c. 18 kilometers

d. 18 miles

43. If Michelle runs at a constant rate of 2.5 meters per second, how long will it take her to run 1 kilometer?

a. 4 minutes

b. 40 minutes

c. 400 seconds

d. 4000 seconds

44. It took T.J. 20 minutes to jog 2 miles. What was his average speed in miles per hour?
　a. 40 miles per hour
　b. 10 miles per hour
　c. 8 miles per hour
　d. 6 miles per hour

45. Sipora drove to Stephanie's house at a constant rate of 45 mph. If Stephanie's house is 220 miles away and Sipora wants to get home in exactly 4 hours, how fast should she drive?
　a. 50 miles per hour
　b. 55 miles per hour
　c. 60 miles per hour
　d. 65 miles per hour

46. Amy can run 8 miles at a constant rate in 40 minutes. Sharon can run 12 miles at a constant rate in an hour. Who has a faster rate?
　a. Amy
　b. Sharon
　c. They both run at the same rate.
　d. It cannot be determined by the information given.

47. Train A travels at 60 mph for 20 minutes. Train B travels at 55 miles per hour for 30 minutes. If both trains are traveling at a constant rate, which train would have traveled a greater distance after the time periods specified?
　a. Train A
　b. Train B
　c. Both trains traveled the same distance.
　d. It cannot be determined by the information given.

48. A train leaves a station traveling west at 60 miles per hour. At the same time, another train heads east on a parallel track, traveling at a rate of 70 miles per hour. If the 2 trains are initially 700 miles apart, how far apart are they after 1 hour?
　a. 630 miles
　b. 610 miles
　c. 570 miles
　d. 560 miles

49. Train A leaves Station A at 6 P.M., traveling east at a constant rate of 70 miles per hour. At the same time, Train B leaves Station B, traveling west at a constant rate of 90 miles per hour. If the two trains pass each other at 8 P.M., then how far apart are the two stations?
　a. 280 miles
　b. 300 miles
　c. 320 miles
　d. 360 miles

50. An eastbound train destined for Stony Brook Station leaves Penn Station at 4 P.M., traveling at a rate of 60 miles per hour. At the same time, a westbound train departs the Stony Brook Station on its way to Penn Station. If the westbound train travels at a constant speed of 70 miles per hour and the two stations are 260 miles apart, then at what time will the two trains pass each other?
　a. 4:30 P.M.
　b. 5:00 P.M.
　c. 5:30 P.M.
　d. 6:00 P.M.

► Answers

1. a. First, calculate the total amount of money: $4,000 + $3,500 + $4,500 = $12,000. He puts 30% of the $12,000, or .30 × $12,000 = $3,600, into the checking account.

2. c. $\frac{1}{8}$ of the $120 went to Suzanne: $\frac{1}{8} \times 120 =$ $15. This means there was 120 − 15 = $105 left; $\frac{1}{4}$ of the $105 went to Darlene: $\frac{1}{4} \times 105 =$ $26.25. Thus, the amount remaining is 105 − 26.25 = $78.75.

3. a. $\frac{1}{3}$ of 12,000 = $\frac{1}{3} \times 12,000 = $4,000 went to checking. $\frac{1}{4}$ of 12,000 = $\frac{1}{4} \times 12,000 = $3,000 went to the CD. And $\frac{1}{8}$ of $12,000 = $\frac{1}{8} \times$ 12,000 = $1,500 went to buy the computer. Thus, the amount left equals 12,000 − 4,000 − 3,000 − 1,500 = $3,500.

4. b. $2\frac{1}{2}$ feet = 2 feet 6 inches. $3\frac{1}{3}$ feet = 3 feet 4 inches. The sum of these values is 5 feet 10 inches.

5. d. Divide the total weight by 3 to figure out how much each of the three reels weighs: 6,720 ÷ 3 = 2,240 pounds each. Next, divide the weight of the reel by $\frac{3.2 \text{ lbs}}{\text{foot}}$: 2,240 pounds ÷ $\frac{3.2 \text{ pounds}}{\text{foot}}$ = 700 feet.

6. c. Five monitors will cost $175 × 5 = $875; three printers will cost $120 × 3 = $360; eight surge suppressors will cost $18 × 8 = $144. Before the discount, this adds to: $875 + $360 + $144 = $1,379; 12% of $1,379 = .12 × 1,379 = $165.48. Thus, the final cost will be $1,379 − 165.48 = $1,213.52.

7. c. A 2:3 ratio is equivalent to an 8:12 ratio. Multiply the $\frac{2}{3}$ ratio by $\frac{4}{4}$ to get $\frac{8}{12}$.

8. b. If 1 inch on the map denotes 1 kilometer, then 3 inches on the map would represent 3 kilometers.

9. d. First set up a proportion: $\frac{27}{3} = \frac{x}{7}$. You can reduce the first fraction: $\frac{9}{1} = \frac{x}{7}$ and then cross multiply: $1(x) = 9(7)$, so $x = 63$.

10. b. To find the distance Mia can hike in 3 hours, first set up the ratio of the distance she can walk in a certain amount of time. 45 minutes is equal to $\frac{3}{4}$ of an hour or 0.75 hours $\frac{1.3 \text{ miles}}{0.75 \text{ hours}}$. Then set up the second ratio, $\frac{d}{3 \text{ hours}}$. Set these 2 ratios equal to each other: $\frac{1.3}{0.75} = \frac{d}{3}$.

11. c. First set up a proportion: $\frac{18}{1} = \frac{x}{6}$. Cross multiplying yields $18 \times 6 = 1 \times x$, and $x = 108$.

12. d. First set up a proportion: $\frac{5}{3} = \frac{x}{18}$. Then, cross multiply: $3x = 18 \times 5$. Then solve for your answer: $3x = 90$, so $x = 30$ minutes.

13. b. 9 to 5 represents an 8-hour work day, less the one hour lunch break yields 7 working hours. Multiply the 7 hours by 2.5 patients per hour = 17.5 patients. Of the choices, 18 patients is the best answer.

14. a. Set up a proportion: $\frac{1.5 \text{ centimeters}}{1 \text{ foot}} = \frac{12 \text{ centimeters}}{? \text{ feet}}$. Cross multiply to get $1.5 \times ? = 12 \times 1$, or $1.5 \times ?$ = 12. Divide both sides by 1.5 to get ? = 8 feet.

15. b. First convert the height of the statue to inches: 305 feet × 12 inches = 3,660 inches. The statue is 3,660 + 1, or 3661, inches tall. Next, set up a proportion: $\frac{1}{60} = \frac{x}{3,661}$. Cross multiply: $60x = 3,661$. Divide both sides by 60: $x = \frac{3,661}{60}$; x is about 61 inches. Convert to feet by dividing by 12: 61 ÷ 12 = 5 r1. Thus, the answer is 5 feet 1 inch, choice **b.**

16. c. Because this is a rate of work problem, consider what fraction of the job would get done in one minute. Scott would get $\frac{1}{30}$ of the job done while Henri would get $\frac{1}{60}$ of the job done in one minute. Together, they would get: $\frac{1}{30} + \frac{1}{60} = \frac{2}{60} + \frac{1}{60} = \frac{3}{60} = \frac{1}{20}$ of the job done in one minute. Therefore, 20 minutes would be needed to pot 100 plants, and 40 minutes to pot all 200 plants.

17. b. Francine has read $\frac{4}{5}$ of 350 pages, or $0.8 \times 350 = 280$. Lydia has read half of that, or 140. Lydia has read 140 pages out of 350, or $\frac{140}{350}$. Reduce to $\frac{2}{5}$.

18. d. This is a two-step problem involving multiplication and subtraction. First, determine the amount of sand contained in the 4 trucks. $\frac{3}{4} \times \frac{4}{1} = \frac{12}{4}$. Next, reduce: $\frac{12}{4} = 3$. Finally, subtract: $3 - 2\frac{5}{6} = \frac{1}{6}$. There is $\frac{1}{6}$ ton more than is needed.

19. c. Semimonthly means twice a month. This means she makes $2 \times \$1,200 = \$2,400$ per month. Multiply by 12 months per year: $12 \frac{\text{months}}{\text{year}} \times \frac{\$2,400}{\text{month}} = \$28,800$ a year.

20. c. If he typically earns $800 a week, he makes $\$800 \div 40$ hours $= \$20$ per hour. This means he will make $1.5 \times 20 = \$30$ for each overtime hour. 10 hours $\times \frac{\$30}{\text{hour}} = \$300$.

21. c. First, add up all the hours he worked: $8 + 5 + 4\frac{1}{2} = 17\frac{1}{2}$ hours. Next, multiply the number of hours he worked by his hourly wage: 17.5 hours $\times \frac{\$22}{\text{hour}} = \$385$.

22. a. Subtract all of the listed deductions and the diversion to yield the net paycheck: $\$2,300 - \$160.45 - \$82.50 - \$73.25 - \$100 = \$1,883.80$.

23. b. They can load 1 truck in the first 4 hours and $\frac{1}{2}$ a truck in the next 2 hours, so they can load $1\frac{1}{2}$ trucks in 6 hours.

24. d. First, if one machine assembles 400 parts in a half hour, it will assemble 800 parts in an hour. Two machines working together will assemble $2 \times 800 = 1,600$ parts per hour. In 5 hours, they will make $5 \times 1,600 = 8,000$ parts. Of these 8,000 parts, 5%, will be defective, so 95% will be nondefective. 95% of 8,000 $= 95\% \times 8,000 = 0.95 \times 8,000 = 7,600$.

25. d. A daily salary is *per day*. She makes $120 per day times 24 days: $\$120 \times 24 = \$2,880$.

26. d. First, add up all of his merchandise sales: $\$825 + \$980 + \$600 = \$2,405$. Next, take 8% of the $2,405: $0.08 \times \$2,405 = \$192.40$. Add the $192.40 commission to his 3 months of pay: $\$192.40 + (3)(\$1,600) = \$192.40 + \$4,800 = \$4,992.40$.

27. b. If 4 machines can complete the job in 6 hours, it will take 1 machine 4 times as long or 24 hours. It would take 3 machines $\frac{1}{3}$ of 24 hrs $= \frac{1}{3} \times 24 = 8$ hours.

28. d. If 16 workers take 10 days to complete a job, 1 worker would take 16 times that amount, or 160 days. It would take 8 workers $160 \div 8 = 20$ days. Also, notice that if the amount of workers is halved, the amount of time will be doubled.

29. a. It would take 1 worker $6 \times 18 = 108$ days. It would take 9 workers $108 \div 9 = 12$ days.

30. c. It would take 1 person $9 \times 12 = 108$ days to complete the job. It would take 36 people 3 days to complete the same job because $108 \div 3 = 36$.

31. c. Anthony can complete $\frac{1}{8}$ of the task in 1 hour. You know this because he completes the entire task in 8 hours. Together, Anthony and Elise complete $\frac{1}{3}$ of the task in 1 hour. (Thus, they are done in 3 hours). Convert both fractions into twenty-fourths. $\frac{8}{24}$ per hour (both) $- \frac{3}{24}$ per hour (just Anthony) $= \frac{5}{24}$ per hour (just Elise). Thus, Elise completes $\frac{5}{24}$ of the task per hour. It will take her $2\frac{4}{5}$ hours to complete the entire task. $\frac{24}{5} = 4\frac{4}{5}$ hours.

32. d. 40 hours of work + 60 hours of work = 100 total hours. Therefore, when considering the percent of work each did, it would be fair to give Rose 40% of the money and Marie 60% of the money. Marie gets 60% of $2,000, or $60\% \times \$2,000 = 0.60 \times \$2,000 = \$1,200$. Alternatively, when combining their efforts, Marie and Rose earned a total of $2,000 for

100 hours of work. This is a rate of $20 per hour. Since Marie worked 60 hours, she gets $60 \text{ hrs} \times \frac{\$20}{\text{hr}} = \$1,200$.

33. c. The ratio of time spent is 18:24, which reduces to 3:4. Use this 3 to 4 ratio in the algebraic equation $3x + 4x = 7x$, where $3x$ is the amount of money Alison gets, $4x$ is the amount of money Artie gets, and $7x$ is the total amount of money (which you know is $7,000). Thus, if $7x$ = $7,000, x = $1,000. Artie's share equals $4x$ or $(4)(\$1,000) = \$4,000$. Alternatively, you can calculate the fractional part of the job that each one worked and then use that fraction to calculate each person's share of the contracted amount. Alison worked 18 hours and Artie worked 24 hours. The combined work time is $18 + 24 = 42$ hours. This means the fractional part of the job for Alison and Artie equals $\frac{18}{42}$ and $\frac{24}{42}$, respectively. Thus, Artie gets $\frac{24}{42}$ of the total $7,000. $\frac{24}{42}$ reduces to $\frac{4}{7}$; $\frac{4}{7}$ of $7,000 = $4,000, choice **c.**

34. b. Tina gets paid $400 semiweekly (2 times a week) so she gets $800 per week. Multiply this weekly amount by the 4 weeks per month: $800 per week $\times$ 4 weeks per month = $3,200 per month. Jim gets paid $1,800 twice a month (semimonthly), so he gets $3,600 per month. This means Jim makes $400 more per month than Tina does.

35. c. Ethan can type 110 reports in 6 hours, so he must type 55 reports in 3 hours. If Kayla types 60 reports and Ethan types 55 reports in 3 hours, the total number equals 115 reports. Now, compare this value with the 375 reports in the question. If they type 115 reports together in 3 hours, $\frac{115}{3} = \frac{375}{x \text{ hours}}$; $\frac{115x}{115} = \frac{3 \times 375}{115}$ and $x = 9.78$

36. c. The person works a 30-hour work week for 52 weeks per year. 30 hours per week $\times$ 52

weeks per year = 1,560 hours. Next, divide the total amount of money by the total amount of hours: $28,000 $\div$ 1,560 = $17.95 per hour.

37. a. Use sixteenths when considering the situation. This means $\frac{1}{16}$ is coming in as $\frac{1}{8} = \frac{2}{16}$ is going out. So every minute the net loss of fluid is $\frac{2}{16} - \frac{1}{16} = \frac{1}{16}$ per minute loss. Since the tank starts out $\frac{1}{2}$ full, it is $\frac{8}{16}$ full. If $\frac{1}{16}$ drains per minute, it will take 8 minutes for the $\frac{8}{16}$ to drain.

38. b. Pipe T fills $\frac{1}{6}$ of the tank every minute. Pipe V empties $\frac{1}{4}$ of the tank per minute. This means the net effect every minute is $\frac{1}{4} - \frac{1}{6} = \frac{3}{12} - \frac{2}{12} = \frac{1}{12}$ of the tank is drained. If $\frac{1}{4}$ of the tank is initially full, this equals $\frac{3}{12}$ full. It will take 3 minutes for these $\frac{3}{12}$ to drain out at a rate of $\frac{1}{12}$ per minute.

39. b. 10,000 liters = 10^4 liters. Since 10^6 liters = 100 times 10^4, the number of grams of pollutant that is removed is 100 times 0.7, or 70.

40. b. $\frac{1}{3}$ gallon is lost per day over the course of a week, or 7 days. So you multiply: $\frac{1}{3}$ gal per day $\times$ 7 days = $\frac{7}{3}$ gal, or $2\frac{1}{3}$ gallons are lost. Notice that it doesn't matter that the tank holds 14 gallons because the amount lost doesn't come close to 14.

41. b. Pipe A fills $\frac{1}{10}$ of the tank every minute. Pipe B empties $\frac{1}{8}$ of the tank per minute. This means the net effect every minute is $\frac{1}{8} - \frac{1}{10} = \frac{5}{40} - \frac{4}{40} = \frac{1}{40}$ of the tank is drained. If $\frac{1}{2}$ of the tank is initially full, this equals $\frac{20}{40}$ full. It will take 20 minutes for the $\frac{20}{40}$ to drain out at a rate of $\frac{1}{40}$ per minute.

42. a. Use the constant rate equation: $D = RT$. Here D = 60 kilometers $\times$ 3 hours = 180 kilometers.

43. c. 1 kilometer = 1,000 meters. Use $D = RT$ with D =1,000, $R = \frac{2.5 \text{ meters}}{\text{second}}$, and T as the unknown. Rearrange $D = RT$ to $T = \frac{D}{R} = \frac{1,000}{2.5}$ = 400 seconds.

44. d. Rearrange $D = RT$ into $R = \frac{D}{T}$. Substitute in the given values: $R = 20$ minutes $= \frac{1}{3}$ hour, $D = 2$ miles into $R = \frac{D}{T}$ and R = 2 miles $\div \frac{1}{3}$ hr = 6 miles per hour.

45. b. Sipora's speed on the way *to* Stephanie's house is irrelevant. To find the speed of her return trip, rearrange $D = RT$ to $R = D \div T = 220 \div 4 = 55$ miles per hour.

46. c. Rearrange $D = RT$ into $R = D \div T$. Amy's rate is $R = 8$ miles $\div 40$ minutes $= 0.2$ miles per minute. Next, calculate Sharon's rate in the same units of miles per minute. This means you need to convert the 1 hour into 60 minutes. Sharon's rate is then $R = 12$ miles $\div 60$ minutes $= 0.2$ miles per minute.

47. b. First, convert minutes to hours: 20 minutes $= \frac{1}{3}$ hour and 30 minutes $= \frac{1}{2}$ hour. Next, calculate the two distances by using $D = RT$. Train A will travel $D = 60 \times \frac{1}{3} = 20$ miles. Train B will travel $D = 55 \times \frac{1}{2} = 27.5$ miles. Thus, Train B travels the greater distance.

48. c. The first train will travel $D = RT = 60 \times 1 = 60$ miles west. The second train will travel $D = RT = 70 \times 1 = 70$ miles east. Thus, if the initial distance between the 2 trains was 700 miles, now the distance is 700 miles $- 60$ miles $- 70$ miles $= 700 - 130 = 570$ miles.

49. c. The total distance covered is equal to the distance that both trains travel. Train A travels east a total of $D = RT = 70 \times 2 = 140$ miles. Train B travels west a total of $D = RT = 90 \times 2 = 180$ miles. Note that $T = 2$ because the trains pass each other after 2 hours. Thus, the total initial distance is 140 miles + 180 miles = 320 miles.

50. d. The total distance will be equal to the distances traveled by both trains throughout the unknown amount of time (T).

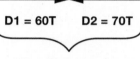

Penn Station SB Station

Train 1   Train 2

D1 = 60T   D2 = 70T

initial distance apart
= 260 miles
= 60T + 70T

initial distance apart = 260 miles
$= 60T + 70T$

Thus, $260 = 60T + 70T = 130T$, and $T = 2$. The trains will pass each other after two hours, so the time will be 6:00 P.M., choice **d.**

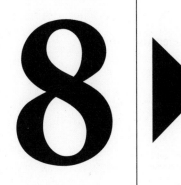

Charts, Tables, and Graphs

When you pick up the newspaper or watch a news report on TV, you'll often see information presented in a graph. More and more, you give and receive information visually. That's one reason you're likely to find graphs on the civil service exam, and a good reason to understand how to read them. This chapter reviews the common kinds of graphs, charts, and tables you should be familiar with before exam day. You will also review mean, median, mode, and probability—math concepts that are frequently used in chart, table, or graph questions.

▶ Pie Charts

Pie charts show how the parts of a whole relate to one another. A pie chart is a circle divided into slices or wedges. Each slice represents a category. Pie charts are sometimes called circle graphs. Let's look at an example of a pie chart and see what kind of information it provides.

Example: The following pie chart represents data collected from a recent telephone survey.

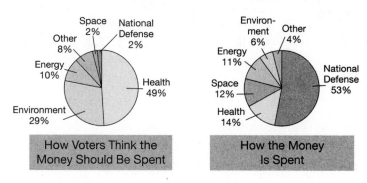

How Federal Dollars Are Spent

Using the "How Federal Dollars Are Spent" pie chart, answer the following questions.

1. Based on the survey, which category of spending best matches the voters' wishes?
2. On which category of spending did the voters want most of the money spent?
3. Which category of spending receives the most federal dollars?
4. To which two categories of spending did voters want the most money to go? Which two categories of spending actually received the most money?

Explanations:

1. Energy: Voters say they would like about 10% of the budget spent on energy and about 11% is spent on energy.
2. Health.
3. National defense.
4. Voters wanted money to go to health and environment. Defense and health received the most money.

▶ Line Graphs

Line graphs show how two categories of data or information (sometimes called **variables**) relate to one another. The data is displayed on a grid and is presented on a scale using a horizontal and a vertical axis for the different categories of information compared on the graph. Usually, each data point is connected together to form a line so that you can see trends in the data and so that you can see how the data changes over time. Often you will see line graphs with *time* on the horizontal axis. Let's look at an example of a line graph and see the kind of information it can provide.

Example: Consider the following information:

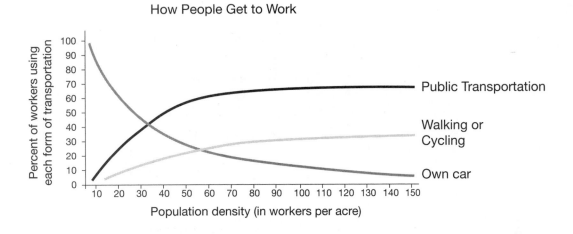

How People Get to Work

Using the "How People Get to Work" line graph, answer the following questions.

1. What variable is shown on the vertical axis? What variable is shown on the horizontal axis?
2. As the population density increases, will more or fewer people drive their own car to work?
3. At about what point in population density does the use of public transportation begin to level off?
4. Which form of transportation becomes less popular as population density increases?

Explanations:

1. Look at the labels. The percent of workers using each form of transportation is shown on the vertical axis. Population density is shown on the horizontal axis.
2. As population density increases, fewer people use their own cars to get to work.
3. At about 60 to 70 workers per acre, the percentage of workers using public transportation begins to level off.
4. Find the line that moves down as population density increases. It's the line labeled "Own car." This is the form of transportation that decreases as population density increases.

▶ Bar Graphs

Like pie charts, **bar graphs** show how different categories of data relate to one another. A bar represents each category. The length of the bar represents the relative frequency of the category, compared to the other categories on the graph. Let's look at an example of a bar graph and see the kind of information it can provide.

Example: The following bar graph compares the 2007 monthly rainfall in Cherokee County with the average monthly rainfall in Cherokee County from 2002–2006.

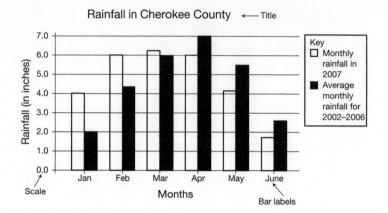

Using the "Rainfall in Cherokee County" bar graph, answer the following questions.

1. What does each bar represent? What is the difference between the shaded bars and the white bars?
2. During which months is the rainfall in 2007 greater than the average rainfall?
3. During which months is the rainfall in 2007 less than the average rainfall?
4. How many more inches of rain fell in April 2007 than in January 2007?
5. How many more inches of rain fell in January 2007 than on average during January 2002–2006?

Explanations:

1. Look at the labels and the key. Each bar represents the number of inches of rainfall during a particular month. From the key, you know that the shaded bars represent the average monthly rainfall for 2002–2006. The white bars represent the monthly rainfall in 2007.
2. Compare the white bars with the shaded bars. Rainfall in 2007 is greater than average during the months that the white bar is taller than the shaded bar for that month. Rainfall in 2007 was greater than the average rainfall during January, February, and March.
3. Compare the white bars with the shaded bars. Rainfall in 2007 is less than the average during the months that the shaded bar is taller than the white bar for that month. Rainfall in 2007 was less than the average rainfall during April, May, and June.
4. Compare the height of the white bars for January and April. In April, 6 inches of rain fell. In January, 4 inches of rain fell. Then subtract: 6 – 4 = 2. So, in April, 2 more inches of rain fell than in January.
5. Compare the height of the shaded bar and the white bar for January. The shaded bar represents 2 inches. The white bar represents 4 inches. Subtract: 4 – 2 = 2. So, two more inches of rain fell in January 2007 than on average during January 2002–2006.

▶ Getting Information from Tables

Tables present information in rows and columns. Rows go across, or horizontally. Columns go up and down, or vertically. The box, or cell, that is made where a row and a column meet provides specific information. When looking for information in tables, it's important to read the table title, the column headings, and the row labels so you understand all of the information. Let's look at some examples of tables and the types of information you might expect to learn from them.

Example:

THE FUJITA-PEARSON TORNADO INTENSITY SCALE		
CLASSIFICATION	WIND SPEED (IN MILES PER HOUR)	DAMAGE
F0	72	Mild
F1	73–112	Moderate
F2	113–157	Significant
F3	158–206	Severe
F4	207–260	Devastating
F5	261–319	Cataclysmic
F6	320–379	Overwhelming

Using the "Fujita-Pearson Tornado Intensity Scale" table, answer the following questions.

1. If a tornado has a wind speed of 173 miles per hour, how would it be classified?
2. What kind of damage would you expect from a tornado having a wind speed of 300 miles per hour?
3. What wind speed would you anticipate if a tornado of F6 were reported?

Explanations:

1. The wind speed for F3 tornados ranges from 158–206 miles per hour.
2. F5 tornados range in wind speed of 261–319 mph and are *cataclysmic.*
3. F6 tornados range from wind speeds of 320–379 miles per hour.

▶ Statistics and Probability

Statistics is a branch of mathematics that involves the study of data. Probability is the study of chance. At times, civil service exam questions will involve charts, tables, and graphs, as well as data and chance—specifically, mean, median, mode, and probability.

When dealing with sets of numbers, there are measures used to describe the set as a whole. These are for example, called measures of central tendency and they include mean, median and mode.

Mean is the average of a set of data. To calculate the mean of a set of data, add up all of the numbers in the set and divide by how many entries are in the set. If you are asked to find the mean of a set of numbers and the set is evenly spaced apart such as 2, 4, 6, 8, 10, 12, 14, the mean is the middle number in this set, because there is an odd number of data items. In this example, the mean is 8. If there is an even number of data items, there are two middle numbers: 4, 8, 12, 16, 20, and 24. In this case, the mean is the average of the two middle numbers. 12 + 16 = 28, and 28 divided by two is 14.

Median is the middle value in a set of numbers that are arranged in increasing or decreasing order. If there are two middle numbers, it is the average of these two. To calculate the median of a set of numbers, first arrange the data in increasing or decreasing order. Find the middle value in a set of an odd number of entries. The median is the mean of the two middle numbers in a set of an even number of entries.

Mode is the value in the set that occurs most often. There can be one mode, several modes, or no mode.

Probability is the likelihood that an event will occur. This event is called a *favorable outcome,* whether it is favorable to the situation or not. For example, find out the probability of rain in the forecast. If the probability of rain is 70%, then 70 out of 100 times it is expected to rain. The rain is considered a favorable outcome in this instance, even if rain is not desired. Probability of, an event is a ratio, expressed as a fraction, decimal, or percent that defines . The notation for the probability of an event is P(event).

In probability problems, you can assume that all outcomes occur at random, unless otherwise noted. If the events described concern dice, assume that the dice always lands "flat" on a number. If the events concern a spinner, assume that the spinner never lands on a dividing line. Also, keep in mind:

The probability of an impossible event is zero. P(impossible) = 0.

The probability of an event that is certain is one. P(event that is certain) = 1.

All probabilities are a number between zero and one. $0 \leq P(event) \leq 1$.

Because an event, E, will either occur or it will not occur, P(E) + P(not E) = 1.

▶ Practice Questions

Use the following chart to answer questions 1 through 5.

NAME	SCORE
Darin	95
Miguel	90
Anthony	82
Christopher	90
Samuel	88

1. What is the mean score of the people listed?
   a. 90
   b. 89
   c. 88
   d. 85

2. What is the median score of the people listed?
   a. 90
   b. 89
   c. 88
   d. 85

3. What is the range of the scores listed?
   a. 90
   b. 50
   c. 24
   d. 13

4. What is the mode of the scores listed?
   a. 90
   b. 89
   c. 88
   d. 85

5. If Anthony's score was incorrectly reported as an 82 when his actual score on the test was a 90, which of the following statements would be true when his actual score is used in the calculations?
   a. The mean, median, range, and mode will change.
   b. The mean, median, and range, will change; the mode will remain the same.
   c. Only the mean and median will change.
   d. None of the above will ocur.

6. The following chart gives the times of four swimmers in their race. Which swimmer had the fastest time?

SWIMMER	TIME (SEC)
Molly	38.51
Jeff	39.23
Asta	37.95
Risa	37.89

   a. Molly
   b. Jeff
   c. Asta
   d. Risa

Use the following information to answer questions 7 through 9.

The table lists the number of members present at the monthly meetings for the Environmental Protection Club.

MONTH	# OF MEMBERS
September	54
October	61
November	70
December	75

7. What was the average monthly attendance over the course of all the months listed?

   a. 71
   b. 65
   c. 61
   d. 56

8. What was the median number of members attending during the course of the four months shown?

   a. 54
   b. 61
   c. 65.5
   d. 70

9. If the data presented in the table were plotted as a bar graph, which of the following represents the data most accurately?

a.

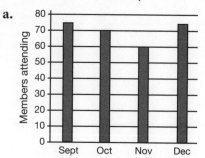

b.

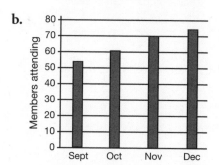

c.

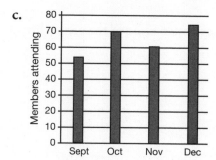

d.

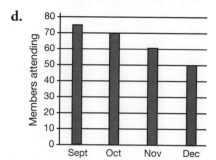

Use the following information to answer questions 10 through 12.

The pie chart shows the Johnson family's monthly budget.

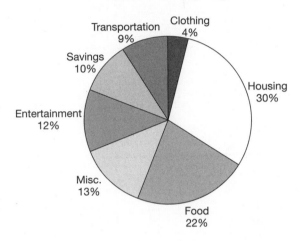

Johnson Family Budget

10. In percent of overall expenses, how much more money is spent on food than on transportation and clothing combined?

a. 9%

b. 11%

c. 13%

d. 22%

11. If the Johnson family budget is $4,000 per month, how much money is spent on housing each month?

a. $800

b. $1,000

c. $1,200

d. $1,400

12. If the Johnson family budget is $4,000 per month, how much money will they save each year?

a. $48,000

b. $4,800

c. $400

d. none of the above

Use the following information to answer questions 13 through 16.

This graph shows the yearly electricity usage for Finnigan Engineering, Inc. over the course of three years for three departments.

13. The electricity cost for Sales during the year 2004 was how much greater than the electricity cost for Customer Service in 2005?

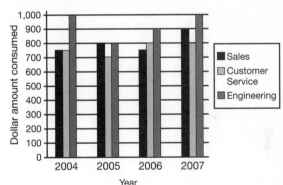

a. $200

b. $150

c. $100

d. $50

14. Which of the following statements is supported by the data?

    a. The Sales Department showed a steady increase in the dollar amount of electricity used during the four-year period.

    b. The Customer Service Department showed a steady increase in the dollar amount of electricity used during the 4-year period.

    c. The Engineering Department showed a steady increase in the dollar amount of electricity used from 2005–2007.

    d. none of the above

15. What was the percent decrease in electricity usage (in dollar amount) from 2004 to 2005 for the Engineering Department?

    a. 25%

    b. 20%

    c. 15%

    d. 10%

16. If the information in the bar graph associated with question 13 is transcribed and a line graph is generated, which of the following line graphs is correct?

a.
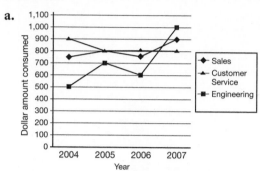

b.
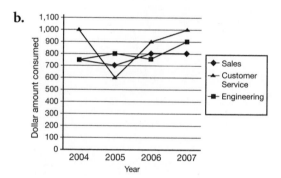

c.
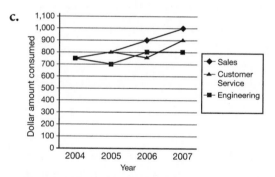

d.
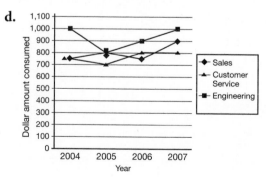

Use the following information to answer questions 17–19.

The table shows the numbers of male and female students involved in several school activities.

ACTIVITY	MALE	FEMALE
Drama	11	13
Journalism	12	10
Science Club	9	11
Debate	12	15

17. Which activity has the lowest ratio of males to females?
   a. Drama
   b. Journalism
   c. Science Club
   d. Debate

18. For all of the students listed, what percent of the students is involved in Debate?
   a. 15%
   b. 20%
   c. 27%
   d. 29%

19. If 3 more males and 4 more females join the Science Club, what percent of the students will be in this club?
   a. 15%
   b. 20%
   c. 27%
   d. 29%

Use the following chart to answer questions 20 through 23.

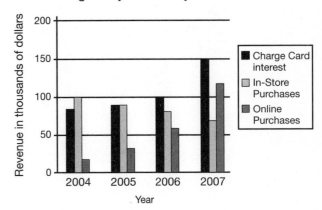

Montgomery Inc. Yearly Profits

20. Based on the chart, which answer choice represents a true statement?
   a. Online Purchases have increased, whereas Charge Card Interest has decreased, over the course of the four years shown.
   b. Charge Card Interest has increased, whereas Online Purchases have decreased, over the course of the four years shown.
   c. In-Store Purchases have increased, whereas Charge Card Purchases have decreased, over the course of the four years shown.
   d. Online Purchases have increased, whereas In-Store Purchases have decreased, over the course of the four years shown.

21. If all of the information on the bar graph was converted into a table, which of the following tables correctly displays the data (with revenue in thousands of dollars)?

a.

	2004	2005	2006	2007
Charge Card Interest	$80	$90	$100	$150
In-Store Purchases	$80	$90	$80	$70
Online Purchases	$15	$60	$30	$120

b.

	2004	2005	2006	2007
Charge Card Interest	$80	$90	$100	$120
In-Store Purchases	$80	$80	$80	$70
Online Purchases	$15	$60	$60	$120

c.

	2004	2005	2006	2007
Charge Card Interest	$80	$90	$100	$150
In-Store Purchases	$100	$90	$80	$70
Online Purchases	$15	$30	$60	$120

d.

	2004	2005	2006	2007
Charge Card Interest	$80	$90	$100	$150
In-Store Purchases	$90	$80	$80	$70
Online Purchases	$15	$30	$60	$120

22. The Online Purchases in 2004 were what fraction of the Charge Card Interest in 2007?
a. $\frac{1}{5}$
b. $\frac{1}{10}$
c. $\frac{1}{4}$
d. $\frac{1}{2}$

23. In-Store Purchases in 2004 made how much more than In-Store Purchases in 2007?
a. $30
b. $60
c. $6,000
d. $30,000

Use the following information to answer questions 24 through 26.

The line graph shows earnings for the three divisions of Steinberg Lumber Company throughout the four quarters in 2007.

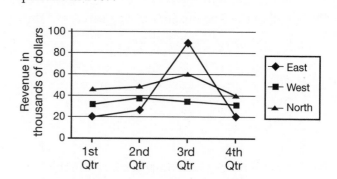

24. Which of the following statements is true?
a. The East Division consistently brought in more revenue than the other 2 divisions.
b. The North Division consistently brought in more revenue than the West Division.
c. The West Division consistently out performed the East Division.
d. Both **b** and **c** are true.

25. What is the percent decrease in revenue for the North Division when analyzing dollar amounts from the 3rd and 4th quarters?

a. $33\frac{1}{3}\%$

b. 40%

c. 50%

d. 60%

26. During the year 2007, Steinberg Lumber secured a major contract with a developer in Canada. The East and North Divisions both supplied lumber for this project. Which of the following statements seems to be supported by the data?

a. The West Division was angry that the other two divisions supplied the lumber for this contract.

b. The next big contract will be covered by the West Division.

c. The contract with the Canadian developer was secured in the third quarter.

d. The contract with the Canadian developer was secured in the fourth quarter.

Use the following information to answer questions 27 through 29.

The pie chart shows the percentage of employees in the various departments of Amelia Computer Consultants, Inc.

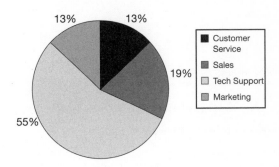

27. Which two departments account for 32% of the employees?

a. Marketing and Tech Support

b. Customer Service and Sales

c. Sales and Tech Support

d. Marketing and Customer Service

28. If the total number of employees is 400, how many employees are in the Tech Support department?

a. 52

b. 76

c. 110

d. 220

29. Suppose that the Customer Service department is expanded by adding 12 new employees. Which of the following statements would be true?

a. Customer Service and Marketing have the same number of employees.

b. The percent of employees in Marketing is now 11%.

c. The percent of employees in sales is now 20%.

d. The percent of employees in Tech Support is now 53%, while the percent of employees in Customer Service is 16%.

30. The chart shows the composition by percent of the human body with respect to various elements.

ELEMENT	PERCENT BY WEIGHT
Carbon	18%
Hydrogen	10%
Oxygen	65%
Other Elements	7%

For a man weighing 260 pounds, how much does the carbon in his body weigh?

a. 46.8 pounds

b. 48.6 pounds

c. 52.4 pounds

d. 54.2 pounds

31. The following chart shows the cost for different categories of UTP cabling. If Athena's office needs to buy 100 feet of UTP cable that can send data at a speed of 75 megabits per second, about how much will she spend?

CATEGORY	CHARACTERISTICS	PRICE PER FOOT
Category 1	Does not support data transmission	$ 0.75
Category 2	Supports data transmission speeds up to 4 megabits per second	$ 1.00
Category 3	Supports data transmission speeds up to 16 megabits per second	$ 1.75
Category 4	Supports data transmission speeds up to 20 megabits per second	$ 2.50
Category 5	Supports data transmission speeds up to 100 megabits per second	$ 3.00

a. $3.00

b. $250

c. $275

d. $300

32. During the year 2007 at Deluxe Vacuum Co., the East and West divisions had equal sales and the North sold the most. Which graph could be the graph of Deluxe's yearly sales for 2007?

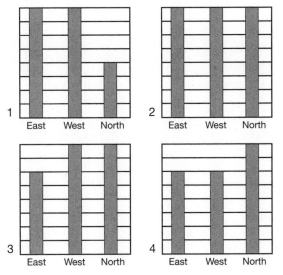

a. 1

b. 2

c. 3

d. 4

Use the following information to answer questions 33 and 34.

Swimming Pool World pledged to donate 3.2% of their sales during the second week of May to the Children's Hospital. Here is their sales chart for May.

MAY SALES	
Week 1	$5,895
Week 2	$73,021
Week 3	$54,702
Week 4	$67,891

33. How much did Swimming Pool World donate to the Children's Hospital?

a. $2,336.67

b. $3,651.05

c. $23,366.72

d. $36,510.50

34. If Swimming Pool World had pledged 1% of sales for the entire month of May, how much would they have donated?

a. about $300 more

b. about $300 less

c. about $500 more

d. about $500 less

35. The following chart shows registration for art classes for Fall 2007.

STUDENTS REGISTERING FOR ART CLASSES	
COURSE	**NUMBER OF STUDENTS**
Stained Glass	21
Beginning Drawing	48
Sculpture	13
Watercolors	18
TOTAL	100

If this is a representative sampling, how many out of 500 students would be expected to choose Stained Glass for their art course?

a. 21

b. 92

c. 105

d. 210

Use the following information to answer questions 36 through 37.

The table shows the rainfall, in inches, over a 5-day period in August for Hilo, Hawaii. It also includes the total rainfall for the year and the average rainfall for a typical year.

	RAINFALL	YEAR	NORMAL
Monday	0.08	90.88	79.15
Tuesday	0.09	90.97	79.16
Wednesday	0.70	91.67	79.17
Thursday	0.19	91.86	79.17
Friday	0.32	92.18	79.50

36. Find the average rainfall for the 5-day period in August.
   a. 1.38 inches
   b. 0.276 inches
   c. 0.32 inches
   d. 0.237 inches

37. Using Monday's reading and rounding off to the nearest whole percent, the year-to-date record is what percent of the normal reading?
   a. 13%
   b. 15%
   c. 87%
   d. 115%

Use the following information to answer questions 38 through 40.

The chart shows the colors of replacement parts for pocket PCs. The total number of parts shipped is 1,650.

BOXED SET OF REPLACEMENT PARTS	
PART COLOR	NUMBER OF PIECES
Green	430
Red	425
Blue	
Yellow	345
TOTAL	1,650

38. If a person randomly grabbed a part out of the box, what is the probability that the part would be blue?
   a. $\frac{1}{4}$
   b. $\frac{1}{9}$
   c. $\frac{1}{12}$
   d. $\frac{3}{11}$

39. Approximately what percent of the total shipment is red?
   a. 18%
   b. 20%
   c. 26%
   d. 30%

40. If the following chart shows the number of replacement parts that were found to be defective, what percent of the new parts is defective?

BOXED SET OF REPLACEMENT PARTS	
PART COLOR	**NUMBER OF DEFECTIVE PIECES**
Green	14
Red	10
Blue	8
Yellow	12

a. $22\frac{1}{3}\%$

b. 18%

c. $8\frac{1}{2}\%$

d. $2\frac{2}{3}\%$

Use the following information to answer questions 41 through 43.

The table lists the size of building lots in the Orange Grove subdivision and the people who are planning to build on those lots. For each lot, installation of utilities costs $12,516. The city charges impact fees of $3,879 per lot. There are also development fees of 16.15 cents per square foot of land.

LOT	AREA (SQ. FT.)	BUILDER
A	8,023	Ira Taylor
B	6,699	Alexis Funes
C	9,004	Ira Taylor
D	8,900	Mark Smith
E	8,301	Alexis Funes
F	8,269	Ira Taylor
G	6,774	Ira Taylor

41. The area of the smallest lot listed is approximately what percent of the area of the largest lot listed?

a. 25%

b. 50%

c. 75%

d. 85%

42. How much land does Mr. Taylor own in the Orange Grove subdivision?

a. 23,066 sq. ft

b. 29,765 sq. ft

c. 31,950 sq. ft

d. 32,070 sq. ft

43. How much will Mr. Smith pay in development fees for his lot?

a. $1,157.00

b. $1,437.35

c. $143,735

d. $274,550

44. Felipe is planning to get wireless Internet service at his house. Two service providers, A and B, offer different rates as shown in the table below. If Felipe plans on using 25 hours of Internet service per month, which of the following statements is true?

INTERNET SERVICE RATES			
PROVIDER	**FREE HOURS**	**BASE CHARGE**	**HOURLY CHARGE**
A	17.5	$20.00	$1.00
B	20	$20.00	$1.50

a. Provider A will be cheaper.

b. Provider B will be cheaper.

c. The providers will cost the same per month.

d. The answer cannot be determined from the information given.

45. Refer to the following table to answer this question. If you take recyclables to the recycler who will pay the most, what is the most money you could get for 2,200 pounds of aluminum, 1,400 pounds of cardboard, 3,100 pounds of glass, and 900 pounds of plastic?

RECYCLER	ALUMINUM	CARDBOARD	GLASS	PLASTIC
X	$.06/ pound	$.03/ pound	$.07/ pound	$.02/ pound
Y	$.07/ pound	$.04/ pound	$.08/ pound	$.03/ pound

a. $409
b. $440
c. $447
d. $485

46. Which of the following brands is the least expensive per ounce?

BRAND	PRICE ($)	WEIGHT (OZ.)
W	0.21	6
X	0.48	15
Y	0.56	20
Z	0.96	32

a. W
b. X
c. Y
d. Z

Use the following information to answer questions 47 through 50.

When an earthquake occurs, some of the energy released travels through the ground as waves. Two general types of waves are generated. One type is called the P wave, and the other is called the S wave. A graph can be made of the travel times of these waves.

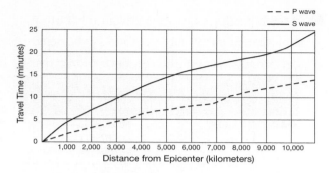

47. How many minutes does it take the S wave to travel 5,500 kilometers?
a. 15 minutes
b. 20 minutes
c. 25 minutes
d. 30 minutes

48. Approximately how many minutes does it take a P wave to travel 8,000 km?
a. 6 minutes
b. 12 minutes
c. 3 minutes
d. 15 minutes

49. An earthquake occurs at noon, and the recording station receives the S wave at 12:04 P.M. How far away is the earthquake?
a. 1,000 kilometers
b. 2,000 kilometers
c. 3,000 kilometers
d. 4,000 kilometers

50. How far away is an earthquake if the difference in arrival time between the P and S waves is 5 minutes?
a. 1,000 kilometers
b. 3,000 kilometers
c. 4,000 kilometers
d. 7,000 kilometers

▶ Answers

1. b. The formula for calculating the mean (average) is:

Mean = $\frac{\text{sum of all values}}{\text{\# of values}}$

The sum of all the values given is: $95 + 90 + 82 + 90 + 88 = 445$. The number of values (scores) is 5. Thus, the mean $= \frac{445}{5} = 89$.

2. a. First, list all of the scores in order: 82, 88, 90, 90, 95. The middle score will be the median, thus 90 is the median.

3. d. The range is calculated by subtracting the lowest score from the highest score. Thus, the range is $95 - 82 = 13$.

4. a. The mode is the score that occurs the most. Here, there are two 90s, thus 90 is the mode.

5. d. Calculate the new median, mode, and range and compare them to the original values. To find the new mean, first add all the scores: $95 + 90 + 90 + 90 + 88 = 453$, and then divide by 5: $453 \div 5 = 90.6$. Next, you can calculate the median and see if it is different: 88, 90, 90, 90, 95. Here you see that the median is the same as it was before, 90. The mode is still 90 because 90 is the score that occurs the most. The range is now $95 - 88 = 7$. Thus, choice **d** is the correct answer.

6. d. The fastest swimmer will have the quickest time. 37.89 is the fastest. Thus, Risa is the fastest swimmer.

7. b. The formula for calculating the mean (average) is:

Mean = $\frac{\text{sum of all values}}{\text{\# of values}}$

The sum of all the values given is: $54 + 61 + 70 + 75 = 260$. The number of values is 4. Thus, the mean $= 260 \div 4 = 65$.

8. c. List all of the values in order: 54, 61, 70, 75. Here, there is an even number of values, so you average the middle 2 numbers. The average of 61 and 70 is $\frac{131}{2} = 65.5$.

9. b. The number of members attending for the four months was: 54, 61, 70, 75, for September, October, November, and December, respectively. This is accurately displayed in choice **b**. Note that choice **b** is also the only choice that depicts the ascending trend. That is to say, the number of members in attendance increases over time.

10. a. 22% is spent on food. When you combine transportation (9%) and clothing (4%), the sum is 13%. Thus, the amount spent on food is $22\% - 13\% = 9\%$ greater.

11. c. Housing is 30% of the monthly budget. 30% of $4,000 is calculated by multiplying: $30\% \times \$4,000 = 0.30 \times \$4,000 = \$1,200$.

12. b. They save 10% of $4,000 each month: $0.10 \times \$4,000 = \$400$. Over the course of a year they will save $400 per month $\times$ 12 months $= \$4,800$.

13. d. The Sales Dept (black bar) spent $750 on electricity in 2004. The Customer Service Dept (lightest bar) spent $700 on electricity in 2005. Thus, the Sales Dept spent $750 - \$700 = \$50$ more.

14. c. The usage for the Engineering Department increases by $100 each year from 2005 through 2007. None of the other statements are supported by the data. Claims of steady increase over the course of four years would be represented as four bars, each with a greater height than the previous one.

15. b. The difference in dollar amounts used is $1,000 - \$800 = 200$. When compared with the original $1,000 consumed, this can be expressed as a percent by equating $\frac{200}{1,000} = \frac{x}{100}$. Thus, $x = 20\%$.

16. d. The line graph in choice **d** accurately displays the data that is obtained from the bar graph.

17. d. The M:F (male to female) ratios are as follows:

Drama: $\frac{11}{13} \approx 0.85$

Journalism: $\frac{12}{10} = 1.2$

Science Club $\frac{9}{11} \approx 0.82$

Debate $\frac{12}{15} = 0.8$

Here, 0.8 is the least value, so a $\frac{12}{15}$ ratio is the smallest M:F ratio listed.

18. d. This question is solved by adding a column and row labeled "Total" onto the side and bottom of the given chart:

ACTIVITY	MALE	FEMALE	TOTAL
Drama	11	13	24
Journalism	12	10	22
Science Club	9	11	20
Debate	12	15	27
TOTAL			93

Now you can see that 27 students out of the 93 total are involved in Debate. $\frac{27}{93} \approx 0.29$. To write these values as a percent, move the decimal point two places to the right and add the percent symbol: 29%.

19. c. Using the new information, our chart becomes:

ACTIVITY	MALE	FEMALE	TOTAL
Drama	11	13	24
Journalism	12	10	22
Science Club	12	15	27
Debate	12	15	27
TOTAL			100

This means that 27 out of 100 students are now in the Science Club. $\frac{27}{100} = 27\%$.

20. d. The black bars (Charge Card) increase from year to year. The lightest bars (In-Store Purchases) decrease from year to year. The gray bars (Online Purchases) increase from year to year. Thus, only choice **d** is correct.

21. c. The black bars (Charge Card) increase from 80 to 90 to 100 to 150. The lightest bars (In-Store Purchases) decrease from 100 to 90 to 80 to 70. The gray bars (Online Purchases) increase from 15 to 30 to 60 to 120. Only choice **c** presents this data correctly.

22. b. In 2004, Online Purchases were at $15,000. In 2007, Chard Card Interest totaled $150,000. Since 15 is $\frac{1}{10}$ of 150, the answer is $\frac{1}{10}$, choice **b.**

23. d. Note that all dollar amounts in the chart are expressed as "Revenue in thousands of dollars." In 2004, the In-Store Purchases were at $100,000. In 2007, the amount is $70,000. Thus, the difference is $30,000. Thus, choice **d,** $30,000, is correct.

24. b. Looking at the graph, you see that the line for *North* (the line with triangular points) is always higher than the line for *West* (the line with the square points). All other statements are not supported by the data in the graph. Thus, only choice **b** is true.

25. a. Here the revenue in thousand of dollars decreases from 60 to 40. Thus, the difference is 20. As compared with the original 60, this represents $\frac{20}{60} = 0.333\ldots$ To express this as a percent, just move the decimal point 2 places to the right: $0.3333 \rightarrow 33\frac{1}{3}\%$.

26. c. Since you are told that this was a "major" contract, the statement best supported by the data is choice **c:** "The contract with the Canadian developer was secured in the third quarter." The data supports this statement because both the East and North Divisions had a significant revenue increase during the third quarter, which might be indicative of having a large contract for that quarter.

27. b. Customer Service (black) accounts are 13% of the total, and Sales (dark gray) accounts are 19% of the total. Together these add to 32%. Since both Marketing and Customer Service are at 13%, either department could be combined with Sales to total 32% of the company employees. Note that only Customer Service and Sales are listed as a choice.

28. d. Tech Support (the lightest) is 55% of the total. 55% of 400 equals $55\% \times 400 = 0.55 \times 400 = 220$. You can save time when answering a question like this by noticing that 55% will be slightly more than $\frac{1}{2}$ the total of 400, so slightly more that 200. Only choice **d** is correct.

29. d. Before the addition of the 12 new customer service representatives, the number of employees in each department was as follows:
Customer Service: $0.13 \times 400 = 52$
Marketing: $0.13 \times 400 = 52$
Sales: $0.19 \times 400 = 76$
Tech Support: $0.55 \times 400 = 220$
The new total is $400 + 12 = 412$. The new number of customer service employees is $52 + 12 = 64$. The percentages are as follows:
Customer Service: $\frac{64}{412} \approx 0.15534 \approx 15.5\ \% \approx 16\%$
Marketing: $\frac{52}{412} \approx 0.12621 \approx 12.6\% \approx 13\%$
Sales: $\frac{76}{412} \approx 0.18447 \approx 18.4\% \approx 18\%$
Tech Support: $\frac{200}{412} \approx 0.53398 \approx 53.4\% \approx 53\%$
Thus, the only choice that would be true is choice **d**.

30. a. Carbon accounts for 18% of body weight. 18% of $260 = 0.18 \times 260 = 46.8$ pounds.

31. d. Since she needs to support a speed of 75 megabits per second, only Category 5 UTP cable can be used. Note that Category 5 "Sup-

ports data transmission speeds up to 100 megabits per second." This cable costs $3 per foot, so 100 feet will cost $100 \times \$3.00 = \$300$.

32. d. The East and West divisions had equal sales, so you need a graph where the bars for East and West are the same height. North sold the most, so you need a graph that also shows North as having the largest bar in the graph. Graph 4 shows this situation. Thus, choice **d** is correct.

33. a. During Week 2, they made $73,021. To find 3.2% of this amount, multiply by 0.032: $0.032 \times \$73,021 = \$2,336.672$. Rounded to the nearest cent, the answer is $2,336.67.

34. b. First, calculate the total by adding up all the dollar amounts:
$5,895
$73,021
$54,702
+ $67,891
$201,509
Next, take 1% of the total by multiplying by 0.01; $0.01 \times \$201,509 = \$2,015.09$. This is about $300 less than the $2,336.67 that they actually donated.

35. c. Since the sampling is representative, this means that the same trend will be seen when a larger sample is considered. Thus, multiply by 5 to see how many students out of 500 will choose stained glass. $5 \times 21 = 105$.

36. b. Add up the values for the 5 days shown: $0.08 + 0.09 + 0.70 + 0.19 + 0.32 = 1.38$. Divide this amount by 5 to get the average: $1.38 \div 5 = 0.276$ inches.

37. d. On Monday, the year to date is 90.88 inches. The normal amount is 79.15. Thus, the year-to-date value is above 100% of the normal value, making choice **d** the only possible correct answer. (Note that $\frac{90.18}{79.15} \approx 1.1482 \approx 114.82\% \approx 15\%$.)

38. **d.** $430 + 425 + 345 = 1,200$ parts are accounted for. Since the total is $1,650$; $1,650 - 1,200 = 450$ blue parts. When randomly picking a part, the chance of getting blue is 450 out of $1,650 = \frac{450}{1,650}$. Simplify the expression: $\frac{450}{1,650} \div \frac{150}{150} = \frac{3}{11}$.

39. **c.** 425 out of 1,650 is red. $\frac{450}{1,650} = 425 \div 1,650 = 0.25757$. To convert to a percent, move the decimal point two places to the right and add the percent symbol: $25.7575\ldots\% \approx 26\%$.

40. **d.** Add a row for the total at the bottom of the given chart:

BOXED SET OF REPLACEMENT PART	
PART COLOR	**NUMBER OF DEFECTIVE PIECES**
Green	14
Red	10
Blue	8
Yellow	12
TOTAL defective	44

44 parts out of 1,650 are defective. $\frac{44}{1,650} = 0.02666$. To express this as a percent, move the decimal point two places to the right and add the percent symbol: $2.66666\ldots\%$. This equals $2\frac{2}{3}\%$.

41. **c.** The smallest lot is 6,699 square feet and the largest lot is 9,004 square feet. 6,699 out of $9,004 = \frac{6,699}{9,004} \approx 0.74400 \approx 74.40\% \approx 74\%$. Thus, choice **c**, 75% is the best approximation.

42. **d.** Look at the chart to see all of the land he owns:

LOT	AREA (SQ. FT.)	BUILDER
A	8,023	Ira Taylor
B	6,699	Alexis Funes
C	9,004	Ira Taylor
D	8,900	Mark Smith
E	8,301	Alexis Funes
F	8,269	Ira Taylor
G	6,774	Ira Taylor

The total amount of land he owns is $8,023 + 9,004 + 8,269 + 6,774 = 32,070$ square feet.

43. **b.** Mr. Smith's lot is 8,900 square feet. You are told "There are also development fees of 16.15 cents per square foot of land." 16.15 cents = $0.1615. Thus, he must pay $0.1615 \times 8,900 = \$1,437.35$ in development fees.

44. **c.** When used for 25 hours per month, Provider A will cost $\$20 + 7.5 \times \$1$ (for the hourly charge above the free hours). This equals $27.50. Provider B will cost $20 plus $5 \times \$1.50$ (for the hourly charge above the free hours). This equals $\$20 + \$7.50 = \$27.50$ as well, so choice **c** is the correct answer.

45. **d.** Since Recycler Y pays more per pound for all four types of recyclables, all four items should be brought there. The aluminum will yield $0.07 \times 2,200 = \$154$. The cardboard will yield $0.04 \times 1,400 = \$56$. The glass will yield $0.08 \times 3,100 = \$248$. The plastic will yield $0.03 \times 900 = \$27$. These add to $485.

46. c. Calculate the price per ounce (oz.) for each brand:

W: $\frac{.21}{6} = 0.035$

X: $\frac{.48}{15} = 0.032$

Y: $\frac{.56}{20} = 0.028$

Z: $\frac{.96}{32} = 0.03$

Thus, brand Y is the least expensive, choice **c**.

47. a. The solid line represents the S wave. This crosses 550 kilometers at time = 15 minutes.

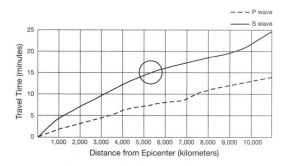

48. b. The P wave is the dashed line. It travels 8,000 kilometers at a point above time = 10, but below time = 15. Hence, a time of 12 minutes is the best answer.

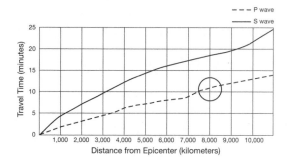

49. a. The S wave was received 4 minutes after the earthquake. Locate 4 minutes on the vertical axis of the graph and then move across until you reach the S-wave graph. Look down to the horizontal axis to see that this means the earthquake is 1,000 kilometer away.

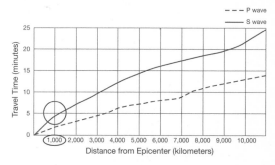

50. b. A difference in time of 5 minutes can be seen by looking at the vertical axis. The vertical axis is marked by 5-minute intervals, so use this distance to judge where the distance (gap) between the waves is also 5 minutes. Look down to see the horizontal axis to note that this time difference occurs at 3,000 kilometers.

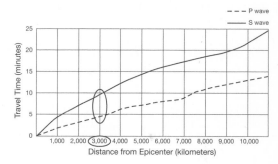

Measurement and Geometry

n the metric system, lengths are calculated in meters, masses are calculated in grams, and volumes are calculated in liters. The prefix of each unit is very important. You should be familiar with the following prefixes:

PREFIX	MEANING	EXAMPLE
milli	$\frac{1}{1,000}$ of	1 milligram is $\frac{1}{1,000}$ of a gram.
centi	$\frac{1}{100}$ of	1 centimeter is $\frac{1}{100}$ of a meter.
deci	$\frac{1}{10}$ of	1 decigram is $\frac{1}{10}$ of a gram.
deca	10 times	1 decameter is 10 meters.
hecto	100 times	1 hectoliter is 100 liters.
kilo	1,000 times	1 kilometer is 1,000 meters.

▶ English Units

The relationships between the English, or customary, units are not as systematic as the relationships between units in the metric system. Here, lengths are measured in inches, feet, yards, and miles. Weights are measured in pounds and ounces. And volumes are measured in cubic inches, cubic feet, and so forth. Here is a chart of common conversions for English units.

COMMON CONVERSIONS	
1 foot = 12 inches	1 cup = 8 fluid ounces
3 feet = 1 yard	1 pint = 2 cups
1 mile = 5,280 feet	1 quart = 2 pints
1 acre = 43,560 square feet	1 gallon = 4 quarts
1 ton = 2,000 pounds	1 pound = 16 ounces
1 gross = 144 units	1 liter = 1,000 cubic centimeters

▶ Converting Units

Conversion factors are an easy way to convert units. For example, using the knowledge that 12 inches = 1 foot, you can generate two conversion factors: $\frac{12 \text{ in.}}{1 \text{ ft.}}$ and $\frac{1 \text{ ft.}}{12 \text{ in.}}$. Suppose you wanted to convert 5 feet into inches. You can use the conversion factor $\frac{12 \text{ in.}}{1 \text{ ft.}}$:

$$5 \text{ ft.} \times \frac{12 \text{ in.}}{1 \text{ ft.}} = 60 \text{ in.}$$

Notice that you crossed out the units you *didn't* want (feet) and ended up with the units you *did* want (inches). Having the feet in the denominator of this conversion factor lets us cross out the "ft." unit in the original 5 feet. In other instances, you may want to cross out inches and convert to feet. The conversion factor to use would be $\frac{1 \text{ ft.}}{12 \text{ in.}}$.

▶ Calculations with Geometric Figures

Perimeter is the distance around a figure. The perimeter of a circle is called its **circumference**. **Area** is a measure of the surface of a two-dimensional figure. **Volume** is a measure of the amount of space inside a three-dimensional shape.

Formula Sheet

You should be familiar with the formulas presented on this formula sheet.

Triangle: $Area = \frac{1}{2}bh$, where b stands for base and h stands for height.

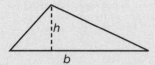

The interior angles of a triangle add to 180°.
The interior angles of a quadrilateral (4-sided polygon) add to 360°.

Square: $Area = s^2$, where s stands for side.

$Perimeter = 4s$

Rectangle: $Area = lw$, where l stands for length and w stands for width.

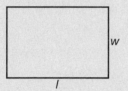

Circle: $Area = \pi r^2$, where r stands for radius.

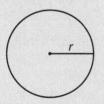

$Circumference = 2\pi r = \pi d$, where d stands for diameter. ($\pi \approx 3.14$ or $\frac{22}{7}$)

Parallelogram: $Area = bh$, where b stands for base and h stands for height.

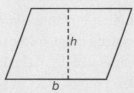

Trapezoid: $Area = \frac{1}{2}h(b_1 + b_2)$, where h stands for height and b stands for base.

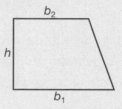

Pythagorean theorem: $a^2 + b^2 = c^2$, where a and b are legs and c is the hypotenuse.

Right circular cylinder: $Volume = \pi r^2 h$, where r stands for radius and h stands for height.

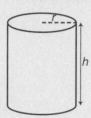

$Total\ Surface\ Area = 2\pi rh + 2\pi r^2$

Rectangular solid: $Volume = lwh$, where l stands for length, w stands for width, and h stands for height.

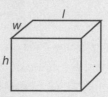

$Total\ Surface\ Area = 2(lw) + 2(hw) + 2(lh)$

▶ Perimeter

Perimeter is an addition concept. It is a linear, one-dimensional measurement of the distance around the outside of a figure. To find perimeter, add up all the lengths of the sides of the figure. Then, name the units. Be alert when working with geometry problems to make sure that the units are consistent. If they are different, a conversion must be made before calculating perimeter.

▶ Area

Area is a measure of how many square units it takes to *cover* a closed figure. Area is measured in square units. Area is a multiplication concept, where two measures are multiplied together. You can also think of units being multiplied together: $cm \times cm = cm^2$, or the words "centimeters squared." Let's look at an example involving area:

Example:

A rectangular swimming pool measures 204 feet long and 99 feet wide. What is the area of the pool in square yards?

Convert both the length and the width into yards:

$204 \text{ ft.} \times \frac{1 \text{ yd.}}{3 \text{ ft.}} = 68 \text{ yd.}$

$99 \text{ ft.} \times \frac{1 \text{ yd.}}{3 \text{ ft.}} = 33 \text{ yd.}$

Next, use the area formula for a rectangle, $A = lw$:

$A = 68 \text{ yards} \times 33 \text{ yards} = 2,244 \text{ square yards.}$

▶ Volume

Volume is a measure of how many cubic units it takes to fill a solid figure. Volume is measured in cubic units. Volume is a multiplication concept, where three measures are multiplied together.

Example:

One cubic centimeter of wood weighs 6 grams. How much would a cube weigh if it measured 10 centimeters on each side?

You are told that the weight is 6 grams per cubic centimeter, or $\frac{6 \text{ g}}{cm^3}$. You need to find out how many cm^3 there are in the bigger cube, which is the volume of the cube. Recall that for a cube, $V = side^3$. The bigger cube has a side = 10, so $V = 10^3 = 1,000 \text{ cm}^3$. Then, to find the weight, you multiply $1,000 \text{ cm}^3 \times \frac{6 \text{ g}}{cm^3} = 6,000 \text{ grams}$.

▶ Practice Questions

1. What is the sum of 3 feet 5 inches, 10 feet 2 inches, and 2 feet 7 inches?
   a. 14 feet 14 inches
   b. 16 feet 4 inches
   c. 15 feet 13 inches
   d. 16 feet 2 inches

2. Three pieces of pipe measure 5 feet 8 inches, 4 feet 7 inches, and 3 feet 9 inches. What is the combined length of all three pipes?
   a. 14 feet
   b. 13 feet 10 inches
   c. 12 feet 9 inches
   d. 12 feet 5 inches

3. How many inches are there in $3\frac{1}{3}$ yards?
   a. 126
   b. 120
   c. 160
   d. 168

4. 76,000 milliliters is equivalent to how many liters?
   a. 7.6 liters
   b. 76 liters
   c. 760 liters
   d. 7,600 liters

5. 2,808 inches is equivalent to how many yards?
   a. 234
   b. 110
   c. 78
   d. 36

6. What is the sum of 5 yards 2 feet, 8 yards 1 foot, 3 yards $\frac{1}{2}$ foot, and 4 yards 6 inches?
   a. 20 yards $\frac{1}{2}$ foot
   b. 20 yards 1 foot
   c. 21 yards 1 foot
   d. 21 yards $\frac{1}{2}$ foot

7. How many yards are in a mile?
   a. 1,760
   b. 4,400
   c. 5,280
   d. 63,360

Use the following chart to answer questions 8 through 10.

ENGLISH—METRIC UNIT CONVERSIONS
LENGTH
1 in. = 2.54 cm
1 yard = .9 m
1 mi. = 1.6 km

8. Convert 3 feet 5 inches into centimeters.
   a. 104.14 centimeters
   b. 65.6 centimeters
   c. 51.3 centimeters
   d. 16.14 centimeters

9. 5,500 yards is equivalent to how many meters?
   a. 13,970 meters
   b. 6,111 meters
   c. 9,800 meters
   d. 4,950 meters

10. 1,280 miles is equal to how many kilometers?
   a. 800 kilometers
   b. 1,152 kilometers
   c. 2,048 kilometers
   d. 3,200 kilometers

11. A child has a temperature of 40 degrees C. What is the child's temperature in degrees Fahrenheit?
$F = \frac{9}{5}C + 32$
   a. 101°
   b. 102°
   c. 103°
   d. 104°

12. If John was waiting for 45 minutes for an appointment with a contractor that lasted 1 hour and 25 minutes, what is the total amount of time spent at the contractor's office?
   a. 2 hour 10 minutes
   b. 2 hour 25 minutes
   c. $2\frac{1}{2}$ hours
   d. 3 hour 10 minutes

13. There are 12 yards of twine on a roll. Danielle cuts off 2 feet of twine for a project. How many *feet* of twine are left on the roll?
   a. 2
   b. 34
   c. 36
   d. 142

Use the following conversion chart to answer questions 14 through 17.

LIQUID MEASURE
8 oz. = 1 c.
1 pt. = 2 c.
1 qt. = 2 pt.
4 qt. = 1 gal.

14. How many ounces are in 2 pints?
   a. 16 ounces
   b. 32 ounces
   c. 44 ounces
   d. 64 ounces

15. 364 ounces is equivalent to how many quarts?
   a. 182 quarts
   b. 91 quarts
   c. 22.75 quarts
   d. 11.375 quarts

16. How many ounces are in 3 gallons?
   a. 384 ounces
   b. 192 ounces
   c. 96 ounces
   d. 48 ounces

17. A 25-gallon tub of fluid will be poured into containers that hold half of a quart each. If all of the containers are filled to capacity, how many will be filled?
   a. 50
   b. 100
   c. 200
   d. 250

18. A rotating door, pictured here, has four sections, labeled *a*, *b*, *c*, and *d*. If section *a* is making a 45 degree angle with wall 1, what angle is section *c* making with wall 2? (Note: Wall 1 and wall 2 are segments of the same line.)

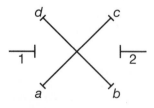

   a. 15 degrees
   b. 45 degrees
   c. 55 degrees
   d. 90 degrees

19. A rectangle has 2 sides equaling 6 feet and 1 yard, respectively. What is the area of the rectangle?

a. 6 square feet

b. 12 square feet

c. 18 square feet

d. 20 square feet

20. A square with $s = 6$ centimeters has the same area of a rectangle with $l = 9$ centimeters. What is the width of the rectangle?

a. 4 centimeters

b. 6 centimeters

c. 8 centimeters

d. 9 centimeters

21. If the area of a circle is 9π square centimeters, what is the circumference?

a. 3π square centimeters

b. 3π centimeters

c. 6π square centimeters

d. 6π centimeters

22. A rectangular tract of land measures 860 feet by 560 feet. Approximately how many acres is this? (1 acre = 43,560 square feet.)

a. 12.8 acres

b. 11.06 acres

c. 10.5 acres

d. 8.06 acres

23. Marguerite is redoing her bathroom floor. Each imported tile measures $1\frac{2}{7}$ inches by $1\frac{4}{5}$ inches What is the area of each tile?

a. $1\frac{8}{35}$ square inches

b. $1\frac{11}{135}$ square inches

c. $2\frac{11}{35}$ square inches

d. $3\frac{3}{35}$ square inches

24. A rectangular swimming pool measures 160 feet long and 80 feet wide. What is the perimeter of the pool in yards?

a. 480

b. 160

c. 240

d. 280

25. In the diagram, the angle x equals how many degrees?

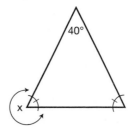

a. 70°

b. 110°

c. 140°

d. 290°

26. If the volume of a cube is 8 cubic inches, what is its surface area?

a. 80 square inches

b. 40 square inches

c. 24 square inches

d. 16 square inches

27. Giorgio is making an "open" box. He starts with a 10 × 7 rectangle, then cuts 2 × 2 squares out of each corner. To finish, he folds each side up to make the box. What is the box's volume?

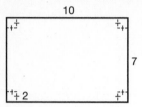

a. 36 units³
b. 42 units³
c. 70 units³
d. 72 units³

28. How many six-inch square tiles are needed to tile the floor in a room that is 12 feet by 15 feet?
a. 180 tiles
b. 225 tiles
c. 360 tiles
d. 720 tiles

Refer to the following polygon to answer questions 29 and 30.

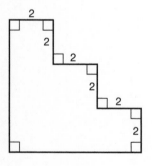

29. What is the perimeter of the polygon?
a. 8 units
b. 12 units
c. 20 units
d. 24 units

30. What is the area of the polygon?
a. 8 square units
b. 12 square units
c. 20 square units
d. 24 square units

31. The standard distance of a marathon is 26.2 miles. If the length of a walker's stride is 1.96 feet, approximately how many steps does this walker take to walk a marathon?

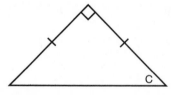

a. 23,527
b. 70,580
c. 138,336
d. 271,139

32. What is the measure of angle *C* in the triangle?

a. 90°
b. 60°
c. 45°
d. 25°

33. How much greater is the area of circle B?

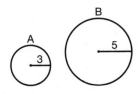

a. 16π square inches

b. 9π square inches

c. 25π square inches

d. 14π square inches

34. *ABCD* is a square and *E* is the midpoint of $\overline{AB}$. Find the area of the shaded region.

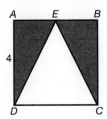

a. 4 square units

b. 6 square units

c. 8 square units

d. 12 square units

35. Two angles in quadrilateral *ABCD* have their measures indicated. The other two angles show variable expressions. What is *x*?

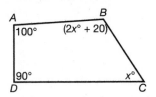

a. 50°

b. 60°

c. 70°

d. 80°

36. One cubic centimeter of clay weighs 3 grams. How much would a cube weigh if it measured 5 centimeters on each side?

a. 15 grams

b. 125 grams

c. 375 grams

d. 75 grams

Use the following information and diagram to answer questions 37–39.

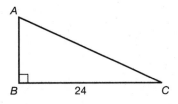

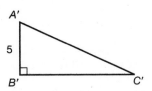

Note: All of the sides of ΔA′B′C′ are half the value of the corresponding sides of ΔABC.

37. Calculate the length of side *A′C′* in triangle ΔA′B′C′.

a. 10

b. 12

c. 13

d. 26

38. The perimeter of ΔABC is how much greater than the perimeter of ΔA′B′C′?

a. 30

b. 40

c. 45

d. 60

39. The area of △*ABC* is how much greater than the area of △*A′B′C′*?

a. 30
b. 40
c. 60
d. 90

40. What is the value of *X* in the following figure?

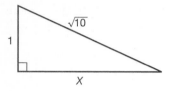

a. 3
b. 4
c. 5
d. 6

41. Find the area of the shaded portion in the figure.

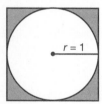

a. π
b. π − 1
c. 2 − π
d. 4 − π

42. What is the area of the shaded part of the circle if the diameter is 6 inches? (Use 3.14 for π.)

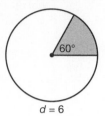

d = 6

a. 4.71 square inches
b. 28.26 square inches
c. 60 square inches
d. 36 square inches

43. A cylindrical can measures 4.2 inches in height. Its circular bases of $\frac{1}{2}$ inch radii are removed, and the cylinder is flattened out. What is the surface area of the flattened-out cylinder? (Use 3.14 for π.)

a. 3.297 square inches
b. 8.54 square inches
c. 12.1 square inches
d. 13.188 square inches

44. A point on the outer edge of a wheel is 2.5 feet from the axis of rotation. If the wheel spins at a full rate of 2,640 revolutions per minute, how many miles will the point on the outer edge of the wheel travel in one hour?

a. 75π
b. 100π
c. 112π
d. 150π

45. What is the perimeter of the shaded area if the shape is a quarter-circle with a radius of 3.5? (Use $\pi = \frac{22}{7}$.)

a. 7 units
b. 11 units
c. 22 units
d. 29 units

46. In the diagram, a half-circle is laid adjacent to a triangle. What is the total area of the shape, if the radius of the half-circle is 3 and the height of the triangle is 4?

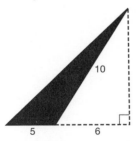

a. $6(\pi + 4)$
b. $6\pi + 12$
c. $6\pi + 24$
d. $\frac{9\pi}{2} + 12$

47. What is the area of the following shaded triangle?

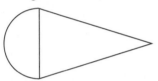

a. 20 square units
b. 25 square units
c. 40 square units
d. 44 square units

48. A triangle has sides that are consecutive even integers. The perimeter of the triangle is 24 inches. What is the length of the shortest side?

a. 10 inches
b. 8 inches
c. 6 inches
d. 4 inches

49. In the following diagram, a circle with an area of 100π square inches is inscribed in a square. What is the length of $\overline{AB}$?

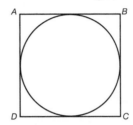

a. 10 inches
b. 20 inches
c. 40 inches
d. 100 inches

50. A bike wheel has a radius of 12 inches. How many revolutions will it take to cover 1 mile? (Use 1 mile = 5,280 feet, and $\pi = \frac{22}{7}$.)

a. 70
b. 84
c. 120
d. 840

► Answers

1. d. First, add up all of the given values:

3 ft. 5 in.
10 ft. 2 in.
+ 2 ft. 7 in.
_____
15 ft. 14 in.

Next, note that 14 inches = 1 foot + 2 inches. This means 15 feet 14 inches = 16 feet 2 inches, choice **d.**

2. a. First, add up all of the given values:

5 ft. 8 in.
4 ft. 7 in.
+ 3 ft. 9 in.
_____
12 ft. 24 in.

Next, note that 24 inches = 2 feet, so 12 feet 24 inches is equivalent to 14 feet.

3. b. Since there are 36 inches per yard, use the conversion factor $\frac{36 \text{ in.}}{1 \text{ yd.}}$, and multiply: $3\frac{1}{3}$ yd. $\times \frac{36 \text{ in.}}{1 \text{ yd.}}$ = $\frac{10}{3}$ yd. $\times \frac{36 \text{ in.}}{1 \text{ yd.}}$ = $\frac{360}{3}$ inches. = 120 inches.

4. b. 1 liter = 1,000 milliliters so you can use the conversion factor $\frac{1 \text{ L}}{1,000 \text{ ml}}$ to convert the milliliters into liters. 76,000 ml $\times \frac{1 \text{ L}}{1,000 \text{ ml}}$ = 76 L.

5. c. Since there are 36 inches per yard, use the conversion factor $\frac{1 \text{ yd.}}{36 \text{ in.}}$ and multiply: 2,808 in. $\times \frac{1 \text{ yd.}}{36 \text{ in.}}$ = 78 yd.

6. c. First, note that 4 yards 6 inches is the same as 4 yards $\frac{1}{2}$ foot, as this will help you combine units. Next, add up all the values:

5 yd. 2 ft.
8 yd. 1 ft.
3 yd. $\frac{1}{2}$ ft.
+ 4 yd. $\frac{1}{2}$ ft.
_____
20 yd. 4 ft.

Next, note that 4 feet = 1 yard + 1 foot. Thus, 20 yards 4 feet can be converted to 21 yards 1 foot.

7. a. 1 mile equals 5,280 feet (memorize this). Since there are 3 feet per yard, use the conversion factor $\frac{1 \text{ yd.}}{3 \text{ ft.}}$ and multiply: 5,280 feet $\times \frac{1 \text{ yd.}}{3 \text{ ft.}}$ = 1,760 yards.

8. a. First, convert 3 feet 5 inches into 36 inches + 5 inches = 41 inches. Next, use the information given in the chart to make a conversion factor. Since 1 inch = 2.54 centimeters, and you want to end up with centimeters, you make a conversion factor with inches in the denominator: $\frac{2.54 \text{ cm}}{1 \text{ in.}}$ Next, multiply: 41 inches $\times \frac{2.54 \text{ cm}}{1 \text{ in.}}$ = 104.14 centimeters.

9. d. The chart shows that 1 yard = .9 meters, so you can write the conversion factor as $\frac{.9 \text{ m}}{1 \text{ yd.}}$ and multiply: 5,500 yd. $\times \frac{.9 \text{ m}}{1 \text{ yd.}}$ = 4,950 meters.

10. c. The chart shows that 1 mile = 1.6 kilometers, so you can write the conversion factor as $\frac{1.6 \text{ km}}{1 \text{ mi.}}$ and multiply: 1,280 miles $\times \frac{1.6 \text{ km}}{1 \text{ mi.}}$ = 2,048 kilometers.

11. d. Substitute 40 in for C in the given equation. Thus, (F = $\frac{9}{5}$ C + 32) becomes F = $\frac{9}{5}$(40) + 32 = (9)(8) + 32 = 72 + 32 = 104 degrees Fahrenheit.

12. a. Line up the units and add:

45 min
+ 1 hr 25 min
_____
1 hr 70 min

Next, note that 70 minutes = 1 hour 10 minutes. Thus, 1 hour 70 minutes = 2 hour 10 minutes.

13. b. First convert the 12 yards into feet: 12 yd. $\times \frac{3 \text{ ft.}}{1 \text{ yd.}}$ = 36 feet at the start. Next, Danielle cuts 2 feet off, so 34 feet are left.

14. b. Using the chart, you can make conversion factors where you will cross off *pints* and end up with *ounces* (oz). Thus, you multiply: 2 pints $\times \frac{2 \text{ c.}}{1 \text{ pt.}} \times \frac{8 \text{ oz.}}{1 \text{ c.}}$ = 32 ounces.

15. d. Using the chart, you can make conversion factors where you will cross off *ounces* (oz) and end up with *quarts* (qt): 364 ounces $\times \frac{1 \text{ c.}}{8 \text{ oz.}} \times \frac{1 \text{ pt.}}{2 \text{ c.}}$ $\times \frac{1 \text{ qt.}}{2 \text{ pt.}} = \frac{364}{32} = 11.375$ quarts.

16. a. Using the chart you can make conversion factors where you will cross off *gallons* and end up with *ounces* (oz): 3 gallons $\times \frac{4 \text{ qt.}}{1 \text{ gal.}} \times \frac{2 \text{ pt.}}{1 \text{ qt.}} \times$ $\frac{2 \text{ c.}}{1 \text{ pt.}} \times \frac{8 \text{ oz.}}{1 \text{ c.}} = 384$ ounces.

17. c. First, convert the gallons into quarts: 25 gallons $\times \frac{4 \text{ qt.}}{1 \text{ gal.}} = 100$ qt. If the fluid will fill 100 one-quart containers, it will then fill 200 $\frac{1}{2}$-quart containers.

18. b. If you draw a line on the diagram to denote the 45° angle mentioned, you can see that the angle section c makes with wall 2 must also be 45°. Recall that opposite angles formed by the intersection of two straight lines are equal:

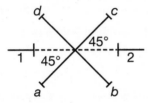

This means that section *c* makes a 45° angle with wall 2.

19. c. First, convert the width (1 yard) into feet: 1 yard = 3 feet. Next, use $A = lw = 6 \times 3 = 18$ square feet. (Note that all of the answer choices are in ft.², so converting to feet is a good idea.)

20. a. The area of the square is $A = s^2 = 6^2 = 36$ square cm. The area of the rectangle must then also be 36 square centimeters. Substituting this into the area formula, along with $l = 9$ you get: $A = lw; 36 = 9 \times w; w = 36 \div 9 = 4$ centimeters.

21. d. You are told that Area = 9π. If $A = \pi r^2$, then $\pi r^2 = 9\pi$, and $r = 3$. Circumference, $C = 2\pi r$ $= 2\pi \times 3 = 6\pi$ centimeters. Remember that perimeters and circumferences are measured

in units (like centimeters) and areas are measured in square units (like square centimeters).

22. b. First, calculate the area in square feet. The area of a rectangle is *lw*, so $A = lw = 860$ feet $\times$ 560 feet = 481,600 square feet. Next, use the conversion factor $\frac{1 \text{ acre}}{43,560 \text{ ft.}^2}$ and multiply: 481,600 ft² $\times \frac{1 \text{ acre}}{43,560 \text{ ft.}^2} \approx 11.056$ acres $\approx$ 11.06 acres.

23. c. Area = *lw*. First, convert the mixed numbers to improper fractions: $1\frac{2}{7}$ inches = $\frac{9}{7}$ inches and $1\frac{4}{5}$ inches = $\frac{9}{5}$ inches. Next, use these fractions in the formula: Area = $lw = \frac{9}{7} \times \frac{9}{5} = \frac{81}{35}$ square inches = $2\frac{11}{35}$ square inches.

24. b. The perimeter of a rectangle is the sum of all its sides: 160 + 160 + 80 + 80 = 480 feet. Next, convert to yards by multiplying 480 with the conversion factor $\frac{1 \text{ yd.}}{3 \text{ ft.}}$: 480 feet $\times \frac{1 \text{ yd.}}{3 \text{ ft.}} = 160$ yards.

25. d. The curved markings indicate that the two bottom angles are equal. You can call these two equal angles *y*. Thus $y + y + 40 = 180$, $2y + 40 = 180$; $2y = 140$; $y = 70$. Angles *x* and *y* form a complete circle (360°). Thus, $x = 360 - y° = 360° - 70° = 290°$.

26. c. The volume formula for a cube is $V = s^3$, so here $s^3 = 8$ and $s = 2$ in. The surface area of one face is $s^2 = 2^2 = 4$ square inches. Since there are six faces, the total surface area is 6 $\times$ 4 square inches = 24 square inches.

27. a. When the 2 $\times$ 2 squares are cut out, the length of the box is 3, and the width is 6. The height is 2:

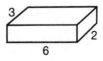

The volume is 3 $\times$ 6 $\times$ 2, or 36.

28. d. Draw yourself a rectangle to represent the 12 feet $\times$ 15 feet floor. Since each tile is 6 inches by

6 inches, or $\frac{1}{2}$ foot by $\frac{1}{2}$ foot, you can see that you could get 24 tiles across the floor, and 30 tiles going down. Now you just multiply 24 by 30 to get the total tiles needed: $24 \times 30 = 720$.

29. d. Fill in the missing sides:

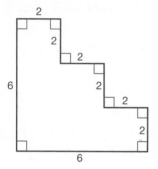

Next, add up all the sides: $P = 6 + 6 + 6(2) = 12 + 12 = 24$ units.

30. d. Divide up the figure into squares as shown:

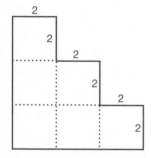

The figure is composed of six squares. The area of each square is $s^2 = 2^2 = 4$. Thus the total area is $6 \times 4 = 24$ square units.

31. b. Convert 26.2 miles to feet, and divide by the length of the walker's stride to find how many steps this walker takes in a marathon: 1 mile = 5,280 feet, so 26.2 miles = 138,336 feet. Divide 138,336 by 1.96 feet per step to get 70,579.6. Round to the nearest whole number to get 70,580 steps.

32. c. The two lines through the sides of the triangle indicate that they are equal. The right angle is 90° and the two angles opposite the two equal sides will be equal. Since the interior angles of

a triangle add to 180°, the two equal angles must add to 180° − 90° = 90°. Thus each angle will be equal to 45°. Thus, angle C = 45°.

33. a. Remember the formula for figuring out the area of a circle: $A = \pi r^2$. Circle A then is $\pi 3^2$ or 9π and circle B is $\pi 5^2$ or 25π, so the area of circle B is 16π greater than circle A.

34. c. To find the area of the shaded region, subtract the area of the triangle from the area of the square. The area of the triangle is $\frac{1}{2}bh = \frac{1}{2}(4)(4) = 8$ square units, and the area of the square is $s^2 = 4^2 = 16$ square units. Thus, the area of the shaded region is $16 - 8 = 8$ square units.

35. a. Set up an equation. (Remember, all the angles added up inside a four-sided figure equal 360°): $90 + 100 + x + 2x + 20 = 360$, which is $3x + 210 = 360$. Subtract 210 from both sides to get $3x = 150$. Divide by 3 to get $x = 50$.

36. c. For this question, you already know that the weight is $\frac{3\,\text{g}}{\text{cm}^3}$. You need to find out how many cubic centimeters there are in the given cube, which is the *volume* of the cube. For a cube, the volume $= side^3$. The given cube has a side $= 5$, so $V = 5^3 = 5 \times 5 \times 5 = 125$. Then, to find the weight you multiply $125 \text{ cm}^3 \times \frac{3\,\text{g}}{\text{cm}^3} = 375$ grams.

37. c. Since $BC = 24$, $B'C'$ will be half that, or 12. Thus, $\triangle A'B'C'$ is a right triangle with legs equaling 5 and 12. You can use the Pythagorean theorem to solve for the hypotenuse: $a^2 + b^2 = c^2$ becomes $5^2 + 12^2 = c^2$, then $25 + 144 = c^2$, then $169 = c^2$, so $c = 13$.

38. a. $\triangle A'B'C'$ is a 5-12-13 right triangle (see answer explanation for question 37) and $\triangle ABC$ is double that, or 10-24-26. Thus, the perimeter of $\triangle A'B'C'$ is $5 + 12 + 13 = 30$, and the perimeter of $\triangle ABC$ is twice that, or 60. Thus, the difference is $60 - 30 = 30$.

39. d. $\Delta A'B'C'$ is a 5-12-13 right triangle (see answer explanation for question 37) and ΔABC is double that, or 10-24-26. The base of $\Delta A'B'C'$ is 24, and its height is 10. Apply the area formula: $A = \frac{1}{2}bh = \frac{1}{2}(24)(10) = 120$ units^2. The base of ΔABC is 12, and its height is 5. Apply the area formula: $A = \frac{1}{2}bh = \frac{1}{2}(12)(5) = 30$ units^2. Thus, the difference is $120 - 30 = 90$ units.

40. a. You can use the Pythagorean theorem to solve for the missing leg: $a^2 + b^2 = c^2$ becomes $12 + x^2 = (\sqrt{10})^2$, then $1 + x^2 = 10$, so $x^2 = 9$, and $x = 3$.

41. d. The shaded area is the difference between the area of the square and the circle. Because the radius is 1, a side of the square is 2. The area of the square is $s^2 = 2^2 = 4$, and the area of the circle is $\pi r^2 = \pi 1^2 = \pi$. Therefore, the answer is $4 - \pi$.

42. a. First, find the area of the circle: Area $= \pi r^2$, or 3.14×9, which equals 28.26 square inches. Then, notice there are 360° in a circle and 60 is one-sixth that ($\frac{60}{360} = \frac{1}{6}$). The shaded area is then only one-sixth the area of the total circle. Divide 28.26 by 6 to get 4.71 square inches.

43. d. After removing the circular bases, you are left with a flat rectangle. Since the height was 4.2 inches, the length of the rectangle is 4.2 inches. Since the circumference of the bases was $C = 2\pi r = 2 \times 3.14 \times \frac{1}{2} = 3.14$ inches, the width of the rectangle is 3.14 inches Thus, the area of the new rectangular figure is $lw = 4.2 \times 3.14 = 13.188$ inches square

44. d. The point lies on the circumference of a circle with a radius of 2.5 feet. Therefore, the distance that the point travels in one rotation is the length of the circumference of the circle, or $2\pi r = 2\pi(2.5) = 5\pi$ feet. Since the wheel spins at 2,640 revolutions per minute, the point travels $2,640 \times 5\pi$ feet per minute $= 13,200\pi$ feet per minute. Multiplying by 60 to find the distance traveled in one hour, you get $60 \times 13,200\pi =$ 792,000π feet per hour. Dividing by 5,280 feet to convert to miles, you get 150π miles per hour.

45. d. The curved length of the perimeter is one quarter of the circumference of a full circle: $\frac{1}{4}$ $2\pi r$, $= 2(\frac{22}{7})(3.5) = 7 \times \frac{22}{7} = 22$. The linear (straight) lengths are radii, so the solution is simply $22 + 2(3.5)$ or 29.

46. d. Because the radius of the hemisphere is 3, and it is the same as half the base of the triangle, the base must be 6. Therefore, the area of the triangle is $\frac{1}{2}bh = \frac{1}{2}(4 \times 6) = 12$. The area of the circle, if it was a whole circle, is πr^2, which equals 9π. Therefore, the area of a half-circle is $\frac{9\pi}{2}$. Adding gives $\frac{9\pi}{2} + 12$.

47. a. To get the height of the triangle (h), using the Pythagorean theorem: $a^2 + b^2 = c^2$ becomes $6^2 + h^2 = 10^2$, then $36 + h^2 = 100$, and $h^2 = 64$, so the height, h, equals 8. Then 5 is plugged in for the base and 8 for the height in the area equation $A = \frac{1}{2}bh$. Thus, $A = \frac{1}{2}(5)(8) = 20$ square units.

48. c. An algebraic equation can be used to solve this problem. The shortest side can be denoted s. Therefore, $s + (s + 2) + (s + 4) = 24$; $3s + 6 = 24$, and $s = 6$.

49. b. If the circle is 100π square inches, its radius must be 10 inches (because $A = \pi r^2$ and here $A = 100\pi$). $\overline{AB}$ is twice the radius, so it is 20 inches.

50. d. The outer edge of the wheel is in contact with the ground. Since you are told to use 1 mile = 5,280 feet, you would be wise to convert the 12 inch radius to 1 foot. You can find the outer edge (circumference) by using $C = 2\pi r = 2(\frac{22}{7})(1) = \frac{44}{7}$ feet. Thus, each time it revolves it covers $\frac{44}{7}$ feet. Divide 5,280 feet by $\frac{44}{7}$ feet to find the number of revolutions in 1 mile: $5,280 \div \frac{44}{7} = 5,280 \times \frac{7}{44} = 840$ revolutions.

Vocabulary Prep for Civil Service Exams

ll civil service exams test vocabulary skills in some form. Nearly all include a section testing your ability to read and understand extended passages. Many also include questions about grammar, vocabulary, and spelling.

There are good reasons for including these skills on civil service exams. To be an effective government employee, you must be able to read and comprehend memos, policy statements, procedural instructions, documents, and reports. Similarly, most positions require you to communicate effectively in writing. You can't do that without some mastery of English vocabulary, grammar, and spelling.

The good news is that these exams test basic skills. No one is going to ask you to read a complicated novel and interpret its symbolism. Nor will a civil service exam ask you to spell *Australopithecus* or to conjugate verbs in the future subjunctive tense (or even to know what the future subjunctive tense is, for that matter). All you need to do is to read a passage and answer some related questions, which will be pretty straightforward, and to recall some fundamental principles of grammar and spelling.

The chapters that follow review the basic skills necessary to pass the vocabulary portion of your civil service exam.

Remember, a rich vocabulary gives you a strong advantage in the workplace. When you have an extensive vocabulary, you can write clear descriptions; you can speak more fluently and with more confidence; you can understand more of what you read; and you can read more sophisticated texts. Achieving a good vocabulary does not come without hard work. Take the time now and make the commitment to improve your verbal skills for your civil service exam.

10 ▶ Vocabulary in Context

The vocabulary section of the civil service exam often includes a section of vocabulary in context questions. For this part of the exam, you will be asked to identify the meanings of vocabulary words used in sentences. Because you will not be able to use a dictionary during the exam, it is important to develop vocabulary strategies that will boost your score and give you the advantage you need.

As you might expect, **vocabulary in context questions** ask you to determine the meanings of particular words. To prepare for this section of the exam, recall the skills you developed at an early age. First, it is a good idea to be an active reader. This is a skill you can practice every day. As you read the daily newspaper, your favorite magazine, or the latest book, have a dictionary handy. Look up as many unfamiliar words as you can so that your bank of vocabulary words becomes as large as possible. Second, be aware that you can use the context of a sentence to help you detect the meaning of a word. Simply put, this means that you can look for clues in and around the vocabulary word.

For practice, try the following exercise to see how this can be done.

As a result of many meetings held by the Human Resources Department, a memo was written to help hiring supervisors present information about new procedures that benefit the company, the staff, and new employees during a new employee orientation seminar. The new procedures create a win-win situation for all concerned, and the Human Resources Department wants to make sure that those people who are instrumental in making the program work have all the information they need. Imagine that your title is Hiring Supervisor, and you receive the following memorandum from the Human Resources Department. Read it carefully. Circle any words that are unfamiliar to you, but do not use a dictionary to look them up just yet.

TO: Hiring Supervisors
FROM: Human Resources
RE: New Employees

In order for new employees to begin work in the office, the *New Employee Introduction Manual* has been compiled. This manual should be distributed to all new hires during an orientation seminar that you will conduct one week before a new employee begins work. During orientation, be sure to point out that not only does the information in the manual inform new employees about office protocol and employee benefits, but it gives them a sense of the new family they are about to join. As you leaf through the manual with new hires, note that the manual begins with basic office etiquette, procedures, and dress codes and then there is a segue to important information about pay schedules and benefits. Explain to your orientation group that with this manual in hand, new employees will have a more global view of the company. They will know what to expect and can ask questions that will make their new position a little more comfortable on the first day. The benefits of the orientation seminar, in addition to the manual, will make our workplace a more cohesive and productive environment for all employees.

As you read, you may have circled *protocol* or *segue*. By looking for context clues—the way the words are used in the paragraph—you can figure out what these words mean.

What does **protocol** *mean?*

Reread the sentence with the word *protocol*.

"During orientation, be sure to point out that not only does the information in the manual inform new employees about office *protocol* and employee benefits, but it gives them a sense of the new family they are about to join."

Even if you have no idea what *protocol* means, you can still tell something about the word by how it is used—by examining the words and ideas surrounding it. This is called determining word meaning through context. Like detectives looking for clues at a crime scene, you must look at the passage for clues that will uncover the definition of the word.

Given the sentence you have here, you can begin to consider the definition of *protocol*. Since the manual informs new employees about office protocol and employee benefits, this tells you that protocol must be a procedure or system designed to make things run smoothly in the office. As you read the next sentence in the memo, you see that the sections of the manual cover many topics: etiquette, procedures, dress codes, salaries, and employee benefits. At this point, you should be able to take a pretty good guess at the definition of the word *protocol*.

→ The best definition of the word *protocol* is
   a. a meeting's agenda.
   b. a code of correct procedure.
   c. a salary schedule.

It cannot be choice **a** because nowhere in the passage does it state that protocol is a list of items covered in a meeting. While a salary schedule, choice **c**, is determined by a certain procedure, it is only part of the scope of an office system. The correct answer is choice **b**, a code of correct procedure.

What does **segue** *mean?*

Look again at the sentence in which *segue* is used.

"As you leaf through the manual with new hires, note that the manual begins with basic office etiquette, procedures, and dress codes and then there is a *segue* to important information about pay schedules and benefits."

Again, even if you have no idea what *segue* means, you can still tell what kind of word it is by the way it is used in the sentence.

→ Because the word *segue* falls between a list of basic office etiquette, procedures, and dress codes *and* important information about pay schedules and benefits, you know this word is
   a. an interference in the sentence.
   b. a transition in the sentence.

There is one very obvious clue. As the hiring supervisor leafs through the manual, he or she pages through all sections of the text, highlighting the basic elements contained in the opening chapters and then notes that the chapters switch or move to important facts about salaries and benefits.

→ *Segue,* in this case, can be defined as
   a. a disorganized flow of ideas.
   b. merely sketchy details and descriptions.
   c. uninterrupted movement from one stage to the next.
   d. wordy and verbose language.

The correct answer is choice **c**, uninterrupted movement from one state to the next. It cannot be choice **b** or **d** because there is no indication that anything in the manual is omitted or for that matter, wordy or verbose. Choice **a** is not a suitable answer because the manual, as it is outlined, appears to be well ordered.

▶ How Much Context Do You Need?

In the previous example, you would still be able to understand the main message of the memorandum even if you did not know—or could not figure out—the meanings of *protocol* and *segue*. In some cases, though, your understanding of a sentence depends on your understanding of a particular word or phrase. For example, can you understand the following sentence without knowing what *adversely* means?

The new policy will *adversely* affect all employees.

You might not understand it in this short sentence, and if you are an employee, you certainly would want to know how you are going to be affected. More defining clues for the word *adversely* will help you know whether it is something good or bad:

The new policy will *adversely* affect all employees; it will freeze their pay, limit their vacation time, and reduce their health benefits.

→ In the sentence, *adversely* most nearly means
  a. mildly or slightly.
  b. regularly or steadily.
  c. negatively or unfavorably.
  d. immediately or swiftly.

The correct answer is choice **c**, negatively or unfavorably. The addition of the second part of the sentence now tells you exactly how the new policy will affect the employees: "It will freeze their pay, limit their vacations, and reduce their benefits." It is not choice **a**, a slight or mild change, nor is it choice **b**, a regular or steady change. You do not know if it is an immediate or swift change, choice **d**, because the sentence says nothing about the time frame in which this change will take place. Remember, good detectives do not make assumptions they are not able to support with facts, and there are no facts in this sentence to support the assumption that the changes will take place immediately. Thus, choice **c** is the best answer.

You may also have noticed that *adversely* is very similar to the word *adversary*. If you know that an *adversary* is a hostile opponent or enemy, then you know that *adversely* is not likely to be something positive. Or, if you know the word *adversity*—hardship or misfortune—then you know that *adversely* must mean something negative or difficult. All of these words share the same root: *advers-*. The only change is in the endings.

Being able to determine the meaning of unfamiliar words from their context is an essential vocabulary skill. Sometimes you will encounter an unfamiliar word whose meaning is indecipherable without a dictionary. More often than not, though, a careful look at the context will give you enough clues to interpret the definition.

▶ Practice Questions

Read the following paragraph. Some words that may be unfamiliar to you are in italics. After you have read and understood the paragraph, explain the context clues that helped you with the meaning of the italicized words. Write your answer on the lines provided on the next page.

Medical researchers can now *verify* that college freshman living in dormitories are at a greater risk of contracting meningitis than other college students. Meningococcal meningitis is a *tenacious* bacterial infection of the membranes around the brain and spinal chord that, if left untreated, can be fatal. Symptoms include fever, neck stiffness, and constant pain from a *chronic* headache. College officials are using this information as an *inducement* for vaccinating incoming freshman. Many universities are now offering this vaccine either free or for a *nominal* fee. The vaccination's *protracted* effectiveness is three to five years.

_____

_____

_____

_____

_____

_____

_____

_____

_____

▶ **Answers**

After reading the paragraph, you learn that a study has been done that shows that college freshman living in dorms have a higher risk of getting meningitis; therefore, you can conclude that *verify* means confirm. Because this disease can be fatal, you can understand that once contracted, it is not easily wiped out; thus, you can infer that *tenacious* means persistent and not easily stopped. Because the symptoms include *constant pain from a chronic headache,* you can deduce that *chronic* means continual. It makes sense that college officials are concerned about the possible outbreak of such a disease on campus and would take measures to prevent its occurrence, so you can infer that *inducement* means encouragement. Students would be encouraged to take the vaccine if it were free or inexpensive; therefore, you can see that *nominal* means a small amount. Finally, you can gather that *protracted* means drawn out by the mention that the vaccine will last from three to five years.

11 ▶ Synonyms and Antonyms

On the civil service exam, your grasp of the English language will be measured with many different types of vocabulary questions. Frequently, synonym and antonym questions are used to assess your vocabulary aptitude. This chapter covers both of these types of questions. In addition, it provides useful tips and practice questions that will help you increase your chance of success on this part of the exam.

A common measure of verbal skills on standardized tests like the civil service exam is the ability to recognize synonyms and antonyms. **Synonyms** are words that share the same meaning or nearly the same meaning as other words. **Antonyms** are words with opposite meanings. Many antonyms seem obvious (*good* and *bad, night* and *day, noisy* and *silent*), but others are not as easily recognizable. This is because many words have more than one meaning. For example, the word *clear* could mean *cloudless* or *transparent* or *unmistakable*. And for each of those meanings, *clear* has an opposite. If an antonym isn't obvious, think about other possible meanings of the word.

Test questions often ask you to find the synonym or antonym of a word. If you are lucky, the word will be surrounded by a sentence that helps you guess what the word means (this is vocabulary in context—see Chapter 10), but the test question could list just a synonym or antonym and four answer choices. In this case, you have to figure out what the word means without any help from context clues.

Questions that ask for synonyms and antonyms can be difficult because they require you to have a relatively large vocabulary. Not only do you need to know the word in question, but you may be faced with four choices that are unfamiliar to you, too. Usually the best strategy is to look at the structure of the word. See if a part of the word—the root—looks familiar. Often you will be able to determine the meaning of a word within the root. (See Appendix 5 for a list of common word roots.) For instance, the root of credible is *cred,* which means to trust or believe. Knowing this, you will be able to understand the meaning of *incredible, sacred,* and *credit.* Looking for related words that have the same root as the word in question can help you choose the correct answer—even if it is by process of elimination.

Another way to dissect meaning is to look for prefixes and suffixes. Prefixes come before the word root, and suffixes are found at the end of a word. Either of these elements can carry meaning or change the use of a word in a sentence. For instance, the prefix can change the meaning of a root word to its opposite: *necessary, unnecessary.*

A suffix like *less* can change the meaning of a noun: *pain* to *painless.* To identify most word parts—word root, prefix, or suffix—the best strategy is to think of words you already know that carry the same root, suffix, or prefix. Let what you know about those words help you find the meaning of words that are less familiar.

▶ Denotation and Connotation

The **denotation** of a word is its dictionary definition. For instance, look at the dictionary definitions for the following words.

procrastination: to postpone or delay needlessly
lazy: to be resistant to work or exertion; slow-moving or sluggish
inactive: not active or tending to be active; not functioning or operating

The **connotation** of a word is its tone. In other words, it is the feeling or emotion you get when you hear a word. Sometimes, the connotation can be favorable or positive. Other times the connotation can be unfavorable or negative. Then again, some words do not arouse any emotion at all and have a neutral connotation.

Look again at the three words just listed. Their connotations are listed here with an explanation for a favorable, unfavorable, or neutral designation.

procrastination—favorable. You have often heard people say that they succumbed to procrastination, and that admission is received sympathetically and somewhat approvingly by others because everyone has procrastinated at one time or another. To admit to this trait is considered acceptable at times.

lazy—unfavorable. Laziness, which is similar in definition to procrastination, is most assuredly unflattering. The connotation or tone of this word brings up feelings that are definitely unappealing.

inactive—neutral. This word does not elicit any favorable or unfavorable emotions. It is considered a neutral word in this group of three, yet its meaning is similar to the others.

▶ Clarity

Mark Twain said, "The difference between lightning and the lightning bug is the difference between the right word and the almost right word." Taking this comment into consideration, it is important to know that there are often many synonyms for one word. It is essential to be as clear as possible when choosing synonyms. While some synonyms can be similar, they are rarely identical. For instance, the words *bountiful, ample, plentiful,* and *glut* suggest abundance. However, one of these words suggests an overabundance. While you can have a bountiful, ample, or plentiful supply of food on the table for Thanksgiving dinner, a glut of food is an excessive amount of food that suggests there will be waste involved. It is important to choose your words carefully.

▶ Practice Questions

For questions 1–15, choose the synonym.

1. Which word means the same as *enthusiastic?*
   a. adamant
   b. available
   c. cheerful
   d. eager

2. Which word means the same as *adequate?*
   a. sufficient
   b. mediocre
   c. proficient
   d. average

3. Which word means the same as *ecstatic?*
   a. inconsistent
   b. positive
   c. wild
   d. thrilled

4. Which word means the same as *affect?*
   a. accomplish
   b. cause
   c. sicken
   d. influence

5. Which word means the same as *continuous?*
   a. intermittent
   b. adjacent
   c. uninterrupted
   d. contiguous

6. Which word means the same as *courtesy?*
   a. civility
   b. congruity
   c. conviviality
   d. rudeness

7. Which word means the same as *frail?*
   a. vivid
   b. delicate
   c. robust
   d. adaptable

8. Which word means the same as *recuperate?*
   a. mend
   b. endorse
   c. persist
   d. worsen

9. Which word means the same as *meager?*
   a. majestic
   b. scarce
   c. tranquil
   d. adequate

10. Which word means the same as *composure?*
   a. agitation
   b. poise
   c. liveliness
   d. stimulation

11. Which word means the same as *eccentric?*
   a. normal
   b. frugal
   c. peculiar
   d. selective

12. Which word means the same as *commendable?*
   a. admirable
   b. accountable
   c. irresponsible
   d. noticeable

13. Which word means the same as *passive?*
   a. inactive
   b. emotional
   c. lively
   d. woeful

14. Which word means the same as *vast?*
   a. attentive
   b. immense
   c. steady
   d. slight

15. Which word means the same as *comply?*
   a. subdue
   b. entertain
   c. flatter
   d. obey

For questions 16–25, choose the word that has the same or nearly the same meaning as the capitalized word.

16. JOURNAL
   a. trip
   b. receipt
   c. diary
   d. list

17. OPPORTUNITY
   a. sensitivity
   b. arrogance
   c. chance
   d. reference

18. INVENT
   a. insert
   b. discover
   c. apply
   d. allow

19. SPHERE
   a. air
   b. spread
   c. globe
   d. enclosure

20. REFINE
   a. condone
   b. provide
   c. change
   d. purify

21. PLEDGE
   a. picture
   b. idea
   c. quote
   d. promise

22. GANGLY
   a. illegally
   b. closely
   c. ugly
   d. lanky

23. SAGE
   a. wise
   b. obnoxious
   c. conceited
   d. heartless

24. NAVIGATE
   a. search
   b. decide
   c. steer
   d. assist

25. DORMANT
   a. hidden
   b. slumbering
   c. rigid
   d. misplaced

For questions 26–40, choose the antonym.

26. Which word means the opposite of *prompt*?
   a. punctual
   b. slack
   c. tardy
   d. regular

27. What word is the opposite of *delay*?
   a. slow
   b. hasten
   c. pause
   d. desist

28. What word is the opposite of *soothe*?
   a. increase
   b. comfort
   c. aggravate
   d. delight

29. Which word means the opposite of *moderate*?
   a. original
   b. average
   c. final
   d. excessive

30. Which word means the opposite of *reveal*?
   a. disclose
   b. achieve
   c. retreat
   d. conceal

31. Which word means the opposite of *initial*?
   a. first
   b. crisis
   c. final
   d. right

32. Which word means the opposite of *brittle*?
   a. flexible
   b. breakable
   c. grating
   d. thin

33. Which word means the opposite of *capable?*
   a. unskilled
   b. absurd
   c. apt
   d. able

34. What word is the opposite of *stray?*
   a. remain
   b. inhabit
   c. wander
   d. incline

35. What word is the opposite of *dainty?*
   a. delicate
   b. coarse
   c. harsh
   d. delicious

36. Which word means the opposite of *craving?*
   a. desire
   b. nonchalance
   c. motive
   d. repugnance

37. Which word means the opposite of *ferocious?*
   a. docile
   b. savage
   c. explosive
   d. noble

38. Which word means the opposite of *grueling?*
   a. effortless
   b. casual
   c. exhausting
   d. empty

39. Which word means the opposite of *forsake?*
   a. admit
   b. abandon
   c. submit
   d. cherish

40. What word is the opposite of *restrain?*
   a. control
   b. liberate
   c. maintain
   d. distract

For questions 41–50, choose the word that has the opposite meaning as the capitalized word.

41. ABSORB
   a. acquire
   b. repel
   c. consume
   d. assist

42. CRITICAL
   a. inimical
   b. judgmental
   c. massive
   d. trivial

43. NIMBLE
   a. sturdy
   b. sluggish
   c. thoughtless
   d. relaxed

44. TRANQUIL
   a. agitated
   b. explicit
   c. assertive
   d. composed

45. SPRIGHTLY
  a. eager
  b. lofty
  c. dull
  d. local

46. INFANTILE
  a. despicable
  b. adolescent
  c. mature
  d. perpetual

47. IMPULSIVE
  a. secure
  b. mandatory
  c. rash
  d. cautious

48. AMIABLE
  a. dangerous
  b. permissive
  c. aloof
  d. congenial

49. COMPETENT
  a. incomplete
  b. intense
  c. inept
  d. massive

50. PROMOTE
  a. explicate
  b. curtail
  c. concede
  d. remote

▶ Answers

1. d. *Enthusiastic* means *eager* or excited.

2. a. If something is *adequate*, it is *sufficient*.

3. d. A person who is *ecstatic* is *thrilled* or exhilarated.

4. d. To *affect* means to *influence*.

5. c. *Continuous* means marked by *uninterrupted* extension in space and time.

6. a. A *courtesy* implies being courteous or mannerly; it is *civility*.

7. b. A *frail* person is weak and *delicate*.

8. a. *Recuperate* means to heal; to *mend*.

9. b. *Meager* and *scarce* both mean lacking.

10. b. If you gain your *composure*, you have *poise*.

11. c. An *eccentric* person is considered to be *peculiar*.

12. a. *Commendable* is the same as *admirable*.

13. a. *Passive* means not active.

14. b. *Vast* means very great in size; *immense*.

15. d. To *comply* is the same as to *obey*.

16. c. A *journal* and a *diary* are both records of daily happenings.

17. c. An *opportunity* to do something is the same as a *chance* to do it.

18. b. *Invent* means to create or to *discover*.

19. c. *Sphere* and *globe* both mean ball or orb.

20. d. To *refine* and to *purify* both mean to remove impurities.

21. d. *Pledge* and *promise* both mean a declaration that one will do something.

22. d. *Gangly* and *lanky* both mean tall, thin, and awkward.

23. a. *Sage* and *wise* both mean intelligent or perceptive.

24. c. To *navigate* and to *steer* both mean to direct a course.

25. b. *Dormant* and *slumbering* both mean sleeping.

26. c. *Prompt* means punctual; *tardy* means late.

27. b. To *delay* is to slow; to *hasten* is to hurry.

28. c. To *soothe* is to comfort; to *aggravate* is to irritate.

29. d. *Moderate* means average; *excessive* means extreme.

30. d. To *reveal* is to disclose; to *conceal* is to hide.

31. c. *Initial* means first; *final* means last.

32. a. *Brittle* means breakable; *flexible* means pliable.

33. a. *Capable* means able; *unskilled* means unable.

34. a. To *stray* is to wander; to *remain* is to stay.

35. b. *Dainty* means delicate; *coarse* means indelicate.

36. d. *Craving* means desire; *repugnance* means aversion.

37. a. *Ferocious* means savage; *docile* means tame.

38. a. *Grueling* means exhausting; *effortless* means easy.

39. d. To *forsake* is to abandon; to *cherish* is to nurture.

40. b. To *restrain* is to control; to *liberate* is to release.

41. b. *Absorb* means to take in or consume; to *repel* is to reject or force away.

42. d. To be *critical* is to be important or vital to something; to be *trivial* is to be unimportant.

43. b. *Nimble* means quick and light in motion; *sluggish* means slow or inactive.

44. a. *Tranquil* means peaceful; *agitated* means disturbed or excited.

45. **c.** *Sprightly* means lively; *dull* suggests a lack or loss of keenness or zest.

46. **c.** *Infantile* means childish, *mature* means grown up.

47. **d.** To be *impulsive* is to be swayed by emotion or to make rash decisions; to be *cautious* is to show forethought.

48. **c.** *Amiable* means friendly; the opposite of friendly is *aloof.*

49. **c.** *Competent* means having adequate abilities; *inept* means incapable or not competent.

50. **b.** To *promote* is to advance someone to a higher rank or to advocate something; to *curtail* is to cut something short.

12 ▶ Reading Comprehension

Because understanding what you read is such a vital skill, most civil service exams include a reading comprehension section that tests your ability to understand what you read. To read effectively, you should be able to find the main idea of a passage, select the topic sentence, locate basic support material or details, discern fact from opinion, and make inferences. This chapter reviews each of these skills.

The reading comprehension portion of the civil service exam is usually presented as a multiple choice test and will ask questions based on brief passages. Reading comprehension questions offer you two advantages as a test taker. First, you do not need any prior knowledge about the topic of the passage. Second, you will be tested only on the information presented in the passage. The disadvantage is that you have to know where and how to find the information you need under certain time constraints and in an unfamiliar text. This somewhat stressful combination makes it easy to choose one of the wrong answer choices, especially since the choices are deliberately designed to mislead you. If you are in a hurry, it is easy to make a mistake.

As you study this reading comprehension section, understand that your vocabulary skills play a vital role when you have to decipher any written text. Sometimes, just one difficult word can skew your understanding of a sentence. Two or three unknown words can make a passage difficult, or even impossible, to interpret. The study of vocabulary in combination with reading comprehension go hand in hand as you continue your test preparation.

The best way to do well on a reading comprehension test is to be very familiar with the kinds of questions that are typically asked, and then to know how to respond to these questions. Questions most frequently ask you to:

- determine the main idea of the passage.
- identify a specific fact or detail in the passage.
- identify the topic sentence.
- discern fact from opinion.
- make an inference based on the passage.
- define a vocabulary word from the passage. (Refer to Chapter 10 to practice this skill.)

Once you know the kinds of questions that will be asked, you can develop some strategies to help you choose correct answers. To do this, you must be a discriminating reader and know where to look for the information, facts, and details you need to help you choose correctly.

One strategy used by many readers is highlighting and underlining. By highlighting or underlining key words and phrases, you can make important details stand out. This helps you quickly find the information later when you need to answer a question or write a summary. To highlight key words and ideas, you must be able to determine which facts and ideas are most important.

Here are three guidelines for highlighting or underlining your text.

1. **Be selective.** If you highlight four sentences in a five-sentence paragraph, this will not help you. The key is to identify what is most important in the paragraph. Ask yourself two questions:
   - What is the main point the author is trying to make—what is the main idea of the paragraph?
   - What information is emphasized or seems to stand out as especially important?
2. **Watch for word clues.** Certain words and phrases indicate that key information will follow. Words and phrases such as *most important, the key is,* and *significantly* are clues to watch out for.
3. **Watch for visual clues.** Key words and ideas are often boldfaced, underlined, or italicized. They may be boxed or repeated in a sidebar as well.

For practice, read the following paragraph and answer the questions that follow. The answer explanation following each type of question—main idea, detail/support material, topic sentence, fact/opinion, and inference—will point out reading comprehension strategies that help you choose the correct answer.

Today's postal service is more efficient and reliable than ever before. Mail that used to take months to move by horse and by foot now moves around the country in days or hours by truck, train, and plane. First class mail usually moves from New York City to Los Angeles in three days or fewer. If your letter or package is urgent, the U.S. Postal Service offers Priority Mail and Express Mail services. Priority Mail offers delivery to most locations in the United States in two to three days or fewer. Express Mail is guaranteed to get your package there overnight. Additionally, the U.S. Postal Service offers lower rates for the same services offered by many competitors.

Main Idea Question

1. What is the main idea of this paragraph?
  a. The U.S. Postal Service offers many services.
  b. Express Mail is a good way to send urgent mail.
  c. First class mail usually takes three days or fewer.
  d. Mail service today is more effective and dependable.

If you selected choice **a**, you would be choosing the subject of the paragraph, not the main idea. The main idea must say something about the subject. To accurately find the main idea of a text, remember that it is usually an *assertion* about the subject. An assertion is a statement that requires evidence or proof to be accepted as true. While the main idea of a passage is an assertion about its subject, it is something more. It is the idea that holds together or controls the passage. The other sentences and ideas in the passage will all relate to that main idea and serve as evidence that the assertion is true.

You might think of the main idea as an umbrella that is held over the other sentences. It must be *general* enough or big enough to cover all of these ideas underneath it (in the paragraph or passage). Choice **b** is too specific to be the main idea; it tells you only about Express Mail. It does not include any information about Priority Mail or first class mail, so it cannot be the main idea of the paragraph. Choice **c** is also too specific. It tells you about first class mail only, so this choice can be excluded. Choice **d** is general enough to encompass the entire passage. The rest of the sentences in the paragraph support the idea that this sentence asserts. Each sentence offers proof that the postal expresses the writer's purpose—to show the efficiency and reliability of today's postal service.

Fact/Detail Question

2. Today's mail is transported by
  a. foot.
  b. horse.
  c. trucks, trains, and planes.
  d. overnight services.

Choices **a** and **b** are mentioned in the paragraph, and you may mistakenly choose one of these if you only scan the paragraph quickly. However, if you read more closely, you will see that in the past, "Mail used to take months to move by horse and by foot," but it "now moves around the country in days or hours by truck, train, and plane," choice **c**. Choice **d** is misleading. Overnight mail services are transported by truck, train, and plane as well.

Topic Sentence Question

3. Of the following sentences, which one is the topic sentence?
  a. Mail that used to take months to move by horse and by foot now moves around the country in days or hours by truck, train, and plane.
  b. Today's postal service is more efficient and reliable than ever before.
  c. If your letter or package is urgent, the U.S. Postal Service offers Priority Mail and Express Mail services.
  d. Express Mail is guaranteed to get your package there overnight.

You will notice that in the paragraph, the main idea is expressed clearly in the first sentence, choice **b**. A sentence such as this one that clearly expresses the main idea of a paragraph or passage is called the **topic sentence**. In many cases, you will find the topic sentence at the beginning of the paragraph, but this is not a hard and fast rule. The topic sentence can be found in the middle or at the end of a paragraph. However, for the sentence to be labeled a topic sentence, it must be an assertion, and it needs proof. The proof is found in the facts and ideas that make up the rest of the paragraph. Choices **a**, **c**, and **d** are sentences that offer specific facts and ideas that support choice **b**.

Fact/Opinion Question

3. "Express Mail is guaranteed to get your package there overnight." This statement is a(n)
   a. fact.
   b. opinion.

   Facts are things known for certain to have happened, to be true, or to exist. **Opinions** are things believed to have happened, believed to be true, or believed to exist. As you can see, the key difference between fact and opinion lies in the difference between believing and knowing. Opinions may be based on facts, but they are still what you think, not what you know. Opinions are debatable; facts are not. The statement in the question, "Express Mail is guaranteed to get your package there overnight," is a fact, so choice **a** is correct.

Inference Question

4. Based on the information in the paragraph, it is safe to say that
   a. it is economical for businesses to take advantage of Express Mail services.
   b. the old-fashioned pony express system of mail delivery did not work.
   c. first class mail service is unreliable.
   d. there is no way to deliver urgent mail.

   An inference is a conclusion that can be drawn based on fact or evidence. You can infer that businesses could take advantage of Express Mail service to speed up deliveries, choice **a**, based on the evidence in the paragraph. "Express Mail is guaranteed to get your package there overnight," justifiably supports this inference. Choices **b**, **c**, and **d** cannot be inferred based on any concrete evidence from the paragraph.

   Knowing that reading comprehension questions can include main idea, topic sentence, detail, fact/opinion, or inference questions is a practical beginning for reading comprehension skills.

▶ Practice Questions

Read the following paragraphs and answer the reading comprehension questions based on your knowledge of the main idea of each paragraph.

If you are a fitness walker, there is no need for a commute to a health club. Your neighborhood can be your health club. You do not need a lot of fancy equipment to get a good workout, either. All you need is a well-designed pair of athletic shoes.

1. This paragraph best supports the statement that
   a. fitness walking is a better form of exercise than weight lifting.
   b. a membership in a health club is a poor investment.
   c. walking outdoors provides a better workout than walking indoors.
   d. fitness walking is a convenient and valuable form of exercise.

Critical reading is a demanding process. To read critically, you must slow down your reading and, with pencil in hand, perform specific operations on the text. Mark up the text with your reactions, conclusions, and questions. In other words, when you read, become an active participant.

2. This paragraph best supports the statement that
   a. critical reading is a slow, dull, but essential process.
   b. the best critical reading happens at critical times in a person's life.
   c. readers should get in the habit of questioning the truth of what they read.
   d. critical reading requires thoughtful and careful attention.

One New York publisher has estimated that 50,000 to 60,000 people in the United States want an anthology that includes the complete works of William Shakespeare. What accounts for this renewed interest in Shakespeare? As scholars point out, his psychological insights into both male and female characters are amazing, even today.

3. This paragraph best supports the statement that
   a. Shakespeare's characters are more interesting than fictional characters today.
   b. people today are interested in Shakespeare's work because of the characters.
   c. academic scholars are putting together an anthology of Shakespeare's work.
   d. New Yorkers have a renewed interest in the work of Shakespeare.

There are no effective boundaries when it comes to pollutants. Studies have shown that toxic insecticides—already banned in many countries—are riding the wind from countries where they remain legal. Compounds such as DDT and toxaphene have been found in remote places like the Yukon and other Arctic regions.

4. This paragraph best supports the statement that
   a. bans on toxins have done little to stop the spread of pollutants.
   b. more pollutants find their way into polar climates than they do into warmer areas.
   c. studies show that many countries have ignored their own anti-pollution laws.
   d. DDT and toxaphene are the two most toxic insecticides in the world.

The Fourth Amendment to the Constitution protects citizens against unreasonable searches and seizures. No search of a person's home or personal effects may be conducted without a written search warrant issued on probable cause. This means that a neutral judge must approve the factual basis justifying a search before it can be conducted.

5. This paragraph best supports the statement that police officers cannot search a person's home or private papers unless they have
   a. legal authorization.
   b. direct evidence of a crime.
   c. read the person his or her constitutional rights.
   d. a reasonable belief that a crime has occurred.

Mathematics allows us to expand our consciousness. Mathematics tells us about economic trends, patterns of disease, and the growth of populations. Math is good at exposing the truth, but it can also perpetuate misunderstandings and untruths. Figures have the power to mislead people.

6. This paragraph best supports the statement that
   a. the study of mathematics is dangerous.
   b. the study of mathematics can be both beneficial and confusing.
   c. the study of mathematics is more important than other disciplines.
   d. the power of numbers is that they cannot lie.

Human technology began with the development of the first stone tools about two and a half million years ago. In the beginning, the rate of development was slow, and hundreds of thousands of years passed without many technological changes. Today, new technologies are reported daily on television and in newspapers.

7. This paragraph best supports the statement that
   a. stone tools were not really technology.
   b. stone tools were in use for two and a half million years.
   c. there is no way to know when stone tools first came into use.
   d. in today's world, new technologies are constantly being developed.

Read the following paragraphs and choose the correct fact or detail to answer the questions.

Ratatouille is a dish that has grown in popularity over the last few years. It features eggplant, zucchini, tomato, peppers, and garlic chopped, mixed, sautéed, and finally, cooked slowly over low heat. As the vegetables cook slowly, they make their own broth, which can be extended with a little tomato paste. The name *ratatouille* comes from the French word *touiller,* meaning to mix or stir together.

8. Which of the following is the correct order of steps for making ratatouille?
   a. Chop vegetables, add tomato paste, stir or mix together.
   b. Mix the vegetables together, sauté them, and add tomato paste.
   c. Cook the vegetables slowly, mix them together, add tomato paste.
   d. Add tomato paste to extend the broth and cook slowly over low heat.

9. Ratatouille can best be described as a
   a. French pastry.
   b. sauce to put over vegetables.
   c. pasta dish extended with tomato paste.
   d. vegetable stew.

After a snow or ice fall, the city streets are treated with ordinary rock salt. In some areas, the salt is combined with calcium chloride, which is more effective in below-zero temperatures and which melts ice better. This combination of salt and calcium chloride is also less damaging to foliage along the roadways.

10. In deciding whether to use ordinary rock salt or the salt and calcium chloride mixture on a particular street, which of the following is NOT a consideration?
    a. the temperature at the time of treatment
    b. the plants and trees along the street
    c. whether there is ice on the street
    d. whether the street is a main or secondary road

11. According to the snow treatment passage, which of the following is true?
    a. If the temperature is below zero, a salt and calcium chloride mixture is effective in treating snow- and ice-covered streets.
    b. Crews must wait until the snow or ice stops falling before salting streets.
    c. Major roads are always salted first.
    d. If the snowfall is light, the city road crews will not salt the streets because this would be a waste of the salt supply.

Many cities have distributed standardized recycling containers to all households. One city attached the following directions: "We prefer that you use this new container as your primary recycling container, as this will expedite pick-up of recyclables. Additional recycling containers may be purchased as needed from the Sanitation Department."

12. According to the passage, each household
    a. may use only one recycling container.
    b. must use the new recycling container.
    c. should use the new recycling container.
    d. must buy a new recycling container.

13. According to the passage, which of the following is true about the new containers?
    a. The new containers are far better than other containers in every way.
    b. The new containers will help increase the efficiency of the recycling program.
    c. The new containers hold more than the old containers did.
    d. The new containers are less expensive than the old.

Read the following paragraphs and choose the topic sentence that best fits the paragraph.

Spices is a pleasant word, whether it connotes fine French cuisine or down-home cinnamon-flavored apple pie. _____. In the past, individuals traveled the world seeking exotic spices for profit and, in searching, have changed the course of history. Indeed, to gain control of lands harboring new spices, nations have actually gone to war.

14. a. The taste and aroma of spices are the main elements that make food such a source or fascination and pleasure.
    b. The term might equally bring to mind Indian curry made thousands of miles away or those delicious barbecued ribs sold down at Harry's.
    c. It is exciting to find a good cookbook and experiment with spices from other lands—indeed, it is one way to travel around the globe.

d. The history of spices, however, is another matter altogether, and it can be filled with danger and intrigue.

It weighs less than three pounds and is hardly more interesting to look at than an overly ripe cauliflower. _____. It has created poetry and music, planned and executed wars, devised intricate scientific theories. It thinks and dreams, plots and schemes, and easily holds more information than all the libraries on Earth.

15. a. The human brain is made of gelatinous matter and contains no nerve endings.
 b. The science of neurology has found a way to map the most important areas of the human brain.
 c. Nevertheless, the human brain is the most mysterious and complex object on earth.
 d. However, scientists say that each person uses only 10% of brainpower over the course of a lifetime.

Gary is a very distinguished-looking man with a touch of gray at the temples. Even in his early fifties, he is still the one to turn heads. He enjoys spending most of his time admiring his profile in the mirror. In fact, he considers his good looks to be his second most important asset in the world. The first, however, is money. He was fortunate enough to be born into a wealthy family, and he loves the power his wealth has given him. _____. He can buy whatever he desires. Gary checks the mirror often and feels great delight with what he sees.

16. a. Gary's gray hair is his worst characteristic.
 b. Conceit is the beginning and the end of Gary's character: conceit of person and situation.
 c. Gary feels blessed to be wealthy and the joy consumes his every thought.
 d. The only objects of Gary's respect are others who hold positions in society above him.

Read the following topic sentences and choose the sentence that best develops or supports the topic sentence.

17. Life on Earth is ancient, and at its first appearance, unimaginably complex.
 a. Scientists place its beginnings at some three billion years ago, when the first molecule floated up out of the ooze with the unique ability to replicate itself.
 b. The most complex life form is, of course, the mammal—and the most complex mammal is humankind.
 c. It is unknown exactly where life started— where the first molecule was "born" that had the ability to replicate itself.
 d. Darwin's theory of evolution was one attempt to explain what essentially remains a great mystery.

18. The continuing fascination of the public with movie star Marilyn Monroe is puzzling, yet it is still strong, even after many decades.
 a. She became a star in the 1950s and died in 1962.
 b. The film that most clearly demonstrates her talent is *The Misfits*.
 c. Her name was originally Norma Jean, but she changed it to Marilyn.
 d. One reason might simply be her life's sad and premature end.

19. One scientific theory of the origin of the universe is the much misunderstood big bang theory.
    a. Physicists now believe they can construct what happened in the universe during the first three minutes of its beginning.
    b. Many scientists believe that, during microwave experiments, you can actually "hear" echoes of the big bang.
    c. The popular notion is that the big bang was a huge explosion in space, but this is far too simple a description.
    d. The big bang theory, if accepted, convinces us that the universe was not always as it is now.

20. There is no instruction by the old bird in the movements of flight, no conscious imitation by the young.
    a. The most obvious way in which birds differ from humans in behavior is that they can do all that they have to do, without ever being taught.
    b. More extraordinary than a bird being able to fly untaught is that it is able to build a nest untaught.
    c. Young birds frequently make their first flights with their parents out of sight.
    d. Young birds brought up by hand in artificial nests will build the proper kind of nest for their species when the time comes.

21. The reintroduced wolves are producing more offspring than expected.
    a. Ranchers and some biologists are protesting the reintroduction of the wolves.
    b. The gray wolf will be taken off the list of endangered species in the northern Rocky Mountains when ten breeding pairs reside in a region for three years.
    c. There are active efforts to reintroduce wolves to national parks in the United States.
    d. The success of an attempt to reintroduce red wolves to parts of North Carolina is not yet clear.

22. The Puritans established a wide variety of punishments to enforce their strict laws.
    a. The Puritans believed that some lawbreakers should be shamed in public by the use of stocks and the pillory.
    b. Disobedient children would feel the sting of the whip.
    c. The Eighth Amendment of the Bill of Rights prohibits cruel and unusual punishment.
    d. Today, many of the punishments used by the Puritans in Massachusetts Bay seem cruel and excessive.

Read the following supporting sentences and choose the sentence that would make the best topic sentence.

23. Irish Catholics continued to fight against British rule.
  a. The struggle today is over the control of these six counties.
  b. For centuries, all of Ireland was ruled by Great Britain.
  c. Six counties in the north—where Protestants outnumber Catholics two to one—remained a part of Great Britain and became known as Northern Ireland.
  d. Political violence has claimed many lives in Northern Ireland.

24. In Oklahoma, a girl is forbidden to take a bite from her date's hamburger.
  a. It is illegal for teenagers to take a bath during the winter in Clinton, Indiana.
  b. On Sunday, children may not spin yo-yos in Memphis, Tennessee.
  c. It may be hard to believe, but these strange laws are still on the books!
  d. It is illegal to parade an elephant down Main Street in Austin, Texas.

25. The hairs themselves are very sensitive.
  a. A cat's whiskers are among the most perfect organs of touch.
  b. The roots are provided with highly sensitive nerve endings.
  c. Serving as feelers, they aid the cat's ability to move in the dark.
  d. This is most important for a cat that does its prowling at night.

26. French explorers probably taught the Inuit Eskimos how to play dominoes.
  a. It was known in 181 A.D. in China.
  b. Also, it was played during the 1700s in Italy.
  c. The game of dominoes has been popular for centuries.
  d. From Italy, it was introduced to the rest of the world.

27. It is a fact that people are now living longer than ever before for many reasons.
  a. Some people in Russia's Caucasus Mountains live to be over one hundred years of age.
  b. No one seems to understand this phenomenon.
  c. Advances in medical science have done wonders for longevity.
  d. The people in this region do not seem to gain anything from medical science.

28. For 16 years, he spread violence and death throughout the west.
  a. Jesse was gunned down on April 3, 1882.
  b. He left a trail of train and bank robberies.
  c. His crimes were committed during the late 1860s.
  d. Jesse Woodson James was the most legendary of all American outlaws.

Read the following questions that ask you to differentiate fact from opinion. Write F in the blank if the statement is a fact and O if it is an opinion.

29. _____ Mr. Orenstein is a terrific boss.

30. _____ Many companies have dress-down days on Fridays.

31. _____ Dress-down days improve employee morale.

32. _____ Wednesday is the fourth day of the week.

33. _____ Wednesday is the longest day of the week.

34. _____ There are many different ways to invest your money to provide for a financially secure future.

35. _____ Many people invest in stocks and bonds.

36. _____ Savings accounts and CDs (certificates of deposit) are the best way to invest your hard-earned money.

37. _____ Stocks and bonds are often risky investments.

38. _____ Savings accounts and CDs are fully insured and provide steady, secure interest on your money.

Read the following paragraphs and respond to the questions.

The use of computer equipment and software to create high quality printing for newsletters, business cards, letterhead, and brochures is called Desktop Publishing, or DTP. The most important part of any DTP project is planning. Before you begin, you should know your intended audience, the message you want to communicate, and what form your message will take.

39. This paragraph best supports the statement that
    a. DTP is one way to become acquainted with a new business audience.
    b. computer software is continually being refined to produce more high quality printing.
    c. the first stage of any proposed DTP project should be organization and design.
    d. the planning stage of any DTP project should not include talking with the intended audience.

Many office professionals have expressed an interest in replacing the currently used keyboard, known as the QWERTY keyboard, with a keyboard that can keep up with technological changes and make offices more efficient. The best choice is the Dvorak keyboard. Studies have shown that people using the Dvorak keyboard can type 20–30% faster and are able to cut their error rate in half. Dvorak puts vowels and other frequently used letters right under the fingers—on the home row—where typists make 70% of their keystrokes.

40. This paragraph best supports the statement that the Dvorak keyboard
   a. is more efficient than the QWERTY.
   b. has more keys right under the typists' fingers than the QWERTY.
   c. is favored by more typists than the QWERTY.
   d. is—on average—70% faster than the QWERTY.

Every year, Americans use over one billion sharp objects to administer health care in their homes. These sharp objects include lancets, needles, and syringes. If not disposed of in puncture-resistant containers, they can injure sanitation workers. Sharp objects should be disposed of in hard plastic or metal containers with secure lids. The containers should be clearly marked and should be puncture resistant.

41. This paragraph best supports the idea that sanitation workers can be injured if they
   a. do not place sharp objects in puncture-resistant containers.
   b. come in contact with sharp objects that have not been placed in secure containers.
   c. are careless with sharp objects such as lancets, needles, and syringes in their homes.
   d. do not mark the containers they pick up with a warning that those containers contain sharp objects.

One of the missions of the Peace Corps is to bring trained men and women to work in countries who need trained professionals in certain fields. People who work for the Peace Corps are volunteers. However, in order to keep the Peace Corps dynamic and vital, no staff member can work for the agency for more than five years.

42. This paragraph best supports the statement that Peace Corps employees
   a. are highly intelligent people.
   b. must train for about five years.
   c. are hired for a limited term of employment.
   d. have both academic and work experience.

More and more office workers telecommute from offices in their own homes. The benefits of telecommuting allow for greater productivity and greater flexibility. Telecommuters produce an average of 20% more than if they were to work in an office. In addition, their flexible schedules allow them to balance their families with their work responsibilities.

43. This paragraph best supports the statement that telecommuters
   a. get more work done in a given time period than workers who travel to the office.
   b. produce a better quality work product than workers who travel to the office.
   c. are more flexible in their ideas than workers who travel to the office.
   d. would do 20% more work if they were to work in an office.

Close-up images of Mars by the Mariner 9 probe indicated networks of valleys that looked like the stream beds on Earth. These images also implied that Mars once had an atmosphere that was thick enough to trap the Sun's heat. If this is true, something must have happened to Mars billions of years ago that stripped away the planet's atmosphere.

44. This paragraph best supports the statement that
   a. Mars once had a thicker atmosphere than Earth does.
   b. the Mariner 9 probe took the first pictures of Mars.
   c. Mars now has little or no atmosphere.
   d. Mars is closer to the Sun than Earth is.

It is a myth that labor shortages today center mostly on computer jobs. Although it is true that the lack of computer-related skills accounts for many of the problems in today's job market, there is a lack of skilled labor in many other fields. There is a shortage of uniformed police officers in many cities and a shortage of trained criminal investigators in some rural areas. These jobs may utilize computer skills, but they are not essentially computer jobs.

45. This paragraph best supports the statement that
   a. people with computer skills are in demand in police and criminal investigator jobs.
   b. unemployment in computer-related fields is not as widespread as some people think.
   c. there is a shortage of skilled workers in a variety of fields, including police work.
   d. trained criminal investigators are often underpaid in rural areas.

The competitive civil service system is designed to give candidates fair and equal treatment and to ensure that federal applicants are hired based on objective criteria. Hiring has to be based solely on a candidate's knowledge, skills, and abilities—sometimes abbreviated as KSA—and not on external factors such as race, religion, or sex. Whereas employers in the private sector can hire employees for subjective reasons, federal employers must be able to justify their decision with objective evidence of candidate qualification.

46. This paragraph best supports the statement that
   a. hiring in the private sector is inherently unfair.
   b. *KSA* is not as important as test scores to federal employers.
   c. federal hiring practices are simpler than those employed by the private sector.
   d. the civil service strives to hire on the basis of a candidate's abilities.

It is well known that the world urgently needs adequate distribution of food, but adequate distribution of medicine is just as urgent. Medical expertise and medical supplies need to be redistributed throughout the world so that people in emerging nations will have proper medical care.

47. This paragraph best supports the statement that
   a. the majority of the people in the world have no medical care.
   b. medical resources in emerging nations have diminished in the past few years.
   c. not enough doctors give time and money to those in need of medical care.
   d. many people who live in emerging nations are not receiving proper medical care.

In the past, suggesting a gas tax has usually been considered a political blunder, but that does not seem to be the case today. Several states are promoting bills in their state legislatures that would cut income or property taxes and make up the revenue with taxes on fossil fuel.

48. This paragraph best supports the statement that
   a. gas taxes produce more revenue than income taxes.
   b. states with low income tax rates are increasing their gas taxes.
   c. state legislators no longer fear increasing gas taxes.
   d. taxes on fossil fuels are more popular than property taxes.

Whether you can accomplish a specific goal or meet a specific deadline depends first on how much time you need to get the job done. What should you do when the demands of the job exceed the time you have available? The best approach is to divide the project into smaller pieces. Different goals will have to be divided in different ways, but one seemingly unrealistic goal can often be accomplished by working on several smaller, more reasonable goals.

49. This paragraph best supports the statement that
   a. jobs often remain only partially completed because of lack of time.
   b. the best way to complete projects is to make sure your goals are achievable.
   c. the best way to tackle large projects is to problem-solve first.
   d. the best approach to a demanding job is to delegate responsibility.

Before you begin to compose a business letter, sit down and think about your purpose for writing the letter. Do you want to request information, order a product, register a complaint, or apply for something? Do some brainstorming and gather information before you begin writing. Always keep your objective in mind.

50. This paragraph best supports the statement that
   a. for many different kinds of writing tasks, planning is an important first step.
   b. business letters are frequently complaint letters.
   c. brainstorming and writing take approximately equal amounts of time.
   d. while some people plan ahead when they are writing a business letter, others do not.

► Answers

1. d. By stating that fitness walking does not require a commute to a health club, the author stresses the convenience of this form of exercise. The paragraph also states that fitness walking will result in a good workout. Choice **a** is incorrect because no comparison to weight lifting is made. Choice **b** may seem like a logical answer, but the paragraph refers only to people who are fitness walkers, so for others, a health club might be a good investment. Choice **c** is not supported by the passage.

2. d. This answer is implied by the whole paragraph. The author stresses the need to read critically by performing thoughtful and careful operations on the text. Choice **a** is incorrect because the author never says that reading is dull. Choices **b** and **c** are not supported by the paragraph.

3. b. The last sentence in the paragraph clearly gives support for the idea that the interest in Shakespeare is due to the development of his characters. Choice **a** is incorrect because the writer never makes this type of comparison. Choice **c** is incorrect because even though scholars are mentioned in the paragraph, there is no indication that the scholars are compiling the anthology. Choice **d** is incorrect because there is no support to show that most New Yorkers are interested in this work.

4. a. The support for this choice is in the second sentence, which states that in some countries toxic insecticides are still legal. Choice **b** is incorrect because even though polar regions are mentioned in the paragraph, there is no support for the idea that warmer regions are not just as affected. There is no support for choice **c**. Choice **d** can be ruled out because there is nothing to indicate that DDT and toxaphene are the most toxic insecticides.

5. a. The second and third sentence combine to give support to choice **a**. The statement stresses that there must be a judge's approval (i.e., legal authorization) before a search can be conducted. Choices **b** and **d** are incorrect because it is not enough for the police to have direct evidence or a reasonable belief—a judge must authorize the search for it to be legal. Choice **c** is not mentioned in the passage.

6. b. This answer is clearly stated in the last sentence of the paragraph. Choice **a** can be ruled out because there is no support to show that studying math is dangerous. Choice **d** is a contradiction to the information in the passage. There is no support for choice **c**.

7. d. The last sentence states that new technologies are reported daily, and this implies that new technologies are being constantly developed. There is no support for choice **a**. With regard to choice **b**, stone tools were first used two and a half million years ago, but they were not necessarily in use all that time. Choice **c** is incorrect because the paragraph states when stone tools first came into use.

8. b. See the second and third sentences for the steps in making ratatouille. Only choice **b** reflects the correct order.

9. d. The main part of the passage describes how to cook vegetables. Only choice **d** indicates that vegetables are included in the dish. The other choices are not reflected in the passage.

10. d. The passage mentions nothing about main or secondary roads.

11. a. The other choices may be true but are not mentioned in the passage.

12. c. The passage indicates that the city prefers, but does not require, the use of the new containers. Also, customers may use more than one container if they purchase an additional one.

13. b. The passage states that the use of the new containers will expedite pick-up of recyclables. This indicates that the new containers will make the recycling program more efficient.

14. d. The mention that searching for spices has changed the course of history and that nations have gone to war over this condiment implies that the subject of the paragraph is history, not cooking, choices **a**, **b**, and **c**. The use of the word *war* involves danger and intrigue, so choice **d** is correct.

15. c. The mention of the amazing things the brain is capable of doing is directly relevant to its mysterious and complex nature. Choices **a**, **b**, and **d** are less relevant and specific.

16. b. Choice **b** addresses both of Gary's vanities: his person and his situation. Choice **a** deals only with Gary's vanity of person. Choice **c** deals only with his vanity of position. Choice **d** is not supported by the passage.

17. a. This choice refers both to age and complexity; choices **b** and **c** refer only to complexity. Choice **d** is less relevant to the topic sentence than the other choices.

18. d. Choice **d** reveals the fascination fans had with Marilyn. Choices **a**, **b**, and **c** are merely facts about Marilyn and are not about people's fascination with her.

19. c. The topic sentence speaks of the big bang theory being much misunderstood, and choice **c** addresses this. The other choices are off topic.

20. a. This choice is a clear comparison between humans and birds: neither one needs

instruction to do what is important to its survival. Choices **b**, **c**, and **d** do not support this topic sentence.

21. b. Because the wolves have produced more offspring than expected, chances are they will be taken off the endangered species list. Choices **a**, **c**, and **d** do not reinforce the context of the topic sentence.

22. d. The topic sentence refers to punishment used in early America. Choice **a** gives a reason for the use of punishment by Puritans. Choices **b** and **c** state why you do not have such punishment today and compares historical punishment with today's sensibility.

23. d. The topic sentence states that violence has claimed many lives in Northern Ireland. Choices **a**, **b**, and **c** only show what led to the situation.

24. c. This choice introduces the idea that some laws are strange. Choices **a**, **b**, and **d** are examples of strange laws, but not the topic sentence.

25. a. This topic sentence states the importance of a cat's whiskers. Choices **b**, **c**, and **d** give other details that do not directly support the topic sentence.

26. c. This choice states the popularity of the game. Choices **a** and **b** state the game's origin. Choice **d** explains how its popularity spread.

27. c. This sentence gives a reason for why people are living longer. Choices **a**, **b**, and **d** are about longevity but are not topic sentences.

28. a. Choice **a** pronounces an end to sixteen years of violence. Choice **b**, **c**, and **d** are facts about James's life.

29. O. This sentence is an opinion because it can be debated. Someone could just as easily take the opposite position.

30. F. This sentence is a fact. It can proven.

31. O. This sentence is an opinion. While it could be a good idea, there are no statistics to prove this.

32. F. This sentence is a fact. Wednesday is the fourth day of the week.

33. O. This sentence is an opinion. While Wednesday may seem longer to some people, it is the same length as any other day of the week.

34. F. This sentence is a fact. There are many opportunities for investment.

35. F. This sentence is a fact. People do invest in stocks and bonds.

36. O. This sentence is an opinion. Savings accounts and CDs do not always earn the highest interest rates.

37. F. This sentence is a fact. The stock market can be uncertain.

38. F. This sentence is a fact. Steady, secure interest can be earned using these methods of investing.

39. c. This sentence indicates the importance of organization and design. Choices **a**, **b**, and **d**, even if true, are not in the passage.

40. a. Choice **a** reflects the idea that the Dvorak keyboard is more efficient than the QWERTY. Choices **b**, **c**, and **d** are not in the passage.

41. b. Choice **b** is the only choice that tells how people should dispose of sharp objects in order to avoid placing sanitation workers in danger. Choices **a**, **c**, and **d** discuss how users should deal with sharp objects.

42. c. The last sentence of the passage supports choice **c**. Choices **a**, **b**, and **d** are not in the passage.

43. a. Choice **a** details the greater productivity of telecommuters. Choices **b**, **c**, and **d** contain words and phrases from the paragraph, but are incorrect.

44. c. Choice **c** indicates that the atmosphere of Mars has been stripped away.

45. c. Choice **c** expresses the overall theme of the paragraph—a shortage of skilled workers in many fields.

46. d. Choice **d** is the best comprehensive statement about the paragraph.

47. d. Choice **d** is implied by the statement that redistribution is needed so that people in emerging nations can have proper medical care. Choices **a**, **b**, and **c** are not mentioned in the paragraph.

48. c. Choice **c** is the best answer because the paragraph indicates that legislators once feared suggesting gas taxes, but now many of them are promoting bills in favor of these taxes. There is no indication that choice **a** is true. Choice **b** is incorrect because the paragraph does not say why more gas taxes are being proposed. There is no support for choice **d**.

49. b. The passage is about making a larger goal more achievable by setting smaller goals. Only choice **b** mentions this.

50. a. Choice **a** is the best overall statement to summarize the message given by the paragraph. Choices **b**, **c**, and **d** do not support the main idea of the paragraph.

13 ▶ Grammar

The ability to write correctly is fundamental for any civil service position. This chapter reviews such grammar essentials as sentence boundaries, capitalization, punctuation, subject-verb agreement, verb tenses, pronouns, and commonly confused words.

There is plenty of writing involved in most civil service jobs. Forms, memos, e-mails, letters, and reports have to be written during the course of every workday, and the grammar section of the written exam helps the government determine whether you have the competence it takes to complete such tasks. As you apply the vocabulary you have learned in this book, it is important to use these words correctly in sentences. Poor usage can get in the way of what you want to say. Correct usage of standard English shows that you have made the effort to understand the conventions of the English language. When English is used according to the conventions that have been established, your words allow the reader—and your employer or supervisor—to understand exactly what you intend to say. Studying the proper ways to use the vocabulary of the English language can give you a good score on the grammar section of the exam and will show that you are indeed capable and proficient as a writer. The tips and exercises in this chapter will help you ensure that you are ready to excel on this portion of the exam.

▶ Complete Sentences and Sentence Fragments

Sentences are the basic units of written language. Complete sentences express a whole thought. They do not leave you guessing about who the subject is, or what action the subject is taking. When you are writing in the workplace, complete sentences are the correct and accepted format for most pieces of information. For that reason, it is important to distinguish between complete sentences and sentence fragments.

A **sentence** expresses a complete thought, while a **fragment** is missing something—it could be a verb or it could be a subject, but the sentence does not express a complete thought. Look at the following examples.

FRAGMENT	COMPLETE SENTENCE
The assistant filing folders.	The assistant was filing folders.
Leaving messages for me.	Janet was always leaving messages for me

The first fragment in this pair of sentences is an example of a sentence that is missing part of its verb. It needs the helping verb *was* before *filing* to make a complete thought. The second fragment has neither a subject nor a verb. Only when a subject and verb are added is this sentence complete.

Look at the following incomplete sentences.

When you saw the tornado approaching.
Before the new house was built in 1972.
Since you are leaving in the morning.

You may have noticed that the fragments have an extra word at the beginning. These words are called **subordinating conjunctions**. When a group of words that would normally be a complete sentence is preceded by a subordinating conjunction, something more is needed to complete the thought. These sentence fragments can easily be corrected:

- When you saw the tornado approaching, you headed for cover.
- Before the new house was built in 1972, the old house was demolished.
- Since you were leaving in the morning, you went to bed early.

Knowing that a subordinating conjunction can signal a sentence fragment, it is a good idea to be familiar with some of the most frequently used subordinating conjunctions. Then you can double-check your work for errors. Use this list as a handy reminder.

after	that
although	though
as	unless
because	until
before	when
if	whenever
once	where
since	wherever
than	while

▶ Run-On Sentences

Run-on sentences are two or more independent clauses (complete sentences) written as though they were one sentence. The main cause of run-on sentences is often faulty punctuation, such as a comma instead of a period between two independent clauses (complete thoughts). End marks like periods, exclamation points, and question marks can solve the run-on sentence problem. Look at the following example.

A complete report has to be submitted every week, it is due on Friday.

This run-on sentence could be corrected in a few different ways. One way is to add a conjunction after the comma and in between the two independent clauses. Words such as *and, or, but, as,* or *because* are **conjunctions** that join sentences.

Using the same sentence as a model, it would be considered correct if you wrote:

A complete report has to be submitted every week, and it is due on Friday.

It would also be correct to delete the comma and separate the two sentences with a semicolon. A **semicolon** indicates that the next part of the sentence is a complete sentence, but it is so closely related to the first that there is no reason to make it into a sentence of its own. So, it would be correct to say:

A complete report has to be submitted every week; it is due on Friday.

The sentence would be correct if you separated the two independent clauses to make two complete sentences. You could rewrite it as follows:

A complete report has to be submitted every week. It is due on Friday.

Last, the sentence would be correct if written with a dash:

A complete report has to be submitted every week—it is due on Friday.

▶ Capitalization

You may encounter questions on your civil service exam that test your ability to use capital letters correctly. If you know the most common capitalization rules, you will be better prepared to correct these errors.

- Capitalize the first word of a sentence. If the first word is a number, write it as a word.
- Capitalize the pronoun *I.*
- Capitalize the first word of a complete quotation: *"What is the address?" she asked.* However, do not capitalize the first word of a partial quotation: *He called me "the best employee" and nominated me for an award.*
- Capitalize proper nouns and proper adjectives. Proper nouns are names of people, places, or things, like *Lyndon B. Johnson; Austin, Texas;* or *Mississippi River.* They are different from common nouns like *president, city, state,* or *river.*
- Proper adjectives are adjectives formed from proper nouns. For instance, if the proper noun is *Japan,* the proper adjective would be *Japanese language.* If the proper noun is *South America,* the proper adjective would be *South American* climate. See the table that follows for examples of proper nouns and adjectives.

CATEGORY	EXAMPLE OF PROPER NOUNS
Days of the week	Friday, Saturday
Months of the year	January, February
Holidays	Christmas, Halloween
Special events	Two Rivers Festival, City Writers' Conference
Names of individuals	John Henry, George Washington
Names of structures	Lincoln Memorial
Buildings	The Empire State Building
Names of trains	Orient Express
Ships	Queen Elizabeth II
Aircraft	Cessna
Product names	Honda Accord
Geographic locations (cities, states, counties, countries, and geographic regions)	Des Moines, Iowa Canada Middle East
Streets	Grand Avenue
Highways	Interstate 29
Roads	Dogwood Road
Landmarks	Continental Divide
Public areas	Grand Canyon, Glacier National Park
Bodies of water	Atlantic Ocean Mississippi River
Ethnic groups	Asian-American
Languages	English
Nationalities	Irish
Official titles (capitalized only when they appear before a person's name—*Marie Hanson, president of the City Council*, vs. *City Council President Marie Hanson*)	Mayor Bloomberg President Johnson
Institutions	Dartmouth College
Organizations	Chrysler Corporation
Businesses	Girl Scouts
Proper adjectives (adjectives formed from proper nouns)	English muffins, French cuisine

▶ Punctuation

A section on the written civil service exam may test your punctuation skills. Knowing how to correctly use periods, commas, and apostrophes will boost your score on the exam.

Periods

If you know the most common rules for using periods, you will have a much easier time spotting and correcting sentence errors.

- Use a period at the end of a sentence that is not a question or an exclamation.
- Use a period after an initial in a name.
    - Example: John F. Kennedy

- Use a period after an abbreviation, unless the abbreviation is an acronym.
    - Abbreviations: Mr., Ms., Dr., A.M., General Motors Corp.; Allied, Inc.
    - Acronyms: NASA, SCUBA, RADAR
- If a sentence ends with an abbreviation, use only one period.
    - Example: *You brought pens, paper, pencils, etc.*

Commas

Commas are more important than many people realize. The correct use of commas helps present ideas and information clearly to readers. Missing or misplaced commas, on the other hand, can confuse readers and convey a message quite different from what is intended. This chart demonstrates just how much impact commas can have on meaning.

There is an indeterminate number of people in this sentence.	My sister Diane John Carey Melissa and I went to dinner.
There are four people in this sentence.	My sister Diane, John Carey, Melissa, and I went to dinner.
There are five people in this sentence.	My sister, Diane, John Carey, Melissa, and I went to dinner.
There are six people in this sentence.	My sister, Diane, John, Carey, Melissa, and I went to dinner.

If you know the most common rules for using commas, you will have a much easier time identifying sentence errors and correcting them.

- Use a comma before *and, but, so, or, for, nor,* and *yet* when they separate two groups of words that could be complete sentences. Example: *The manual listed the steps in sequence, and that made it easy for any reader to follow.*

- Use a comma to separate items in a series. Example: *The student driver stopped, looked, and listened when she approached the railroad tracks.*
- You may wonder if the comma after the last item in a series is really necessary. This is called a series comma, and is used to ensure clarity.
- Use a comma to separate two or more adjectives modifying the same noun. Example: *The hot, black, rich coffee was just what I needed on Monday*

morning. (Notice that there is no comma between *rich*—an adjective—and *coffee*—the noun it describes.)

- Use a comma after introductory words, phrases, or clauses in a sentence. Example of an introductory word: *Usually, the secretary reads the minutes of the meeting.* Example of an introductory phrase: *During her lunch break, she went shopping.* Example of an introductory clause: *After you found the source of the problem, it was easily rectified.*

- Use a comma after a name followed by Jr., Sr., M.D., Ph.D., or any other abbreviation. Example: *The ceremony commemorated Martin Luther King, Jr.* Remember that commas should be on both sides of an abbreviation—*The life of Martin Luther King, Jr., was the subject of the documentary.*

- Use a comma to separate items in an address. Example: *The package was addressed to 1433 West G Avenue, Orlando, Florida 36890.*

- Use a comma to separate a day and a year, as well as after the year when it is in a sentence. Example: *I was born on July 21, 1954, during a thunderstorm.*

- Use a comma after the greeting of a friendly letter and after the closing of a letter. Example of a greeting: *"Dear Uncle John,."* Example of a closing: *"Sincerely yours,."*

- Use a comma to separate contrasting elements in a sentence. Example: *Your speech needs strong arguments, not strong opinions, to convince me.*

- Use commas to set off **appositives**—words or phrases that explain or identify the noun in a sentence. Example: *My dog, a dachshund, is named Penny.*

Apostrophes

Apostrophes are used to show ownership or relationships, to show where letters have been omitted in a contraction, and to form the plurals of numbers and letters.

If you know the most common rules for using apostrophes, you will have a much easier time spotting and correcting punctuation errors.

- Use an apostrophe in contractions. This tells the reader that a letter has been omitted.
  - Example: do not = don't
  - I will = I'll
  - it is = it's
- Use an apostrophe to form the plural of numbers and letters.
  - Example: There are two o's and two m's in the word roommate.
  - She chose four a's on the multiple choice exam.
- Use an apostrophe to show possession.

POSSESSION		
SINGULAR NOUNS RULE: ADD 'S	**PLURAL NOUNS ENDING IN S RULE: ADD '**	**PLURAL NOUNS NOT ENDING IN S RULE: ADD 'S**
boy's	boys'	men's
child's	kids'	children's
lady's	ladies'	women's

▶ Verbs

The **subject** of a sentence—who or what the sentence is about, the person or thing performing the action—should agree with its verb in number. Simply put, this means that if a subject is singular, the verb must be singular; if the subject is plural, the verb must be plural. If you are unsure whether a verb is singular or plural, use this simple test. Fill in the blanks below using the verb *speak*. Be sure that it agrees with the subject.

He _____. (The correct form of the verb in this sentence would be singular because the subject—*he*—is singular. The sentence, written correctly, would be: He *speaks.*)

They _____. (The correct form of the verb in this sentence would be plural because the subject—*they*—is plural. The sentence, written correctly, would be: They *speak.*)

Try this simple test with other verbs such as *sing, write, think,* or *plan* if you are confused about subject/verb agreement. Notice that a verb ending with *s* is usually a sign of the singular form of the verb, and there would be a singular subject in the sentence. Similarly, a subject ending with *s* is the sign of a plural subject, and the verb in the sentence would be plural.

If a sentence includes a **verb phrase** (a main verb and one or more helping verbs), the **helping verb** (a verb that helps the main verb express action or make a statement) has to agree with the subject.

Example: The **gymnast is** performing.
The **gymnasts are** performing.

The new **schedule has interfered** with our plans.
The new **schedules have interfered** with our plans.

▶ Agreement When Using Pronoun Subjects

Few people have trouble matching noun subjects and verbs, but pronouns are sometimes difficult for even the most sophisticated writers. Some pronouns are always singular; others are always plural. Still others can be either singular or plural, depending on the usage.

These pronouns are always singular:

each	everyone
either	no one
neither	one
anybody	nobody
anyone	someone
everybody	somebody

For example, you would say "Neither of them *has* been to Chicago"—not "Neither of them *have* been to Chicago." *Neither* is the subject, so the verb must be singular.

The indefinite pronouns *each, either,* and *neither* are most often misused. You can avoid a mismatch by mentally adding the word *one* after the pronoun and removing the other words between the pronoun and the verb. Look at the following examples.

Each of the men wants his own car.
Each **one** of the men wants his own car.

Either of the sales clerks knows where the sale merchandise is located.
Either **one** of the sales clerks knows where the sale merchandise is located.

It is important to note that a subject is never found in a prepositional phrase. Any noun or pronoun found in a prepositional phrase is the object of the preposition, and this word can never be the subject of the sentence. Try to filter out prepositional phrases when looking for the subject of a sentence. Using the two sentences as models, note the prepositional phrases in bold. When you have identified these phrases, you will have a much easier time finding the subject of the sentence.

Each **of the men** wants his own car.
Either **of the sales clerks** knows where the sale merchandise is located.

These kinds of sentences may sound awkward because many speakers misuse these pronouns, and you may be used to hearing them used incorrectly. To be sure that you are using them correctly, the substitution trick—inserting *one* for the words following the pronoun—will help you avoid making an error.

Some pronouns are always plural and require a plural verb. They are:

both	many
few	several

Other pronouns can be either singular or plural:

all	none
any	some
most	

The words or prepositional phrases following these pronouns determine whether they are singular or plural. If what follows the pronoun is plural, the verb must be plural. If what follows is singular, the verb must be singular.

All of the **work is** finished.
All of the **jobs are** finished.
Is any of the **pizza** left?
Are any of the **pieces** of pizza left?

None of the **time was** wasted.
None of the **minutes were** wasted.

▶ Agreement When Using Subjects Joined by *and*

If two nouns or pronouns are joined by *and,* they require a plural verb.

He **and** she want to buy a new house.
Bill **and** Verna want to buy a new house.

▶ Agreement When Using Subjects Joined by *or* or *nor*

If two nouns or pronouns are joined by *or* or *nor,* they require a singular verb. Think of them as two separate sentences, and you will never make a mistake in agreement.

He **or** she wants to buy a new house.
He wants to buy a new house.
She wants to buy a new house.

Neither Portuguese **nor** Dutch is widely spoken today.
Portuguese is not widely spoken today.
Dutch is not widely spoken today.

▶ Verb Tense

The tense of a verb tells the reader when the action occurs, occurred, or will occur. **Present tense verbs** let the reader imagine the action as it is being read. **Past tense verbs** tell the reader what has already happened. **Future tense verbs** tell the reader what will happen.

Read the three paragraphs that follow. The first is written in the present tense, the second in the past tense, and the third in the future tense. Notice the difference in the verbs; they are highlighted so that you can easily see them.

1. To plan for growth in the small city, a city planner **is hired** to speak to the town council. The city planner **presents** a map of the city where some public buildings **are located**. Each of the squares on the map **represents** one city block. Street names **are labeled**. Arrows on streets **indicate** that the street **is** one way only in the direction of the arrow. Two-way traffic **is** allowed on streets with no arrows. This plan **alleviates** traffic in the downtown area.

2. To plan for growth in the small city, a city planner **was hired**. The city planner **presented** a map of the city where some public buildings **were located**. Each of the squares on the map **repre-sented** one city block. Street names **were labeled**. Arrows on streets **indicated** that the street **was** one way only in the direction of the arrow. Two-way traffic **was** allowed on streets with no arrows. This plan **alleviated** traffic in the downtown area.

3. To plan for growth in the small city, a city planner **will be hired**. The city planner **will present** a map of the city where some public buildings **will be located**. Each of the squares on the map **will represent** one city block. Street names **will be labeled**. Arrows on streets **will indicate** that the street **will be** one way only in the direction of the arrow. Two-way traffic **will be allowed** on streets with no arrows. This plan **will alleviate** traffic in the downtown area.

It is easy to distinguish present, past, and future tense by trying the word in a sentence beginning with *today* (present tense), *yesterday* (past tense), or *tomorrow* (future tense).

PRESENT TENSE TODAY, I _____	PAST TENSE YESTERDAY, I _____	FUTURE TENSE TOMORROW, I _____
drive	drove	will drive
think	thought	will think
rise	rose	will rise
catch	caught	will catch

The important thing to remember about verb tense is to be consistent. If a passage begins in the present tense, keep it in the present tense unless there is a specific reason to change—to indicate that some action occurred in the past, for instance. If a passage begins in the past tense, it should remain in the past tense. Similarly, if a passage begins in the future tense, it should remain in the future tense. Verb tense should never be mixed as it is in the following sample.

Incorrect

The doorman **opens** the door and **saw** the crowd of people.

Correct

Present Tense: The doorman **opens** the door and **sees** the crowd of people.

Past Tense: The doorman **opened** the door and **saw** the crowd of people.

Future Tense: The doorman **will open** the door and **will see** the crowd of people.

Sometimes it is necessary to use a different verb tense in order to clarify when an action took place. Read the following sentences and their explanations.

1. The game warden **sees** the fish that you **caught**. (The verb *sees* is in the present tense and indicates that the action is occurring in the present. The verb *caught* is in the past tense and indicates that the fish were caught at some earlier time.)

2. The house that **was built** over a century ago **sits** on top of the hill. (The verb *was built* is in the past tense and indicates that the house was built in the past. The verb *sits* is in the present tense and indicates that the action is still occurring.)

▶ Pronouns

Using a single pronoun in a sentence is usually easy to do. In fact, most people would readily be able to identify the mistakes in the following sentences.

Me went to the movie with **he**.

My instructor gave **she** a ride to the class.

Most people know that *me* in the first sentence should be *I* and that *he* should be *him*. In the second

sentence, *she* should be *her*. Such errors are easy to spot when the pronouns are used alone in a sentence. The problem occurs when a pronoun is used with a noun or another pronoun. See if you can spot the errors in the following sentences.

The director rode with Jerry and **I**.

Belle and **him** are going to the company picnic.

The errors in these sentences are not as easy to spot as those in the sentences using a single pronoun. In order to remedy this problem, you can turn the sentence with two pronouns into two separate sentences. Then the error becomes very obvious.

The director rode with Jerry.

The director rode with **me** (not *I*).

Belle is going to the company picnic.

He (not *him*) is going to the company picnic.

To help you move through this grammar problem with ease, you should know that **subject pronouns**—those that are the subject in a sentence or the predicate nominative—are in the nominative case. (A **predicate nominative** is a noun or pronoun that is the same as the subject. For example: *It was I.* In this sentence, the subject *it* is the same as the pronoun *I*.) Subjective pronouns are *I, he, she, we,* and *they.*

Objective pronouns—those that are the object of a preposition or the direct/indirect object of the sentence—are in the objective case. (A **direct object** is the word that receives the action of the verb or shows the result of the action. It answers the question *who* or *whom.* For example: *She went with me.* An **indirect object** is the word that comes before the direct object. It tells *to whom* or *for whom* the action of the verb is done. For example: *She gave* **me** *some flowers on my birthday.*)

Objective pronouns are *me, him, her, us,* and *them. You* and *it* do not change their forms, so there is no need to memorize case for those words. Knowing when to use objective pronouns can become problematic when they are used in compounds such as:

She directed her comments to Margaret and **me**.

A simple way to find the correct pronoun is to test each one separately.

She directed her comments to Margaret.
She directed her comments to **me**.

▶ Pronoun Agreement

Using singular and plural pronouns can be a problem at times. Like subjects and verbs, pronouns must match the number of the nouns they represent. If the noun that a pronoun represents is singular, the pronoun must be singular. On the other hand, if the noun a pronoun represents is plural, the pronoun must be plural.

Sometimes a pronoun represents another pronoun. If so, either both pronouns must be singular or both pronouns must be plural. Consult the lists of singular and plural pronouns you saw earlier in this chapter.

The **doctor** must take a break when **she** is tired. (singular)
Doctors must take breaks when **they** are tired. (plural)

One of the girls misplaced **her** purse. (singular)
All of the girls misplaced **their** purses. (plural)

If two or more singular nouns or pronouns are joined by *and,* use a plural pronoun to represent them.

If **he and she** want to join us, **they** are welcome to do so.
Mark and Jennifer planned a meeting to discuss **their** ideas.

If two or more singular nouns or pronouns are joined by *or,* use a singular pronoun. If a singular and a plural noun or pronoun are joined by *nor,* the pronoun should agree with the closest noun or pronoun it represents.

The **bank or the credit union** can lend money to **its** patrons.
The **treasurer or the assistant** will loan you **his** calculator.

Neither **the soldiers nor the sergeant** was sure of **her** location.
Neither **the sergeant nor the soldiers** was sure of **their** location.

▶ Commonly Confused Words

The following word pairs are often misused in written language. By reading the explanations and looking at the examples, you can learn to use these words correctly every time.

Its/It's

Its is a possessive pronoun and shows that something belongs to *it. It's* is a contraction for *it is* or *it has.* The only time you should ever use *it's* is when you can also substitute the words *it is* or *it has.*

The dog knows *its* way home.
It's only fair that I should do the dishes for you tonight.

Who/That

Who refers to people. *That* refers to things.

There is the man *who* helped me find my wallet. The office worker *who* invented White-Out was very creative.

This is the house *that* my sister bought. The book *that* I need is no longer in print.

There/Their/They're

Their is a possessive pronoun that shows ownership. *There* is an adverb that tells where an action or item is located. *They're* is a contraction for the words *they are.* It is easy to remember the differences if you remember these tips.

- *Their* means belonging to them. Of the three words, *their* can be most easily transformed into the word *them.* Extend the *r* on the right side and connect the *i* and the *r* to turn *their* into *them.* This clue will help you remember that *their* means that it belongs to *them.*
    - *Their* coats should be hanging on racks by the door.
- If you examine the word *there,* you can see that it contains the word *here.* Whenever you use *there,* you should be able to substitute *here,* and the sentence should still make sense.
    - She told me to wait over *there* for the next available salesperson.
- Imagine that the apostrophe in *they're* is actually a very small letter *a.* Use *they're* in a sentence only when you can substitute *they are.*
    - Yes, *they're* coming to dinner with us next Saturday night.

Your/You're

Your is a possessive pronoun that means something belongs to you. *You're* is a contraction for the words *you are.* The only time you should use *you're* is when you can substitute the words *you are.*

Your name will be the next one called. *You're* the next person to be called.

To/Too/Two

To can be used as a preposition or an infinitive.

- A **preposition** shows relationships between other words in a sentence.
    - Example: *My car is in the employee parking lot.* The word *in* shows the relation of *my car* to *parking lot.* The meaning of the sentence would be different if another preposition such as *on, over,* or *beside* were used. Other examples: *to* the office, *in* the red, *to* my home, *beside* the table, *over* the top, *at* his restaurant, *to* our disadvantage, *in* an open room, *by* the door
- An **infinitive** is *to* followed by a verb. For example: *to* talk, *to* deny, *to* see, *to* find, *to* advance, *to* read, *to* build, *to* want, *to* misinterpret, *to* peruse
    - Example; *To find* the correct answer, I did some very careful thinking.

Too means *also.* To see if you are using the correct spelling of the word *too,* substitute the word *also.* The sentence should still make sense. Example: *I did not know that you wanted to go too.*

Too can also mean *excessively.*

It was *too* hot inside the car.

Two is a number, as in one, *two.* If you memorize this, you will never misuse this form.

There are only *two* people in our party.

▶ Practice Questions

*For questions 1–8, look for run-on sentences or sentence fragments. Choose the answer choice that does NOT express a correct, complete sentence. If there are no mistakes, select choice **d**.*

1. a. Manuel wanted to complete all of his courses so he could get his degree.
 b. She couldn't believe the premise of the story.
 c. The train leaving the station.
 d. no mistakes

2. a. At the end of the day, they hoped to be finished with all tasks.
 b. When will you teach me how to cook like you do?
 c. I can't wait Janet can't either.
 d. no mistakes

3. a. The medieval literature class was very interesting.
 b. The children in the park, including all of the girls on the swings.
 c. Christina is an excellent elementary school teacher.
 d. no mistakes

4. a. Sandra Day O'Connor was the first woman to serve on the U.S. Supreme Court.
 b. You visited the presidential library of Lyndon B. Johnson.
 c. I saw Dr. Sultana because Dr. Das was on vacation.
 d. no mistakes.

5. a. What is the best route to Philadelphia?
 b. The artichokes cost more than the asparagus does.
 c. Turn off the television it's time for dinner!
 d. no mistakes.

6. a. Baseball is the national pastime of the United States.
 b. Ernest Hemingway won the Nobel Prize for Literature.
 c. The rest of the story coming to you later.
 d. no mistakes.

7. a. The sky was a brilliant blue this morning.
 b. John is an avid stamp collector.
 c. Elvis Presley's home is in Memphis, Tennessee.
 d. no mistakes

8. a. If you see a grizzly bear, do not make any sudden movements.
 b. The county executive a person who works very hard.
 c. The national park system in the United States preserves land for all to enjoy.
 d. no mistakes

For questions 9–13, choose the sentence that uses commas correctly.

9. a. Ecstatic the winner, hugged her coach.
 b. My best friend, James is always on time.
 c. As far as I know, that room is empty.
 d. Maureen my cousin, is going to Hawaii in August.

10. a. Concerned about her health, Jessica made an appointment to see a doctor.
   b. Those sneakers are available in black tan red, and white.
   c. After, checking our equipment you began our hiking trip.
   d. Exhausted I climbed, into bed.

11. a. Hoping for the best, I called Dan.
   b. You visited England, France Spain, and Italy.
   c. You can have chocolate ice cream or, you can have a dish of vanilla pudding.
   d. Timothy, however will attend a community college in the fall.

12. a. Max was the most physically fit and he won the 5K, race.
   b. Shortly she will answer, all messages.
   c. My physician, Dr. O'Connor, told me I was very healthy.
   d. Bonnie was outgoing friendly, and sociable.

13. a. After his vacation to the Caribbean Art, decided to learn scuba diving.
   b. I like jazz, classical, and blues music.
   c. My good friend, Melanie sent me a picture of her new puppy.
   d. The abundant, blue, violets were scattered everywhere in the woodland garden.

*For questions 14–19, choose the sentence or phrase that has a mistake in capitalization or punctuation. If you find no mistakes, select choice **d**.*

14. a. My favorite season is Spring.
   b. Last Monday, Aunt Ruth took me shopping.
   c. You elected Ben as treasurer of the freshman class.
   d. no mistakes

15. a. He shouted from the window, but you couldn't hear him.
   b. NASA was launching its first space shuttle of the year.
   c. The boys' wore identical sweaters.
   d. no mistakes

16. a. Occasionally someone will stop and ask for directions.
   b. When you come to the end of Newton Road, turn left onto Wilson Street.
   c. Lauren's father is an auto mechanic.
   d. no mistakes

17. a. That book must be yours.
   b. This is someone elses coat.
   c. Don B. Norman was one of the founders of the community.
   d. no mistakes

18. a. The US flag should be flown proudly.
   b. She served eggs, toast, and orange juice for breakfast.
   c. He wanted turkey, lettuce, and mayonnaise on his sandwich.
   d. no mistakes

19. **a.** Dear Anne,

b. Sincerely, yours

c. Yours truly,

d. no mistakes

For questions 20–25, choose the correct verb form.

20. I am trying to become more skilled at weaving before winter _____

a. arrived.

b. will have arrived.

c. will arrive.

d. arrives.

21. While trying to _____ his cat from a tree, he fell and hurt himself.

a. be rescuing

b. have rescued

c. rescue

d. rescuing

22. The volunteers from the fire department _____ quickly and extinguished a fire on North Country Road.

a. will respond

b. responded

c. will have responded

d. have responded

23. In Tuesday's paper, the owner of the supermarket was recognized for helping a customer who _____ on the icy sidewalk.

a. falls

b. would fall

c. had fallen

d. has fallen

24. The people who bought this old lamp at the antique auction _____ very smart.

a. was

b. were

c. is

d. has been

25. I _____ her speak on Friday night about the advantages of organic gardening.

a. will have heard

b. would hear

c. would have heard

d. will hear

For questions 26–30, choose the correct pronoun form.

26. That snappy looking sports car belongs to my sister and _____.

a. I

b. me

c. mine

d. myself

27. The person _____ made this delicious cheesecake has my vote.

a. that

b. which

c. who

d. whose

28. George and Michael left _____ backpacks in the car.

a. his

b. their

c. there

d. its

29. You arranged the flowers and placed
_____ in the center of the table.

   a. them

   b. this

   c. it

   d. that

30. _____ met more than ten years
ago at a mutual friend's birthday party.

   a. Her and I

   b. Her and me

   c. She and me

   d. She and I

*For questions 31–40, find the sentence that has a mistake in grammar or usage. If there are no mistakes, select choice **d**.*

31. a. Have you ever read the book called *The Firm?*

   b. She urged me not to go.

   c. Stop, look, and listen.

   d. no mistakes

32. a. Three's a crowd.

   b. If you're not sure, look in the dictionary.

   c. They weren't the only ones that didn't like the movie.

   d. no mistakes

33. a. Anne will leave first and Nick will follow her.

   b. Maya Angelou, a famous poet, recently spoke at our school.

   c. The clerk asked for my address and phone number.

   d. no mistakes

34. a. That parrot doesnt talk.

   b. Don't spend too much money.

   c. You waited until he stopped to make a phone call.

   d. no mistakes

35. a. Alberto laughed loudly when he saw us.

   b. They're looking for another apartment.

   c. The first house on the street is there's.

   d. no mistakes

36. a. I love the fireworks on the Fourth of July.

   b. The dog's barking woke us from a sound sleep.

   c. My grandparents live in Dallas, Texas.

   d. no mistakes

37. a. Ursula has broke one of your plates.

   b. The sun rose from behind the mountains.

   c. Don't spend too much time on that project.

   d. no mistakes

38. a. She believed in keeping a positive attitude.

   b. After you sat down to eat dinner, the phone rung.

   c. Sign all three copies of the form.

   d. no mistakes

39. a. The Adirondack Mountains are in New York.

   b. President Carter returned control of the Panama Canal to Panama.

   c. She missed the bus and arrives late.

   d. no mistakes

40. a. The childrens books are over there.
   b. There is not enough paper in the printer for the entire document.
   c. What's the weather forecast for today?
   d. no mistakes

*For questions 41–45, choose the sentence that does not use the correct form of the commonly confused word. If there are no mistakes, select choice **d**.*

41. a. If it's nice weather tomorrow, I plan to go for a hike.
   b. Some analysts think the stock market has seen it's best days.
   c. It's usually a good idea to purchase life insurance.
   d. no mistakes

42. a. She spoke too quickly to the group in the lobby.
   b. Can you attend this morning's meeting too?
   c. Save all of your files in to or three folders.
   d. no mistakes

43. a. When will you bring you're pictures to work?
   b. It is your responsibility to arrange the details.
   c. If you're planning to attend, please let me know in advance.
   d. no mistakes

44. a. Only their supervisor can answer those questions.
   b. There is a phone call for you.
   c. They're are only two ways to handle that situation.
   d. no mistakes

45. a. They are the ones who deserve all the credit.
   b. This is the house that I told you about.
   c. Marie sent a gift to her grandmother, who is in the hospital.
   d. no mistakes

For questions 46–50, choose the sentence that is correct in both grammar and punctuation.

46. a. The trip was scheduled for Friday the family was excited.
   b. The trip was scheduled for Friday, and the family was excited.
   c. The trip was scheduled for. Friday the family was excited.
   d. The trip, was scheduled for Friday, and the family was excited.

47. a. They finished their lunch. Left the building. And returned at 1:30.
   b. They finished their lunch, left the building, and returns at 1:30.
   c. They finished their lunch, left the building, and returned at 1:30.
   d. They finished their lunch, left the building, and returning at 1:30.

48. a. Searching for her keys, Kira, knew she would be late.
   b. Searching for her keys Kira knew she would be late.
   c. Searching, for her keys and Kira knew she would be late.
   d. Searching for her keys, Kira knew she would be late.

49. **a.** The longtime residents in the community were proud of there school district.

b. The longtime residents in the community were proud of their school district.

c. The longtime residents in the community was proud of their school district.

d. The longtime residents in the community, were proud of their school district.

50. **a.** Lisa, Dara, and Amy wanted to work together on the committee.

b. Lisa Dara and Amy wants to work together on the committee.

c. Lisa, Dara, and Amy wanting to work together on the committee.

d. Lisa, Dara, and Amy have wants to work together on the committee.

► Answers

1. **c.** This is a sentence fragment.
2. **c.** This is a run-on sentence.
3. **b.** This is a sentence fragment.
4. **d.** There are no mistakes.
5. **c.** This is a run-on sentence.
6. **c.** This is a sentence fragment.
7. **d.** There are no mistakes.
8. **b.** This is a sentence fragment.
9. **b.** The commas set off an introductory phrase.
10. **a.** The comma sets off an introductory clause.
11. **a.** The comma sets off an introductory phrase.
12. **c.** The comma sets off the appositive in the sentence.
13. **b.** The commas separate items in a series.
14. **a.** *Spring* should not be capitalized.
15. **c.** The word *boys'* should not show possession; no apostrophe is needed.
16. **a.** A comma is need to set off the introductory word, *occasionally*.
17. **b.** An apostrophe is needed before the last *s* in the word *elses* to show possession.
18. **a.** There should be periods after the abbreviation *U.S.*
19. **b.** The comma should be placed after the word *yours*.
20. **d.** This sentence is in the present tense.
21. **c.** The infinitive form of the verb is used in this sentence.
22. **b.** This sentence is in the past tense.
23. **c.** This sentence needs a verb that is in the past tense.
24. **b.** *Were* is in agreement with the plural subject *people*.
25. **d.** This sentence is in the future tense.
26. **b.** The correct form of the pronoun is *me* (objective case).

27. **c.** The correct pronoun is *who* because it refers to a person.
28. **b.** The pronoun *their* agrees with the plural subject, *George and Michael*.
29. **a.** The pronoun *them* agrees with the plural noun *flowers*.
30. **d.** *She and I* is the subject of the sentence, so the subjective case is needed.
31. **d.** There are no mistakes.
32. **c.** The word *that* should be *who* because it refers to people.
33. **a.** There should be a comma before the conjunction *and* in this sentence to separate two complete thoughts.
34. **a.** The contraction *doesn't* should have an apostrophe.
35. **c.** The correct possessive pronoun is *theirs*, not *there's*.
36. **d.** There are no mistakes.
37. **a.** The correct verb form is *has broken*.
38. **b.** The correct verb form is *rang*.
39. **c.** Both verbs, *missed and arrives* should be in the past tense.
40. **a.** An apostrophe should be added before the *s* in *children's* to make it possessive.
41. **b.** This sentence requires the possessive form (with no apostrophe), *its*.
42. **c.** The required form of this word is the number *two*.
43. **a.** This sentence should use the possessive form of the word *your*.
44. **c.** This sentence should use the adverb *there*.
45. **d.** There are no mistakes.
46. **b.** This choice uses the comma and the conjunction correctly. Choice **a** is a run-on sentence. Choice **c** contains sentence fragments. Choice **d** misuses commas.

47. c. The word *returned* is in the past tense, as are *finished* and *left.* Choice **a** contains sentence fragments. Choices **b** and **d** misuse verb tense.

48. d. The comma in this sentence correctly separates the introductory phrase. Choices **a** and **c** misuse commas. Choice **b** lacks punctuation.

49. b. This sentence uses the correct form of *their,* the correct verb, and the correct punctuation.

The word *there* is used incorrectly in choice **a**. Choice **c** uses verb tense incorrectly. Choice **d** is an example of comma misuse.

50. a. This sentence uses the correct punctuation in a series and the correct verb form. Choices **b**, **c,** and **d** misuse commas and verb tense.

14 ▶ Spelling

Because accurate spelling is such an essential and important communication skill, it is always tested on the civil service exam. In this chapter, you will find spelling rules, test tips, and practice exercises that will make the spelling section of the exam easier for you.

There is no "quick fix" for spelling. The secret to correct spelling is memorization. If you take the time to commit the words you encounter every day to memory, not only will you excel on this section of the exam, but your correspondence and written work will be more clear and effective and look more professional.

Spelling tests are usually given in multiple-choice format. Typically, you will be given several possible spellings for a word and asked to identify the one that is correctly spelled. This can be a difficult task, even for the best speller, because you must be able to see very subtle differences between word spellings. The best way to prepare for a spelling test is to put your memorization skills into high gear, have a good grasp of spelling rules, and know the exceptions to those rules. The fundamental rules and their exceptions are outlined here.

SPELLING RULES AND EXCEPTIONS

THE RULE	THE EXCEPTION
Use *i* before *e*—as in *piece*.	Use *i* before *e* except after *c*—as in *receive* or *conceive*—or when *ei* sounds like a—as in *neighbor* or *weigh*.
When adding prefixes, do not change the spelling of the word—as in *unnecessary* or *misspell*	none
When adding suffixes, do not change the spelling of the word—as in *finally* or *usually*.	When a word ends in *y*, change the *y* to *i* before adding *ness* or *ly*—as in *heaviness* or *readily*. One-syllable words ending in *y* generally remain the same—as in *dryness* or *shyly*.
Drop the final *e* before adding a suffix that begins with a vowel—as in *caring* or *usable*.	Keep the final *e* to retain the soft sound of *c* or *g* preceding the *e*—as in *noticeable* or *courageous*.
Keep the final *e* before a suffix beginning with a consonant—as in *careful* or *careless*.	Words like *truly*, *argument*, *judgment*, or *acknowledgment* are exceptions.
When words end in *y* and a consonant precedes the *y*, change the *y* to *i* before adding a suffix with *i*—as in *hurried* or *funnier*.	none
When a suffix begins with a vowel, double the final consonant before the suffix if the word has only one syllable—as in *planning*—or if the word ends with a single consonant preceded by a single vowel—as in *forgetting*.	If the accent is not on the last syllable, do not add a double consonant—as in *canceled* or *preferable*.
When spelling the plural form of a noun, add an *s*—as in *books* or *letters*. add an *es*—as in *boxes* or *lunches*. Nouns are normally made plural by adding an *s*. An *es* is added when there is an extra sound heard in words that end in *s*, *sh*, *ch*, or *x*—as in *dresses*, *birches*, *bushes*, or *boxes*.	none
If the noun ends in a *y*, change the *y* to an *i* and add *es*—as in *salaries* or *ladies*.	If the noun ends in *y* and is preceded by a vowel, just add *s*—as in *attorneys* or *monkeys*.
If a noun ends in *f* or *fe*, add an *s*—as in *chiefs* or *roofs*.	Some nouns that end in *f* or *fe* are formed by changing the *f* to *v* and adding *s* or *es*—as in *knives* or *leaves*.

THE RULE	THE EXCEPTION
If a noun ends in *o* and is preceded by a vowel, add an *s*—as in *pianos* or *radios*	Some nouns that end in *o* preceded by a consonant are formed by adding *es*—as in *potatoes* or *tomatoes*.
Plural or compound nouns can be spelled with an *s* or an *es*—as in *bookmarks* or *mailboxes*.	Some plural nouns are irregular nouns and have to be memorized—as in *children, men,* or *women*.
When a noun and a modifier make a compound noun, the noun is made plural—as in *sisters-in-law* or *passers-by*.	A few compound nouns are irregular—as in *six year olds* or *drive-ins*. Some nouns take the same form in the singular and the plural—as in *deer, species,* or *sheep*.
Numbers, letters, signs, and words that take the shape of words are spelled with an apostrophe and an *s*—*She received all A's on her report card* or *There are two o's and two m's* in roommate.	none
	Some foreign words are formed as they are in their original language—as in *alumni* or *data*. Some foreign words may be spelled as they are in the original language or by adding *s* or *es*—as in *appendixes/appendices* or *indexes/indices*. Some foreign words are formed according to the ending of the word: *singular ending in *is* plural ending in *es*—as in *analysis/analyses* or *crisis/crises*. *singular ending in *um* plural ending in *a*—as in *curriculum/curricula*. *singular ending in *on* plural ending in *a*—as in *criterion/criteria*. *singular ending in *eau* plural ending in *eaux*—as in *beau/beaux*. *singular ending in *a* plural ending in *ae*—as in *formula/formulae*. *singular ending in *us* plural ending in *i*—as in *stimulus/stimuli*.
When using *-cede, -ceed,* or *-sede*, memorize the following: There is only one English word ending in *sede*—*supersede*. There are only three common verbs ending in *ceed*—*exceed, proceed,* and *succeed*. Other words that have the same sound end in *cede*—*secede, precede,* and *concede,* for example.	

- Sound out the word in your mind. Remember that long vowels inside words usually are followed by single consonants—as in *sofa*, *total*, or *crime*. Short vowels inside words usually are followed by double consonants—as in *dribble*, *scissors*, or *toddler*.
- Give yourself auditory (listening) clues when you learn words. Say *Wed-nes-day* or *lis-ten* or *bus-i-ness* to yourself so that you remember to add the silent letters when you write the word.
- Look at each part of the word. See if there is a root, prefix, or suffix that will always be spelled the same way. For example, in the word *uninhabitable*, *un*, *in*, and *able* are always spelled the same. *Habit* is a self-contained root word that is easy to spell.

Memorize as many spelling rules as you can and know the exceptions to the rules.

▶ Using Spelling Lists

When you apply to take your civil service exam, you may be given a list of spelling words to study. If so, here are some suggestions to make your studying a little easier and quicker.

- Cross out or discard any words that you already know for certain. Do not let them get in the way of the words you need to study.
- Divide the list into groups to study. The groups can be bunched as three, five, or seven words. Consider making flash cards for the words that you find the most difficult.
- Say the words as you read them. Spell them out in your mind so you can "hear" the spelling.
- Highlight or circle the tricky elements in each word.
- Quiz yourself and then check your spelling.

If you do not receive a list of spelling words to study, the following list is a good one to use. These words are typical of the words that appear on spelling exams.

achievement	doubtful	ninety
allege	eligible	noticeable
anxiety	enough	occasionally
appreciate	enthusiasm	occurred
asthma	equipped	offense
arraignment	exception	official
autonomous	fascinate	pamphlet
auxiliary	fatigue	parallel
brief	forfeit	personnel
ballistics	gauge	physician
barricade	grieve	politics
beauty	guilt	possess
beige	guarantee	privilege
business	harass	psychology
bureau	hazard	recommend
calm	height	referral
cashier	incident	rehearsal
capacity	indict	salary
cancel	initial	schedule

circuit	innocent	seize
colonel	irreverent	separate
comparatively	jeopardy	specific
courteous	knowledge	statistics
criticism	leisure	surveillance
custody	license	suspicious
cyclical	lieutenant	tentative
debt	maintenance	thorough
definitely	mathematics	transferred
descent	mortgage	withhold

▶ Homophones

Words that sound alike but have different meanings are called **homophones** or **homonyms**. The following chart shows some of the most common homophones for you to study. It is best to study the spellings and the definitions until you have each word memorized.

HOMOPHONES

ad: a shortened form of *advertisement*
add: to combine to form a sum

affect: to influence
effect: outcome or result

allowed: permitted
aloud: using a speaking voice

bare: without covering
bear: a large furry animal; to tolerate

board: a group of people in charge; a piece of wood
bored: to be tired of something

brake: to slow or stop something
break: to split or crack

build: to construct
billed: presented a statement of costs

cite: to quote as an authority or example
sight: ability to see; a scene
site: place or setting of something

council: a group that advises

counsel: advice; to advise

dew: moisture

do: to make or carry out

due: owed

fair: consistent with the rules; having a pleasing appearance; moderately good

fare: transportation charge; food and drink; to get along

for: because of or directed to

fore: located at or toward the front

four: a number between three and five

grate: reduce to fragments; make a harsh, grinding sound; irritate or annoy

great: very large in size

hear: to listen to

here: a specific place

heard: the past tense of *hear*

herd: a large group of animals

hole: an opening

whole: entire or complete

hour: 60 minutes

our: a pronoun showing possession

knew: past tense of *know*

new: recent

know: to understand

no: not permitted

lead: first or foremost position; a margin; information pointing toward a clue

led: past tense of *lead*

leased: rented for a specific time period

least: lowest in importance or rank

lessen: made fewer in amount or quantity

lesson: exercise in which something is learned

made: past tense of *make*

maid: a servant

meat: the edible part of an animal

meet: come together

passed: the past tense of *pass*

past: previous, beforehand

peace: free from war

piece: a part of something

plain: level area; undecorated; clearly seen

plane: flat and even; a tool used to smooth wood; a shortened form of *airplane*

rain: water falling in drops

reign: period during which a monarch rules

right: correct or proper

rite: a ritual or ceremony

write: to record in print

role: function or position; character or part played by a performer

roll: to move forward by turning over

scene: the place something happens

seen: form of the verb *see*

soar: to fly or rise high into the air

sore: painful

stair: part of a flight of steps

stare: to look directly and fixedly

sweet: having a sugary taste

suite: series of connected rooms

their: ownership of something

there: a place

they're: a contraction of *they are*

threw: the past tense of *throw*; an act of motion

through: by means of; among or between

tide: variation of the level of bodies of water caused by gravitational forces

tied: the past tense of *tie*

to: indicates direction

too: also

two: the number after one

vary: to change

very: complete; extremely

ware: articles of the same general kind, e.g., *hardware, software*

wear: to have or carry on the body

where: location or place

weather: condition of the atmosphere

whether: a possibility

wood: material that trees are made of

would: form of the verb *will*

► Practice Questions

For questions 1–14, choose the correctly spelled word.

1. It is my _____ that municipal employees handle their jobs with great professionalism.
a. beleif
b. bilief
c. belief
d. beleaf

2. The accounting firm was _____ for fraudulent practices.
a. prosecuted
b. prossecuted
c. prosecutted
d. prosecuited

3. Every _____ has to be handled differently.
a. sittuation
b. situation
c. situachun
d. sitiation

4. It was a _____ day for the department's annual picnic.
a. superb
b. supperb
c. supurb
d. sepurb

5. To be elected _____, candidates must have a solid background in law enforcement.
a. sherrif
b. sherriff
c. sherif
d. sheriff

6. To be hired for the job, he needed to have _____ ability.
a. mechinical
b. mechanical
c. mechenical
d. machanical

7. The agents were searching for _____ cargo on the airplane.
a. elicitt
b. ellicit
c. illicet
d. illicit

8. There will be an immediate _____ into the cause of the accident.
   a. inquiry
   b. inquirry
   c. enquirry
   d. enquery

9. The union workers' contract could not be _____ before the calendar year ended.
   a. terminated
   b. termenated
   c. terrminated
   d. termanated

10. A _____ can be obtained at the town hall.
   a. lisense
   b. lisence
   c. lycence
   d. license

11. In many states, passing a road test requires drivers to _____ park.
   a. paralel
   b. paralell
   c. parallal
   d. parallel

12. The paramedics attempted to _____ the victim.
   a. stabilize
   b. stablize
   c. stableize
   d. stableise

13. The attorney asked a question that was _____ to the case; the judge overruled it.
   a. irelevent
   b. irelevant
   c. irrelevant
   d. irrelevent

14. The mayor highlighted the _____ statistics during her campaign speech.
   a. encouredging
   b. encouraging
   c. incurraging
   d. incouraging

*For questions 15–36, choose the misspelled word. If there are no mistakes, select choice **d**.*

15. a. radios
   b. leaves
   c. alumni
   d. no mistakes

16. a. anouncement
   b. advisement
   c. description
   d. no mistakes

17. a. omission
   b. aisle
   c. litrature
   d. no mistakes

18. a. informal
   b. servent
   c. comfortable
   d. no mistakes

19. a. vegetable
   b. width
   c. variation
   d. no mistakes

20. a twentieth
   b. fortieth
   c. ninetieth
   d. no mistakes

21. a. association
   b. unecessary
   c. illegal
   d. no mistakes

22. a. villin
   b. volunteer
   c. voracious
   d. no mistakes

23. a. hindrence
   b. equipped
   c. possessive
   d. no mistakes

24. a. procedure
   b. judgment
   c. testamony
   d. no mistakes

25. a. explicit
   b. abduct
   c. rotate
   d. no mistakes

26. a. through
   b. threw
   c. thorough
   d. no mistakes

27. a. quantaty
   b. quality
   c. quaint
   d. no mistakes

28. a. requirement
   b. reverence
   c. resistent
   d. no mistakes

29. a. incorporate
   b. contridict
   c. exhale
   d. no mistakes

30. a. pertain
   b. reversel
   c. memorization
   d. no mistakes

31. a. marshal
   b. martial
   c. tyrenny
   d. no mistakes

32. a. optimum
   b. palpable
   c. plunder
   d. no mistakes

33. a. ravinous
   b. miraculous
   c. wondrous
   d. no mistakes

34. **a.** phenomonal

    b. emulate

    c. misconception

    d. no mistakes

35. **a.** mischief

    b. temperture

    c. lovable

    d. no mistakes

36. **a.** stadium

    b. competitor

    c. atheletic

    d. no mistakes

For the questions 37–50, choose the correct homophone.

37. My favorite _____ is peach pie with vanilla ice cream.

    a. desert

    b. dessert

38. While nuclear energy is efficient, storing nuclear _____ is always a problem.

    a. waste

    b. waist

39. The price for the carpet was _____.

    a. fair

    b. fare

40. This is the _____ of the new art museum.

    a. sight

    b. cite

    c. site

41. Come _____ the park later this evening to see the sunset.

    a. buy

    b. bye

    c. by

42. This is the _____ book George has read.

    a. fourth

    b. forth

43. The acoustics in the auditorium made it easy for the audience to _____ the melodic sounds of the soloist.

    a. here

    b. hear

44. Our choice to stay in the comfortable, cozy _____ house was a good decision.

    a. guessed

    b. guest

45. Have dinner with us at the restaurant; we'll meet you _____.

    a. they're

    b. their

    c. there

46. May I have a _____ of cheese?

    a. piece

    b. peace

47. All children have the _____ to an education.

    a. write

    b. rite

    c. right

48. It is a good idea to exercise on a _____ bicycle during inclement weather.
   a. stationery
   b. stationary

49. At the beach, we went digging for clams and _____.
   a. mussels
   b. muscles

50. We _____ the exit and had to turn around.
   a. past
   b. passed

► Answers

1. **c.** belief
2. **a.** prosecuted
3. **b.** situation
4. **a.** superb
5. **d.** sheriff
6. **b.** mechanical
7. **d.** illicit. This word should not be confused with *elicit,* which means to draw out or extract.
8. **a.** inquiry
9. **a.** terminated
10. **d.** license
11. **d.** parallel
12. **a.** stabilize
13. **c.** irrelevant
14. **b.** encouraging
15. **d.** no mistakes
16. **a.** announcement
17. **c.** literature
18. **b.** servant
19. **d.** no mistakes
20. **d.** no mistakes
21. **b.** unnecessary
22. **a.** villain
23. **a.** hindrance
24. **c.** testimony
25. **d.** no mistakes
26. **d.** no mistakes
27. **a.** quantity
28. **c.** resistant
29. **b.** contradict
30. **b.** reversal
31. **c.** tyranny
32. **d.** no mistakes
33. **a.** ravenous
34. **a.** phenomenal
35. **b.** temperature
36. **c.** athletic
37. **b.** *Dessert* is an after-dinner treat; a *desert* is an arid land.
38. **a.** *Waste* means material that is rejected during a process; the *waist* is the middle of the body.
39. **a.** *Fair* means equitable; a *fare* is a transportation fee.
40. **c.** *Site* refers to a place; *cite* means to refer to; *sight* is the ability to see.
41. **c.** *By* means near; *bye* is used to express farewell; *buy* means to purchase.
42. **a.** *Fourth* refers to the number four; *forth* means forward.
43. **b.** *Hear* means to perceive sound with the ear; *here* is a location, place, or position.
44. **b.** A *guest* is one who is a recipient of hospitality. *Guessed* is the past tense of *guess.*
45. **c.** *There* refers to a place; *their* is a possessive pronoun; *they're* is a contraction for *they are.*
46. **a.** A *piece* is a portion; *peace* means calm or quiet.
47. **c.** A *right* is a privilege; to *write* is to put words on paper; a *rite* is a ceremonial ritual.
48. **b.** *Stationary* means standing still; *stationery* is writing paper.
49. **a.** *Mussels* are marine animals; *muscles* are body tissues.
50. **b.** *Passed* is the past tense of *pass; past* means a time gone by.

Test Time!

Don't close this book and run away just yet. "Test time" should not be a phrase that inspires sweaty palms and nervous stomachs. The practice tests in this section are intended to gauge your skills before you sit down to take the civil service exam. By knowing in what areas you are strong *and* in what areas you are rusty, you will be better prepared on the day of the official civil service exam. Like any scout will tell you, it's best to be prepared!

After reviewing Sections 1 through 3 in this book, you should be able to put all that you have learned together and tackle these questions. Allow yourself about two hours to complete Practice Test 1. After you are done, be sure to check your answers against the answer section. Then, reevaluate questions you answered incorrectly by going back and studying the necessary material from earlier chapters. You can make flashcards for math formulas or tricky vocabulary concepts.

Then try your skills again—take Practice Test 2. Again, if there are topics with which you are not comfortable, make sure you review these sections before the official test day. Good luck!

15 ▶ Practice Test 1

1. If a piece of packaging foam is .05 in. thick, how thick would a stack of 350 pieces of foam be?
  a. 7,000 in.
  b. 700 in.
  c. 175 in.
  d. 17.5 in.

2. 30% of what number equals 60% of 9,000?
  a. 18,000
  b. 5,400
  c. 2,400
  d. 1,620

3. Three pieces of wood measure 4 yd. 1 ft. 3 in., 5 yd. 2 ft. 4 in., and 4 yd. 1 ft. 5 in. lengthwise. When these boards are laid end to end, what is their combined length?
  a. 14 yd. 2 ft.
  b. 14 yd. 1 ft. 11 in.
  c. 13 yd. 2 in.
  d. 13 yd. 2 ft.

4. Select the answer choice that best completes the following sequence.

  a.
  b.
  c.
  d.

5. During a relay race, markers will be placed along a roadway at 0.2-mile intervals. If the entire roadway is 10,560 feet long, how many markers will be used?
  a. 10
  b. 100
  c. 20
  d. 200

6. If it takes 27 nails to build 3 boxes, how many nails will it take to build 7 boxes?
  a. 64
  b. 72
  c. 56
  d. 63

7. The average purchase price (arithmetic mean) of four shirts is $9. If one shirt was priced at $15, and another at $7, what might be the prices of the other two shirts?
  a. $4 and $3
  b. $7 and $15
  c. $9 and $9
  d. $10 and $4

8. What percent of $\frac{3}{8}$ is $\frac{1}{2}$?
  a. 25%
  b. $33\frac{1}{3}\%$
  c. 75%
  d. $133\frac{1}{3}\%$

9. A large bag of cement mix weighs $38\frac{1}{2}$ pounds. How many quarter-pound bags of mix can be made from this large bag?
  a. fewer than 10 bags
  b. 16 bags
  c. 80 bags
  d. 154 bags

10. Use $(F = \frac{9}{5}C + 32)$ to convert 15° C into the equivalent Fahrenheit temperature.
  a. 59°
  b. 60°
  c. 62°
  d. 65°

11. What is the perimeter of the shaded area if the shape is a quarter circle with a radius of 8?

  a. 2π
  b. 4π
  c. $2\pi + 8$
  d. $4\pi + 16$

12. Select the answer choice that best completes the following sequence.
  CMM, EOO, GQQ, _____, KUU
  a. GRR
  b. GSS
  c. ISS
  d. ITT

13. How many ounces are in 5 pints?
  a. 10 oz.
  b. 20 oz.
  c. 40 oz.
  d. 80 oz.

14. A rod that is 3.5×10^7 cm is how much shorter than a rod that is 7×10^{14} cm?
  a. 20,000,000 times shorter
  b. 4,000,000 times shorter
  c. 50,000 times shorter
  d. 20,000 times shorter

15. Joel had to insert form letters into 800 envelopes. In the first hour he completed $\frac{1}{8}$ of the total. In the second hour he completed $\frac{2}{7}$ of the remainder. How many envelopes does he still have to fill?
  a. 300
  b. 400
  c. 500
  d. 700

16. Jen's median bowling score is greater than her mean bowling score for 5 tournament games. If the scores of the first four games were 140, 192, 163, and 208, which could have been the score of her fifth game?
  a. 130
  b. 145
  c. 168
  d. 177

17. An 18-gallon barrel of liquid will be poured into containers that each hold half a pint of fluid. If all of the containers are filled to capacity, how many will be filled?
  a. 36
  b. 72
  c. 144
  d. 288

18. Select the answer choice that best completes the sequence.
  Ô Ö ⊘ ⊗ l ◯ ◯ ⊗ ⊘ l Ô __ __ ⊘
  a. ⊘ ◯
  b. Ô ⊗
  c. ⊗ Ö
  d. Ô ⊘

19. In a box of 300 nails, 27 are defective. If a nail is chosen at random, what is the probability that it will NOT be defective?

a. $\frac{27}{100}$

b. $\frac{91}{100}$

c. $\frac{27}{300}$

d. $\frac{91}{300}$

20. When Christian and Henrico work together, they can complete a task in 6 hours. When Christian works alone, he can complete the same task in 10 hours. How long would it take for Henrico to complete the task alone?

a. 45

b. 30

c. 15

d. 10

21. The square root of 52 is between which two numbers?

a. 6 and 7

b. 7 and 8

c. 8 and 9

d. none of the above

22. Juliet made $12,000 and put $\frac{3}{4}$ of that amount into an account that earned interest at a rate of 4%. After 3 years, what is the dollar amount of the interest earned?

a. $10,080

b. $10,800

c. $1,800

d. $1,080

23. If the area of a circle is 16π square inches, what is the circumference?

a. 2π inches

b. 4π inches

c. 8π inches

d. 12π inches

24. Select the answer choice that best completes the sequence.

QAR, RAS, SAT, TAU, _____

a. UAV

b. UAT

c. TAS

d. TAT

25. A container was filled $\frac{1}{3}$ of the way with fluid. Damian added 24 liters more, filling the container to full capacity. How many liters are in the container now?

a. 12 L

b. 30 L

c. 36 L

d. 48 L

26. Bolts cost $4 per 10 dozen and will be sold for 10 cents each. What is the rate of profit?

a. 200%

b. 150%

c. 100%

d. 75%

27. Select the answer choice that best completes the sequence.

    a. ☒ ☒

    b. ◣ ▶

    c. ◩ ☒

    d. ▶ ☒

28. $6,000 is deposited into an account. If interest is compounded semiannually at 2% for 6 months, then what is the new amount of money in the account?

    a. $120

    b. $6,120

    c. $240

    d. $6,240

Use the following information to answer questions 29–32.

A forest fire engulfed the Wildlife Preserve in Blackhill County in 2003. Since then, park rangers have kept track of the number of forest animals living in the forest. The following is a graph of how many deer, foxes, and owls were reported during the years following the fire.

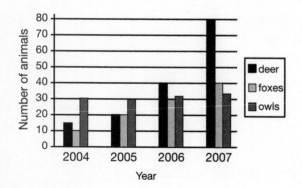

29. Which of the following statements appears to be true for the years shown?

    a. The fox population doubled every year since 2004.

    b. The deer population doubled every year since 2005.

    c. The owl population showed neither a steady increase nor a steady decrease.

    d. Both **b** and **c** are true.

30. Which statement might explain the data presented in the graph?

    a. The owl population was greatly reduced by the fire and thus the trend shows a steady increase in this population during the years of recovery.

    b. The owls were able to fly away from the fire, thus the owl population does not show the pattern of recovery that the deer and fox population exhibit.

    c. Factors independent of the fire are causing a steady decline in the owl population.

    d. A steep decline in the owl population can be attributed to illness.

31. The growth of the deer population from 2006–2007 was how much greater than the growth of the fox population for the same year?

    a. 10

    b. 20

    c. 30

    d. 40

32. What was the percent increase in deer from 2004–2005?

    a. $33\frac{1}{3}\%$

    b. 50%

    c. $\frac{3}{4}\%$

    d. $\frac{1}{3}\%$

33. A square with 8 in. sides has the same area of a rectangle with a width of 4 in. What is the length of the rectangle?

a. 8 in.

b. 12 in.

c. 16 in.

d. 64 in.

34. A rectangular tract of land measures 440 feet by 1,782 feet. What is the area in acres? (1 acre = 43,560 square feet.)

a. 14 acres

b. 16 acres

c. 18 acres

d. 20 acres

35. What is the mode of the following numbers?

12, 9, 8, 7, 8, 9, 5, 9

a. 7

b. 8.375

c. 9

d. 9.5

36. The largest sector of the pie chart below has a central angle equal to approximately how many degrees?

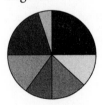

a. 15 degrees

b. 45 degrees

c. 90 degrees

d. 180 degrees

37. The following chart shows the monthly attendance for union meetings over the course of four months. Which two months had the same number of members attending?

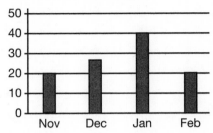

a. November and December

b. December and February

c. November and February

d. December and January

38. If the radius of a cylindrical tank is 7 cm and its volume is 1,540 cm^3, what is the height in cm?

a. 10 cm

b. 15.4 cm

c. 10π cm

d. 15.4π cm

39. If Martin exchanges 120 quarters, 300 dimes, 600 nickels, and 500 pennies for bills, he may get

a. 4 20-dollar bills, 2 10-dollar bills, and 1 5-dollar bill.

b. 3 20-dollar bills, 1 10-dollar bill, and 1 5-dollar bill.

c. 2 50-dollar bills and 1 20-dollar bill.

d. 1 50-dollar bill, 2 20-dollar bills, and 1 5-dollar bill.

40. Brian jogged 12 miles. For the first 2 miles, his pace was 3 mph. For the next 3 miles, his pace was 5 mph. For the remainder of his jog, his pace was 4 mph. What was his approximate average speed?
   a. 3.98 mph
   b. 6.86 mph
   c. 7.2 mph
   d. $2\frac{2}{3}$ mph

Choose the correct vocabulary word to complete each of the following sentences.

41. The newspaper _____ the statement made in the article because it was incorrectly stated.
   a. abolished
   b. invalidated
   c. retracted
   d. annulled

42. The proposition was read, and the committee was asked to vote on the issue; Connor decided to _____ from the vote.
   a. tackle
   b. undermine
   c. abstain
   d. destabilize

43. Typically, computer designs reach _____ within six months.
   a. division
   b. discord
   c. obsolescence
   d. secrecy

44. For information about making a sound investment, you should get advice from a(n) _____.
   a. prospectus
   b. entrepreneur
   c. teller
   d. cashier

45. The new senator was considered a _____ because she refused to follow her party's platform on nearly every issue.
   a. mentor
   b. maverick
   c. protagonist
   d. visionary

46. School calendars were originally based on a(n)_____ lifestyle, where all family members needed to be available to help in the fields.
   a. business
   b. technological
   c. scientific
   d. agrarian

47. The project seemed both _____ and beneficial, and the office staff supported it enthusiastically.
   a. implacable
   b. feasible
   c. savory
   d. irreparable

48. Judith, a _____ young worker, diligently replaced all of the research files at the end of every day.
   a. erudite
   b. insightful
   c. meticulous
   d. sagacious

49. His _____ behavior made him seem childish and immature.
   a. beguiling
   b. receding
   c. forlorn
   d. puerile

50. The _____ young woman gave generously to many worthy causes.
   a. incisive
   b. benevolent
   c. gregarious
   d. personable

51. _____, the pediatric nurse fed the premature baby.
   a. Carelessly
   b. Precariously
   c. Gingerly
   d. Wantonly

52. The furniture in the attic turned out to be a veritable _____ of valuable antiques.
   a. reproof
   b. bonanza
   c. censure
   d. rubble

53. Choosing to _____ her estate to the literacy foundation, she was able to help those who could not read.
   a. confiscate
   b. eliminate
   c. bequeath
   d. extract

54. Her haughty and _____ manner was not appealing to her constituents.
   a. poignant
   b. nocturnal
   c. amicable
   d. supercilious

55. _____ donations from a generous but anonymous benefactor were received every year at the children's hospital.
   a. Magnanimous
   b. Parsimonious
   c. Prudent
   d. Diplomatic

Read the passage and respond to the questions that follow.

Today, bicycles are elegantly simple machines that are common all over the globe. Many people ride bicycles for recreation while others use them as a means of transportation. The first bicycle, called a draisienne, was invented in Germany in 1818 by Baron Karl de Draid de Sauerbrun. Because it was made of wood, the draisienne was not very durable, nor did it have pedals. Riders moved it by pushing their feet against the ground.

In 1839, Kirkpatrick Macmillan, a Scottish blacksmith, invented a much better bicycle. Macmillan's machine had tires with iron rims to keep them from getting worn down. He also used foot-operated cranks similar to pedals so his bicycle could be ridden at a quick pace. It did not look much like the modern bicycle because its back wheel was substantially larger than its front wheel. Although Macmillan's bicycle could be ridden easily, they were never produced in large numbers.

In 1861, Frenchman Pierre Michaux and his brother Ernest invented a bicycle with an improved crank mechanism. They called their bicycle a velocipede, but most people called it a bone shaker because of the jarring effect of the wood and iron frame. Despite the unflattering nickname, the velocipede was a hit and the Michaux family made hundreds of the machines annually. Most of them were for fun-seeking young people.

Ten years later, James Starley, an English inventor, made several innovations that revolutionized bicycle design. He made the front wheel many times larger than the back wheel, put a gear on the pedals to make the bicycle more efficient, and lightened the wheels by using wire spokes. Although this bicycle was much lighter and less tiring to ride, it was still clumsy, extremely top-heavy, and ridden mostly for entertainment.

It was not until 1874 that the first truly modern bicycle appeared on the scene. Invented by another Englishman, H. J. Lawson, this safety bicycle would look familiar to today's cyclists. The safety bicycle had equalized wheels, which made it much less prone to toppling over. Lawson also attached a chain to the pedals to drive the rear wheel. By 1893, the safety bicycle had been further improved with air-filled rubber tires, a diamond-shaped frame, and easy braking. With the improvements provided by Lawson, bicycles became extremely popular and useful for transportation. Today they are built, used, and enjoyed all over the world.

56. There is enough information in this passage to show that
  a. several people contributed to the development of the modern bicycle.
  b. only a few velocipedes built by the Michaux family are still in existence.
  c. for most of the nineteenth century, few people rode bicycles just for fun.
  d. bicycles with wheels of different sizes cannot be ridden easily.

57. The first person to use a gear system on bicycles was
  a. H. J. Lawson.
  b. Kirkpatrick Macmillan.
  c. Pierre Michaux.
  d. James Starley.

58. This passage was most likely written in order to
  a. persuade readers to use bicycles for transportation.
  b. describe the problems that bicycle manufacturers encounter.
  c. compare bicycles used for fun with bicycles used for transportation.
  d. tell readers a little about the history of the bicycle.

59. Macmillan added iron rims to the tires of his bicycle to
  a. add weight to the bicycle.
  b. make the tires last longer.
  c. make the ride less bumpy.
  d. made the ride less tiring.

60. Read the following sentence from the fourth paragraph:

> Ten years later, James Starley, an English inventor, made several innovations that *revolutionized* bicycle design.

As it is used in the sentence, the word *revolutionized* most nearly means

a. canceled.

b. transformed.

c. maintained.

d. preserved.

61. Which of the following statements from the passage represents the writer's *opinion*?

a. The safety bicycle would look familiar to today's cyclists.

b. Two hundred years ago, bicycles did not even exist.

c. The Michaux brothers called their bicycle a velocipede.

d. Macmillan's machine had tires with iron rims.

Read the directions for each of the following questions and select the word *that is the synonym or antonym for the word provided.*

62. A synonym for *apathetic* is

a. pitiable.

b. indifferent.

c. suspicious.

d. evasive.

63. A synonym for *surreptitious* is

a. expressive.

b. secretive.

c. emotional.

d. artistic.

64. An antonym for *deterrent* is

a. encouragement.

b. obstacle.

c. proponent.

d. discomfort.

65. An antonym for *impertinent* is

a. reverential.

b. rude.

c. relentless.

d. polite.

66. A synonym for *animated* is

a. abbreviated.

b. civil.

c. secret.

d. lively.

67. A synonym for *augment* is

a. repeal.

b. evaluate.

c. increase.

d. criticize.

68. An antonym for *ludicrous* is

a. absurd.

b. somber.

c. reasonable.

d. charitable.

69. An antonym for *archaic* is

a. tangible.

b. modern.

c. ancient.

d. haunted.

70. A synonym for *vindictive* is
a. outrageous.
b. insulting.
c. spiteful.
d. offensive.

Answer each of the following grammar and usage questions.

71. Which of the following sentences uses the correct pronoun form?
a. Do you think you will work with Jason or I on this project?
b. Do you think you will work with Jason or me on this project?
c. Do you think you will work with Jason or she on this project?
d. Do you think you will work with Jason or he on this project?

72. Which of the following sentences is correctly punctuated?
a. Charlotte, who ran in the Boston Marathon last year will compete in this years New York City Marathon.
b. Charlotte who ran in the Boston Marathon, last year, will compete in this year's New York City Marathon.
c. Charlotte who ran in the Boston Marathon last year, will compete in this years New York City Marathon.
d. Charlotte, who ran in the Boston Marathon last year, will compete in this year's New York City Marathon.

73. Which of the following sentences is capitalized correctly?
a. The Governor gave a speech at the fourth of July picnic, which was held at morgan's beach.
b. The Governor gave a speech at the Fourth of July picnic, which was held at Morgan's beach.
c. The governor gave a speech at the Fourth of July picnic, which was held at Morgan's Beach.
d. The governor gave a speech at the fourth of july picnic, which was held at Morgan's Beach.

74. Which of the following sentences uses the correct verb form?
a. Before I learned to read, my sister takes me to the public library.
b. Before I learned to read, my sister will take me to the public library.
c. Before I learned to read, my sister took me to the public library.
d. Before I learned to read, my sister has took me to the pubic library.

75. Which of the following sentences shows subject/verb agreement?
a. The art professor, along with several of her students, is planning to attend the gallery opening tomorrow evening.
b. The art professor, along with several of her students, are planning to attend the gallery opening tomorrow evening.
c. The art professor, along with several of her students, plan to attend the gallery opening tomorrow evening.
d. The art professor, along with several of her students, have planned to attend the gallery opening tomorrow evening.

76. In which of the following sentences is the verb NOT in agreement with the subject?
  a. Where are the forms you want me to fill out?
  b. Which is the correct form?
  c. Here is the forms you need to complete.
  d. There are two people who still need to complete the form.

77. In which of the following sentences is the pronoun NOT correct?
  a. Francine can run much faster than me.
  b. Erin and Bob are painting the house by themselves.
  c. Five members of the team and I will represent our school.
  d. Our neighbors gave us some tomatoes from their garden.

78. Which of the following sentences uses the correct verb form?
  a. Only one of the many problems were solved.
  b. Only one of the many problems was solved.
  c. Only one of the many problems been solved.
  d. Only one of the many problems are solved.

79. Which of the following sentences uses punctuation correctly?
  a. Dr. Richard K Brown, CEO of the company, will speak to the scientists at Brookhaven National Laboratory on Wed at 9:00 A.M.
  b. Dr Richard K Brown, C.E.O. of the company, will speak to the scientists at the Brookhaven National Laboratory on Wed. at 9:00 A.M.
  c. Dr. Richard K. Brown, C.E.O. of the company, will speak to the scientists at the Brookhaven National Laboratory on Wed. at 9:00 A.M.
  d. Dr. Richard K. Brown, C.E.O. of the company, will speak to the scientists at the Brookhaven National Laboratory on Wed at 9:00 A.M.

80. Which of the following sentences is NOT a run-on sentence?
  a. He was from a small town, he moved to a very large city.
  b. He was from a small town he moved to a very large city.
  c. He was from a small town, but he moved to a very large city.
  d. He was from a small town but he moved to a very large city.

Choose the correctly spelled word to complete each of the following sentences.

81. Each of the new employees has similar _____.
  a. asspirations
  b. asparations
  c. aspirrations
  d. aspirations

82. The president and the vice president were a _____ pair.
  a. compatible
  b. compatable
  c. commpatible
  d. compatibel

83. I was skeptical of the claims made by the _____ salesman.
  a. loquatious
  b. loquacious
  c. loquacius
  d. loquecious

84. Who is your immediate _____?
   a. supervisor
   b. supervizor
   c. superviser
   d. supervizer

85. There are two types of _____:
   viral and bacterial.
   a. neumonia
   b. pnumonia
   c. pnemonia
   d. pneumonia

*Choose the misspelled word in the following questions. If there are no mistakes, select choice **d**.*

86. **a.** illuminate
   b. enlighten
   c. clarify
   d. no mistakes

87. **a.** abolish
   b. forfit
   c. negate
   d. no mistakes

88. **a.** zoology
   b. meterology
   c. anthropology
   d. no mistakes

89. **a.** ajournment
   b. tournament
   c. confinement
   d. no mistakes

90. **a.** vague
   b. trepidation
   c. vengence
   d. no mistakes

► Answers

1. d. To solve, multiply the thickness of each piece of foam by the total number of pieces; $.05 \times 350 = 17.5$ in.

2. a. "30% of what number equals 60% of 9,000?" can be written mathematically as $.30 \times x = .60 \times 9{,}000$. Dividing both sides by .30 will yield
$$\frac{x}{.30} = \frac{(.60)(9{,}000)}{.30} = \frac{5{,}400}{.30} = 18{,}000$$

3. a. First, line up all of the units and add:

   4 yd. 1 ft. 3 in.
   5 yd. 2 ft. 4 in.
   +4 yd. 1 ft. 5 in.
   13 yd. 4 ft. 12 in.

Next, note that 12 in. = 1 ft., so 13 yd. 4 ft. 12 in. is the same as 13 yd. 5 ft., and that 3 ft. = 1 yd., so 5 ft. = 1 yd. + 2 ft. Ultimately, you can rewrite the entire length as 14 yd. 2 ft.

4. d. The amount of the shaded area changes from $\frac{1}{4} \rightarrow \frac{1}{2} \rightarrow \frac{1}{4}$
Thus, you need to find the answer that is $\frac{1}{4}$ shaded followed by $\frac{1}{2}$ shaded. Choice **d** is correct.

5. a. 5,280 feet = 1 mile, so 10,560 feet = 2 miles. To solve, divide the total 2 mile distance by the interval, .2 miles: $2 \div .2 = 10$.

6. d. First set up a proportion: $\frac{27}{3} = \frac{x}{7}$. You can reduce the first fraction: $\frac{9}{1} = \frac{x}{7}$ and then cross multiply: $1(x) = 9(7)$, so $x = 63$.

7. d. If the cost of four shirts averaged out to $9, then the sum of all four shirts was $4 \times 9 = \$36$. (Note that the sum of all 4 shirts must equal $36 in order for the average to equal 9: Average = sum $\div$ 4 = 36 $\div$ 4 = 9.) Of the $36 total, $22 is accounted for (one shirt was $15, and another $7), leaving $14 unaccounted for. Only choice **d** adds to $14.

8. d. Recall that "What percent" can be expressed as $\frac{x}{100}$. The question "What percent of $\frac{3}{8}$ is $\frac{1}{2}$?" can be expressed as: $\frac{x}{100} \times \frac{3}{8} = \frac{1}{2}$. This simplifies to $\frac{3 \times x}{800} = \frac{1}{2}$. Cross multiplying yields $6 \times x = 800$. Dividing both sides by 6 yields $x = 133\frac{1}{3}\%$.

9. d. Divide $38\frac{1}{2}$ by $\frac{1}{4}$. By expressing $38\frac{1}{2}$ as its equivalent 38.5, you get: $38.5 \div \frac{1}{4} = 38.5 \times \frac{4}{1} = 154$ bags.

10. a. Substitute 15° C in for the variable C in the given equation. Thus, $F = \frac{9}{5}C + 32$ becomes $F = \frac{9}{5}(15) + 32 = (9)(3) + 32 = 27 + 32 = 59$ degrees Fahrenheit.

11. d. The perimeter of the curved length is a quarter of the circumference of a whole circle when $r = 8$. Since $C = 2\pi r$ and you want a quarter of this value, solve $\frac{1}{4} \times 2 \times \pi \times r = \frac{1}{4} \times 2 \times \pi \times 8 = 4\pi$. The two straight edges are radii and are each 8 units long. Thus, the total perimeter = $4\pi + 8 + 8 = 4\pi + 16$.

12. c. The first letter of each triplet changes by skipping 1 letter : C ➔ E ➔ G ➔ I ➔ K. Thus, the first letter in the missing triplet is I. The last 2 letters of each triplet follow the same pattern (skip 1 letter): MM ➔ OO ➔ QQ ➔ SS ➔ UU. Thus, the answer is ISS.

13. d. Using the knowledge that 1 pt. = 2 c. and 1 c. = 8 oz., you can use a series of conversion factors to eliminate pints and keep ounces. Thus, you multiply: $5 \text{ pt.} \times \frac{2 \text{ c.}}{1 \text{ pt.}} \times \frac{8 \text{ oz.}}{1 \text{ c.}} = 80$ oz.

14. a. To find how many "times shorter" the first rod is, divide: $\frac{7 \times 10^{14}}{3.5 \times 10^{7}}$
$= 2 \times 10^{14-7} = 2 \times 10^{7} = 20{,}000{,}000$ times shorter.
Hint: Treat their division like two separate division operations, $7 \div 3.5$ and $10^{14} \div 10^{7}$. But you must remember that the dividends

are multiplied together in the end. Also, to divide 10^{14} by 10^7, subtract the exponents.

15. c. Joel starts with 800 envelopes to fill. During the first hour he filled $\frac{1}{8}$ of the 800: $\frac{1}{8} \times 800 = 100$. He then had $800 - 100 = 700$ left to fill. In the second hour he filled $\frac{2}{7}$ of the remaining 700; $\frac{2}{7} \times 700 = 200$ filled in the second hour. After two hours, Joel has $700 - 200 = 500$ remaining.

16. d. The mean is found by adding up the numbers and dividing by the number of values. The median is found by listing all of the numbers in order and taking the middle value. To find the solution, try out each answer choice to see if it works. A score of 130 would give a mean of 167 and a median of 163. A score of 145 would give a mean of 169 and a median of 163. A score of 168 would give a mean of 174 and a median of 168. A score of 177 would give a mean of 176 and a median of 177. 177 is the only one that has a median greater than the mean:
Median = 140 163 **177** 192 208
Mean = $(140 + 163 + 177 + 192 + 208) \div 5 = 880 \div 5 = \mathbf{176}$

17. d. Using the knowledge that 1 gal. = 4 qt. and 1 qt. = 2 pt., you can generate a series of conversion factors and multiply them so that you can cross out the units you do not want (gal.) and keep the units you do want (pt.): 18 gal. $\times \frac{4 \text{ qt.}}{1 \text{ gal.}} \times \frac{2 \text{ pt.}}{1 \text{ qt.}} = 144$ pints. Next, remember you are looking for half-pints. 144 pints will fill 288 half-pint containers.

18. d. This is an alternating series. The first and third segments are repeated. The second segment is a reverse of the other two.

19. b. If 27 of the 300 are defective, then $300 - 27 = 273$ are not defective. Thus, the probability of selecting a nail that is not defective will be

273 out of 300:
$\frac{273}{300} = \frac{91}{100}$

20. c. Christian can complete $\frac{1}{10}$ of the task in 1 hour (you assume this because he completes the entire task in 10 hours). Together, Christian and Henrico complete $\frac{1}{6}$ of the task in 1 hour. Convert both fractions into thirtieths. $\frac{5}{30}$ per hour (both men) $- \frac{3}{30}$ per hour (just Christian) $= \frac{2}{30} = \frac{1}{15}$ per hour (just Henrico). Since Henrico completes $\frac{1}{15}$ of the task per hour, it will take him 15 hours to complete the entire task when working alone.

21. b. $7^2 = 49$ and $8^2 = 64$. So the square root of 52 will equal a number that is between 7 and 8.

22. d. Use the formula $I = PRT$, which means *Interest = principal × rate of interest × time*, where principal equals your original amount of money (in dollars), and time is in years. Here the original amount of money (P) is $9,000 because she put $\frac{3}{4}$ of the $12,000 into the account. $I = .04$ and $T = 3$ years. Substituting into $I = PRT$, you get $I = (9000)(.04)(3) = \$1,080$.

23. c. You are told that Area = 16π. Since $A = \pi r^2$, $16 = r^2$, and $r = 4$. Use this r in the circumference formula: Circumference $= C = 2\pi r = 2\pi \times 4 = 8\pi$ inches.

24. a. The first letter in each triplet progresses from Q → R → S → T, so the next triplet will begin with U. The second letter of each triplet is a constant: A. The third letter of each triplet progresses from R → S → T → U, so the third letter in the next triplet will be V. Thus, the answer is UAV.

25. c. 24 L represents $\frac{2}{3}$ of the whole capacity. You can ask yourself "$\frac{2}{3}$ of what number is 24?" This can be expressed mathematically as $\frac{2}{3} \times x = 24$; $x = 24 \div \frac{2}{3} = 24 \times \frac{3}{2} = 36$ L.

26. a. 10 dozen bolts = $10 \times 12 = 120$ bolts. When they are all sold, the amount collected is $\$.10 \times 120 = \$12$. Since the 10 dozen cost $4, the profit is $\$12 - \$4 = \$8$. Next, to find the rate of profit, set up a proportion:
$$\frac{\$8 \text{ profit}}{\text{initial } \$4} = \frac{x}{100}$$
Cross multiply to get $(100)(8) = (4)(x)$, or $800 = (4)(x)$. Divide both sides by 4 to get $x = 200$. Thus, the rate of profit is 200%.

27. a. As the series progresses, the amount of shading changes from $\frac{1}{2} \rightarrow \frac{3}{4} \rightarrow$ whole $\rightarrow$ none $\rightarrow$ $\frac{1}{4} \rightarrow \frac{1}{2} \rightarrow \frac{3}{4} \rightarrow$ whole. So the next two terms will be: none $\rightarrow \frac{1}{4}$.

28. b. Because the interest is compounded semiannually (twice a year), after half a year (6 months) the amount of interest earned $I = PRT = 6{,}000 \times .02 \times \frac{1}{2} = \$120$. Now the account has $\$6{,}000 + \$120 = \$6{,}120$ in it.

29. d. The fox population (lightest bars) went up by 10 animals each year. Thus, choice **a** is incorrect. The deer population (black bar) doubled every year since 2005 ($20 \rightarrow 40 \rightarrow 80$). The owl population stayed around 30, showing neither an increase nor a decrease. Thus, both **b** and **c** are true statements, making choice **d**, "Both **b** and **c** are true," the correct answer.

30. b. The owl population is essentially maintaining its size. There is not a steady increase (**a** is incorrect), a steady decline (**c** is incorrect), or a steep decline (**d** is incorrect). Thus, choice **b** is the correct answer.

31. c. The deer (black bar) went from 40 in 2006 to 80 in 2007. That is an increase of 40 deer. The fox population (lightest bar) grew from 30 in 2006 to 40 in 2007. That is an increase of 10. Thus the difference in growth is $40 - 10 = 30$.

32. a. The deer (black bar) increased from 15 in 2004 to 20 in 2005. This is a change of 5 deer.

When compared to the initial 15, 5 out of 15 represents $\frac{5}{15} = \frac{x}{100}$; $x = 33\frac{1}{3}\%$.

33. c. The area of the square is $A = side^2 = s^2 = 8^2 = 64$ in.^{2}. The area of the rectangle must then also be 64 in.^{2}. Substituting this area and the given width $w = 4$ into the area formula, you get: $A = lw$; $64 = l \times 4$; $l = 64 \div 4 = 16$ in.

34. c. First, calculate the area in square feet: Area $= lw = 440$ ft. $\times 1782$ ft. $= 784{,}080$ ft.^{2}. Next convert to acres by using the conversion factor $\frac{1 \text{ acre}}{43{,}560 \text{ ft.}^2}$ and multiply: $784{,}080$ ft.$^2 \times \frac{1 \text{ acre}}{43{,}560 \text{ ft.}^2} = 18$ acres.

35. c. The mode is the number that occurs the most. You are given:
12, **9**, 8, 7, 8, **9**, 5, **9**.
Note that 9 occurs the most and is the mode.

36. c. The largest sector takes up a quarter of the pie chart (the black sector). The interior angles of a circle add to 360 degrees and $\frac{1}{4}$ of $360 = \frac{1}{4} \times 360 = 90$ degrees.

37. c. The attendance for both November and February was 20 members each. You can tell that this is true because the bars for these months are the same height.

38. a. If you use $\pi = \frac{22}{7}$, and the formula $V = \pi r^2 h$, you get $1{,}540 = \frac{22}{7} \times 7^2 \times h$. This simplifies to $1{,}540 = 154 \times h$. Dividing both sides by 154 yields $h = 10$ cm.

39. d. Multiply the number of coins by the value of the coin:
120 quarters $= 120 \times \$.25 = \$30$
300 dimes $= 300 \times \$.10 = \$30$
600 nickels $= 600 \times \$.05 = \$30$
500 pennies $= 500 \times \$.01 = \$5$
Next, add all of the dollar amounts up: $\$30 + \$30 + \$30 + \$5 = \$95$. The only choice that represents $95 is **d**: 1 50-dollar bill, 2 20-dollar bills, and 1 5-dollar bill.

40. **b.** To find the average speed, you must use $D = RT$ (*Distance* = *Rate* (Time) with the total distance and the total time as D and T respectively. You are given the total distance of 12 miles. You need the total time. This can be found by using the information in the question. The formula $D = RT$ can be rewritten as $T = \frac{D}{R}$. Making a chart for yourself will help you stay organized:

INFO	TIME
2 mi. @ 3 mph	$T = \frac{D}{R} = \frac{2}{3} = \frac{40}{60}$
3 mi. @ 5 mph	$T = \frac{D}{R} = \frac{3}{5} = \frac{36}{60}$
7 mi. @ 4 mph	$T = \frac{D}{R} = \frac{7}{4} = \frac{105}{60}$

Total time $= \frac{181}{60}$ hr ≈ 3.02 hr

Now you can use the total time and total distance in the formula $D = RT$. Since you want R, you can rearrange this formula to $R = D \div T$. Thus, you have $R = D \div T = 12 \div 3.02$ hr ≈ 3.98 mph.

41. **c.** To *retract* something is to take it back or disavow it. This is the term usually applied to withdrawing something erroneous or libelous printed in a newspaper.

42. **c.** To *abstain* means to refrain from something by one's own choice.

43. **c.** *Obsolescence* is the state of being outdated.

44. **a.** A *prospectus* is a published report of a business and its plans for a program or offering.

45. **b.** A *maverick* is a political independent, nonconformist, or free spirit.

46. **d.** *Agrarian* means having to do with agriculture or farming.

47. **b.** To be *feasible* is to be practical, manageable, convenient, or serviceable.

48. **c.** *Meticulous* means extremely and excessively concerned with details.

49. **d.** *Puerile* means to be of or like a child; to be boyish, trifling, or silly.

50. **b.** A *benevolent* person is one who is charitable, giving.

51. **c.** To handle a baby *gingerly* would be to handle it delicately and with great caution.

52. **b.** A *bonanza* is a source of great wealth or prosperity.

53. **c.** To *bequeath* something is to pass it to another when you die.

54. **d.** To be *supercilious* means to show arrogant superiority and disdain for those one views as unworthy.

55. **a.** *Magnanimous* donations are noble in mind or heart.

56. **a.** Each paragraph of the passage describes an inventor whose inventions became more and more advanced. There is no evidence to support choice **b**. Choices **c** and **d** are incorrect because they both make statements that, according to the passage, are untrue.

57. **d.** The fourth paragraph states that James Starley added a gear to the pedals.

58. **d.** The passage gives the history of the bicycle. Choice **a** is incorrect because few opinions are included in the passage. There is no support for choices **b** and **c**.

59. **b.** This information is clearly stated in the second paragraph. The iron rims kept the tires from wearing down, and the tires lasted longer. Choice **a** is incorrect because although the iron rims probably did make the machine heavier, that was not Macmillan's goal. Choice **c** is incorrect because no information is given about whether iron-rimmed or wooden tires moved more smoothly. There is no support for choice **d**.

60. **b.** Based on the paragraph, this is the only possible choice. Starley *revolutionized* the bicycle;

he made many innovative changes, thereby transforming the form and shape of the bicycle. Based on the context, the other choices are incorrect.

61. a. This is the only choice that states an opinion. The writer cannot be certain that the safety bicycle would look familiar to today's cyclists; it is his or her opinion that this is so. The other choices are presented as facts.

62. b. To be *apathetic* is to show little emotion or interest; to be *indifferent* is to have no particular interest or concern.

63. b. *Surreptitious* is acting in a stealthy or *secretive* manner.

64. a. A *deterrent* prevents or discourages; *encouragement* inspires or heartens.

65. d. Someone who is *impertinent* is rude; someone who is *polite* is courteous.

66. d. To be *animated* is to be filled with activity or vigor; *lively* is to be filled with energy.

67. c. To *augment* means to *increase* or expand in size or extent.

68. c. To be *ludicrous* is to be absurd; to be *reasonable* is to be rational.

69. b. *Archaic* means ancient or outdated; *modern* is current or contemporary.

70. c. To be *vindictive* is to be vengeful; to be *spiteful* means to be malicious

71. b. *Jason or me* is the object of the sentence; the objective pronoun *me* is used.

72. d. In this sentence, the appositive—*who ran in the Boston Marathon last year*—describes Charlotte and is separated from the rest of the sentence with commas. The word *year's* is possessive and has an apostrophe.

73. c. All proper nouns—*Fourth of July* and *Morgan's Beach*—are capitalized correctly in this sentence.

74. c. This sentence is in the past tense and uses the verb *took*.

75. a. The subject of the sentence, *art professor*, is singular and takes the singular verb *is planning*.

76. c. The subject *forms* should take the plural verb *are*, not the singular *is*.

77. a. If completed, the sentence would read, *Francine can run much faster than I can run;* therefore, the subjective pronoun *I* should be used.

78. b. The subject of the sentence *one* takes the singular verb *was solved*.

79. c. Periods are correctly placed after all abbreviations in this sentence.

80. c. This sentence has a comma before the conjunction *but*, which correctly connects the two complete thoughts in the sentence.

81. d. aspirations

82. a. compatible

83. b. loquacious

84. a. supervisor

85. d. pneumonia

86. d. no mistakes

87. b. forfeit

88. b. meteorology

89. a. adjournment

90. c. vengeance

16 ▶ Practice Test 2

1. What is the mode of the following numbers?

12, 9, 8, 7, 7, 2, 9, 5, 7

a. 5

b. 7

c. 8

d. 9

Use the following chart to answer questions 2 and 3.

METRIC UNITS TO ENGLISH UNITS CONVERSIONS
1 cm = .39 in.
1 m = 1.1 yd.
1 km = .6 mi.

2. 3.5 ft. is equivalent to approximately how many meters?

a. 4 m

b. 3.85 m

c. 3.18 m

d. 18 m

3. 5 yd. 2 ft. is equivalent to approximately how many centimeters?

a. 523 cm

b. 79.56 cm

c. 52.3 cm

d. 6.63 cm

4. Select the answer choice that best completes the sequence.

VAB, WCD, XEF, _____, ZIJ

a. AKL

b. UHG

c. YGH

d. GHW

5. 20% of what number equals 40% of 120?

a. 48

b. 96

c. 200

d. 240

6. The ratio of multimedia designers to graphic designers at a production house is 2:1. If the combined number of multimedia designers and graphic designers is 180, and half of the multimedia designers are women, how many women multimedia designers are there?

a. 60

b. 80

c. 90

d. 120

7. If a map drawn to scale shows 5.2 cm between two points and the scale is 1 cm = 1.5 km, how far apart are the two points in meters?

a. 7.8

b. 780

c. 7,800

d. 78,000

8. Use $F = \frac{9}{5}C + 32$ to convert 113° F into the equivalent Celsius temperature.

a. 38°

b. 45°

c. 54°

d. 63°

9. Damian earns a semimonthly salary of $2,300. What is his yearly salary?

a. $55,200

b. $34,000

c. $27,600

d. $24,000

10. It took Amanda 45 minutes to jog 3 miles at a constant rate. Find her rate in mph.

  a. 3 mph

  b. 4 mph

  c. 10 mph

  d. 15 mph

11. What percent of $\frac{1}{8}$ is $\frac{1}{32}$?

  a. 35%

  b. 30%

  c. 20%

  d. 25%

12. Nicole bought Blue Diamond stock at $15 per share. After six months, the stock is worth $20 per share. This represents a percent increase of

  a. 25%.

  b. 30%.

  c. $33\frac{1}{3}$%.

  d. 75%.

13. One construction job can be completed by 15 workers in 8 days. How many days would if take 20 workers to complete the job?

  a. 4 days

  b. 6 days

  c. 8 days

  d. 10 days

14. 3 pieces of wood measure 8 yd. 2 ft. 1 in., 6 yd. 1 ft. 9 in., and 3 yd. 1 ft. 7 in. length. When these boards are laid end to end, what is their combined length?

  a. 18 yd. 17 in.

  b. 18 yd. 5 ft.

  c. 18 yd. 2 ft. 5 in.

  d. 18 yd. 5 in.

15. What percent of $\frac{3}{16}$ is $\frac{1}{64}$?

  a. 5%

  b. $8\frac{1}{3}$%

  c. 33%

  d. 80 %

Use the following information to answer questions 16–18.

1,200 new nursing students were asked to complete a survey in which they were asked which type of nursing they would like to pursue. The data was used to make the following pie chart.

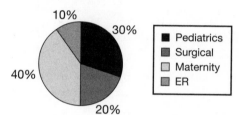

Nursing Survey

16. How many nursing students would like to pursue pediatrics?

  a. 360

  b. 400

  c. 600

  d. 800

17. Half of the nurses who indicated that would like to pursue surgical nursing also noted that they would like to transfer to a sister school across town. How many students indicated that they would like to make such a transfer?

  a. 240 students

  b. 120 students

  c. 60 students

  d. 10 students

18. If the same color scheme is used, which of the following bar graphs could represent the same data as the pie chart?

a.

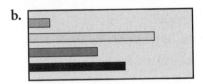

b.

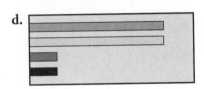

c.

d.

19. $(8^5 \times 3^4) \div (8^3 \times 3^2)$ is equivalent to

a. 576.

b. 420.

c. 376.

d. 256.

20. Pipe A leads into a tank and Pipe B drains the tank. Pipe A can fill the entire tank in 1 hour. Pipe B can drain the entire tank in 45 minutes. At a certain point in time, the valves leading to both pipes are shut and the tank is $\frac{1}{2}$ full. If both valves are opened simultaneously, how long will it take for the pipe to drain?

a. $\frac{1}{2}$ hr

b. 1 hr

c. $1\frac{1}{2}$ hr

d. $1\frac{3}{4}$ hr

21. Select the answer choice that best completes the sequence.

B_2CD, _____, BCD_4, B_5CD, BC_6D

a. B_2C_2D

b. BC_3D

c. B_2C_3D

d. BCD_7

22. Select the answer choice that best completes the sequence.

Ⅰ ⌐⊓ ☐☐☐ ⊔ __

a. ☐☐

b. ∟☐

c. Ⅰ⊓

d. ⌐Ⅰ

23. The reduced price of a computer is $1,250 after a 20% deduction is applied. The original price was

a. $250.

b. $1,000.

c. $1,562.50.

d. $6,250.

24. Three cylindrical solids with $r = \sqrt{7}$ m and $h = 1$ m are packed into a rectangular crate with $l = 10$ m, $w = 9$ m, and $h = 1.2$ m. The empty space will be filled with shredded paper. What volume will the shredded paper occupy?

a. 86 m^2

b. 66π m^2

c. 42π m^3

d. 42 m^3

25. External hard drives cost $280 each. When more than 30 drives are purchased, a 10% discount is applied to each drive's cost. How much money will 40 drives cost (excluding tax)?

   a. $7,000

   b. $8,200

   c. $10,080

   d. $ 11,200

26. Select the answer choice that best completes the following sequence.

   BOC, COB, DOE, EOD, _____

   a. FOG

   b. DOG

   c. DOF

   d. FOE

27. Which of the following is longest?

   (1 cm = 0.39 inches)

   a. 1 meter

   b. 1 yard

   c. 32 inches

   d. 85 centimeters

28. $\frac{2}{5}\% =$

   a. $\frac{1}{250}$

   b. .4

   c. $\frac{1}{25}$

   d. 04

29. A box contains 23 iron washers, 15 steel washers, and 32 aluminum washers. If a washer is chosen at random, what is the probability that a steel washer will be chosen?

   a. $\frac{3}{14}$

   b. $\frac{23}{70}$

   c. $\frac{32}{70}$

   d. $\frac{15}{7}$

30. If the volume of a cube is 27 cubic centimeters, what is its surface area?

   a. 3 cm^2

   b. 6 cm^2

   c. 9 cm^2

   d. 54 cm^2

Use the following information to answer questions 31–33.

This graph shows the number of inches of rain for five towns in Suffolk County during spring 2007.

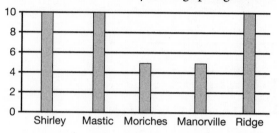

31. What was the median number of inches for the five towns?

   a. 5

   b. 8

   c. 9

   d. 10

32. What was the mode?

   a. 5

   b. 8

   c. 9

   d. 10

33. What was the average number of inches for the season shown?

   a. 5

   b. 8

   c. 9

   d. 10

34. When expressed as a percent, $\frac{9}{17}$ is most accurately approximated as
a. .0053%.
b. 45.2 %.
c. 50%.
d. 52.9%.

35. The length of a rectangle is equal to 3 inches more than twice the width. If the width is 2 in., what is the area of the rectangle?
a. 7 square inches
b. 14 square inches
c. 18 square inches
d. 21 square inches

36. Kira's register contains 10 20-dollar bills, 3 5-dollar bills, 98 1-dollar bills, 88 quarters, 52 dimes, 200 nickels, and 125 pennies. How much money is in the register?
a. $351.45
b. $351.20
c. $350
d. $345.51

37. Select the answer choice that best completes the sequence.
DEF, DEF_2, DE_2F_2, _____, $D_2E_2F_3$
a. DEF_3
b. D_3EF_3
c. D_2E_3F
d. $D_2E_2F_2$

38. Hannah's yard is square. A lamp is placed in the center of her yard. The lamp shines a radius of 10 feet on her yard, which is 20 feet on each side. How much of the yard, in square feet, is NOT lit by the lamp?
a. 400π
b. $40 - 10\pi$
c. $400 - 10\pi$
d. $400 - 100\pi$

39. Chris drove for 100 miles. During the first 45 miles, he drove at a rate of 75 mph. During the next 45 miles, he drove at a rate of 50 mph. For the last 10 miles, he drove at a rate of 25 mph. What was his approximate average rate for the whole trip?
a. 40 mph
b. 53 mph
c. 55 mph
d. 60 mph

40. What is the area of the shaded figure inside the rectangle?

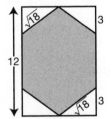

Note: Figure not drawn to scale.
a. 18
b. 36
c. 54
d. 60

Choose the correct vocabulary word for each of the following sentences.

41. Portland's oldest citizen was _____; he refused to leave his home, even when he was warned of rising floodwaters.
a. recitative
b. redundant
c. repatriated
d. recalcitrant

42. Michael and Brenda had such terrific
_____; they always seemed to know, with-
out being told, what the other felt.
a. altercation
b. equilibrium
c. rapport
d. symmetry

43. The politician's _____ voice
detailed the many projects he planned to tackle
once he was in office.
a. clamorous
b. flocculent
c. affable
d. fervent

44. The audience puzzled over the
_____ remark made by the may-
oral candidate.
a. obvious
b. cryptic
c. shrewd
d. conniving

45. She shed _____ tears when she
heard the tragic news.
a. copious
b. scant
c. nonchalant
d. genteel

46. After graduation, Charles requested a(n)
_____ so that he did not have to
pay his school loans immediately.
a. surrogate
b. deferment
c. tincture
d. improvement

47. The nonprofit agency bought office supplies
using a tax _____ number.
a. liability
b. exempt
c. information
d. accountability

48. With this group of _____ person-
alities, she was sure her party would be a success.
a. scintillating
b. mundane
c. irradiated
d. burnished

49. Her _____ remarks were not taken
seriously by anyone on the nominating
committee.
a. porous
b. obsessive
c. frivolous
d. durable

50. A key reference book detailing eyewitness
accounts had to have _____
updates when new information surfaced.
a. subsequent
b. personable
c. rote
d. steadfast

51. The National Parks Service, in
_____ with its mission, preserves
the great outdoors for all to enjoy.
a. contention
b. amnesty
c. conflict
d. accordance

52. The exhibit at the botanical gardens is an unusual collection of cacti and other _____ from around the world.

   a. perennials

   b. succulents

   c. annuals

   d. tubers

53. Although the freeway system continues to grow, it often cannot keep pace with a _____ population.

   a. burgeoning

   b. beckoning

   c. capitulating

   d. exasperating

54. With admirable _____, the renowned orator spoke to the crowd gathered in the lecture hall.

   a. toil

   b. ado

   c. finesse

   d. tedium

55. The _____ advice offered by his friend saved him from making a grave mistake.

   a. insensitive

   b. judicious

   c. metaphorical

   d. unorthodox

Read the passage and respond to the questions that follow.

Although many companies offer tuition reimbursement, most companies reimburse employees only for classes that are relevant to their position. This is a very limiting policy. A company that reimburses employees for all college credit courses—whether job-related or not—offers a service not only to the employees, but to the entire company and greater community.

One good reason for giving employees unconditional tuition reimbursement is that it shows the company's dedication to its employees. In today's economy, where job security is a thing of the past and employees feel more and more expendable, it is important for a company to demonstrate to its employees that it cares. The best way to do this is with concrete investments in the employees and their futures.

In turn, this dedication to the betterment of company employees will create greater employee loyalty. A company that releases funds to pay for the education of its employees will get its money back by having employees stay with the company longer. Employee turnover will be reduced because even the employees who do not take advantage of the tuition reimbursement program will be more loyal to their company—just knowing that their company cares enough to pay for their education invokes loyalty.

Most importantly, the company that has an unrestricted tuition reimbursement program will have higher quality employees. Although these companies do indeed run the risk of losing money on an employee who goes on to another job in a different company as soon as he or she gets a degree, more often than not, the employee will stay with the company. And even if employees do leave after graduation, it generally takes several years to complete any degree program. If the employee leaves upon graduation, the employer will have had a more sophisticated, more intelligent, and therefore more valuable and productive employee during that employee's tenure with the company. If the employee stays, that education will doubly benefit the company. Not only is the employee more educated, but now that employee can be promoted, and the company does not have to fill a high-level vacancy from the outside. Vacancies can be filled by people who already know the company well.

Though unconditional tuition reimbursement requires a significant investment on the employer's part, it is perhaps one of the wisest investments a company can make.

56. According to the passage, unconditional tuition reimbursement is good for which of the following reasons?
   a. Employees get a cheaper education.
   b. Employees become more valuable.
   c. Employees can find better jobs.
   d. Employers lose a great deal of money.

57. Which of the following statements from the passage is NOT an opinion?
   a. The best way to do this is with concrete investments in them.
   b. Most importantly, the company that has an unrestricted tuition reimbursement program will have higher quality employees.
   c. Although many companies offer tuition reimbursement, most companies only reimburse employees for classes that are relevant to their position.
   d. A company that puts out funds to pay for the education of its employees will get its money back by having employees stay with the company longer.

58. The author's reason for writing this passage was to
   a. entertain the reader.
   b. narrate a story.
   c. explain tuition reimbursement.
   d. persuade the reader.

59. The writer most likely uses the word *wisest* in the last sentence, rather than words such as *profitable, practical,* or *beneficial,* because
   a. wisdom is associated with education, the subject of the passage.
   b. the writer is trying to appeal to people who are already highly educated.
   c. education could not be considered practical.
   d. the word *beneficial* is too abstract for readers to comprehend.

60. Which of the following words best describes the tone of this passage?
   a. insincere
   b. deceitful
   c. optimistic
   d. cynical

61. The passage suggests that, compared to employees of companies that offer unconditional tuition reimbursement, employees of companies that do not offer this benefit are
   a. less loyal.
   b. more likely to be promoted.
   c. not as smart.
   d. more likely to stay with the company.

62. In paragraph two, the word *expendable* most nearly means
   a. expensive.
   b. flexible.
   c. replaceable.
   d. extraneous.

63. The main idea of the passage is that
   a. companies should reimburse employees for work-related courses.
   b. both companies and employees would benefit from unconditional tuition reimbursement.
   c. companies should require their employees to take college courses.
   d. by insisting on a college degree, companies will be better able to fill vacancies from within.

Read each question and select the word that is the synonym or antonym for the word provided.

64. An antonym for *disperse* is
   a. gather.
   b. agree.
   c. praise.
   d. satisfy.

65. A synonym for *droll* is
   a. forget.
   b. charm.
   c. sedate.
   d. absurd.

66. A synonym for *commendable* is
   a. admirable.
   b. accountable.
   c. irresponsible.
   d. noticeable.

67. An antonym for *prevarication* is
   a. accolade.
   b. veracity.
   c. deprecation.
   d. mendacity.

68. An antonym for *mirth* is
   a. pallor.
   b. solemnity.
   c. penury.
   d. lethargy.

69. A synonym for *domain* is
   a. entrance.
   b. rebellion.
   c. formation.
   d. territory.

70. An antonym for *orient* is
   a. confuse.
   b. arouse.
   c. deter.
   d. simplify.

Answer each of the following grammar and usage questions.

71. Which of the following sentences uses capitalization correctly?
   a. Last Thursday, my Mother, my Aunt Barbara, and I went to the museum to see an exhibit of African art.
   b. Last Thursday, my mother, my Aunt Barbara, and I went to the museum to see an exhibit of African art.
   c. Last Thursday, my mother, my aunt Barbara, and I went to the Museum to see an exhibit of African art.
   d. Last Thursday, my mother, my aunt Barbara, and I went to the museum to see an exhibit of African Art.

72. Which of the following sentences uses periods correctly?

   a. Dr Harrison will speak at the hotel in Chicago, Ill, on thurs at 3:00 P.M.

   b. Dr. Harrison will speak at the hotel in Chicago, Ill, on Thurs at 3:00 P.M.

   c. Dr Harrison will speak at the hotel in Chicago, Ill, on Thurs. at 3:00 P.M.

   d. Dr. Harrison will speak at the hotel in Chicago, Ill., on Thurs. at 3:00 P.M.

73. Which of the following sentences is NOT a complete sentence?

   a. Hearing the thunder, the lifeguard ordered us out of the water.

   b. Turn off the lights.

   c. Sunday afternoon spent reading and playing computer games.

   d. I was surprised to see that my neighbor had written a letter to the editor.

74. Which of the following sentences is a complete sentence?

   a. The newspapers are supposed to be delivered by 7:00, but I am usually finished before 6:45.

   b. I called the delivery service this morning, they told me the shipment would arrive on time.

   c. Look in the closet you should find it there.

   d. I was the first to sign the petition Harry was the second.

75. Which of the following sentences uses the correct verb form?

   a. Margaret brang a cake so that everyone in the office could help celebrate her birthday.

   b. Margaret brought a cake so that everyone in the office could help celebrate her birthday.

   c. Margaret bring a cake so that everyone in the office could help celebrate her birthday.

   d. Margaret had brung a cake so that everyone in the office could help celebrate her birthday.

76. Which of the following sentences shows subject/verb agreement?

   a. Neither of the dogs have been to obedience training.

   b. Neither of the dogs were to obedience training.

   c. Neither of the dogs is been to obedience training.

   d. Neither of the dogs has been to obedience training.

77. Which of the following sentences shows subject/verb agreement?

   a. One of the customers have complained about poor service.

   b. Neither of the customers have complained about poor service.

   c. Each of the customers have complained about poor service.

   d. Some of the customers have complained about poor service.

78. Which of the following sentences does NOT use the italicized pronoun correctly?

  a. Alicia and *me* want to spend Saturday at Six Flags Amusement Park.

  b. Either Sam or William will bring *his* CD player to the party.

  c. She and *I* will work together on the project.

  d. Why won't you let *her* come with us?

79. Which of the following sentences uses the italicised pronouns correctly?

  a. Four band members and *me* were chosen to attend the state competition; one of *you* will do the driving.

  b. Four band members and *me* were chosen to attend the state competition; one of *us* will do the driving.

  c. Four band members and *I* were chosen to attend the state competition; one of *we* will do the driving.

  d. Four band members and *I* were chosen to attend the state competition; one of *us* will do the driving.

*Choose the misspelled word in the following questions. If there are no mistakes, select choice **d**.*

80. **a.** embarrassment
  b. accomodate
  c. weird
  d. no mistakes

81. **a.** inadvertant
  b. occasion
  c. liquefy
  d. no mistakes

82. **a.** tyranny
  b. dessicate
  c. subpena
  d. no mistakes

83. **a.** dictionary
  b. auditorium
  c. biology
  d. no mistakes

84. **a.** geometry
  b. perimeter
  c. circumferance
  d. no mistakes

85. **a.** general
  b. corporal
  c. lieutenant
  d. no mistakes

Choose the correct spelling of the word for the following sentences.

86. Do you think I should run for a seat on the city _____?

  a. counsel
  b. council

87. The amount for the carpet was a _____ price.

  a. fair
  b. fare

88. This problem is _____ complex.

  a. two
  b. to
  c. too

89. My grandmother is an _____ historian.

   a. imminent

   b. immanent

   c. eminent

90. _____ only four o'clock in the afternoon.

   a. It's

   b. Its

▶ Answers

1. b. To find the mode, see which number occurs the most: 12, 9, 8, **7**, **7**, 2, 9, 5, **7**. Thus, 7 is the mode.

2. c. You should know that 3 ft. = 1 yd. and the chart tells you that 1 m = 1.1 yd. Thus, you can create conversion factors that let you cross off *feet* and end up with *meters*: $3.5 \text{ ft.} \times \frac{1 \text{ yd.}}{3 \text{ ft.}} \times \frac{1 \text{ m}}{1.1 \text{ yd.}} \approx 3.18 \text{ m}$.

3. a. 5 yd. = 15 ft., so 5 yd. 2 ft. = 17 ft. Next, using the fact that 1 ft. = 12 in. and 1 cm = .39 in., you can create conversion factors that let you cross off *feet* and end up with *cm*: $17 \text{ ft.} \times \frac{12 \text{ in.}}{1 \text{ ft.}} \times \frac{1 \text{ cm}}{.39 \text{ in.}} \approx 523 \text{ cm}$.

4. c. The first term of each triplet represents the alphabet in sequence: V ➜ W ➜ X ➜ Y ➜ Z. Thus, the first letter of the missing triplet is Y. The second and third letters of the triplets follow the pattern of skipping one letter. Thus, the second term of the missing triplet will be: A ➜ C ➜ E ➜ G ➜ I. And the third term of the missing triplet will be: B ➜ D ➜ F ➜ H ➜ I. Therefore, the answer is YGH.

5. d. "20% of what number equals 40% of 120?" can be written mathematically as $.20 \times x = .40 \times 120$. Dividing both sides by .20 yields: $x = \frac{(.40)(120)}{.20} = 240$

6. a. You are told that the ratio of multimedia designers to graphic designers at a production house is 2:1. Thus, $\frac{2}{3}$ of the 180 total must be multimedia designers. $\frac{2}{3}$ of $180 = \frac{2}{3} \times 180 = 120$ multimedia designers. Half of these are women, so there are 60 women multimedia designers.

7. c. First use a proportion to get the real-life value: $\frac{1 \text{ cm}}{1.5 \text{ km}} = \frac{5.2 \text{ cm}}{x \text{ km}}$; $x = 1.5 \times 5.2 = 7.8 \text{ km}$. Next, convert kilometers to meters by multiplying by $\frac{1,000 \text{ m}}{1 \text{ km}}$: $7.8 \text{ km} \times \frac{1,000 \text{ m}}{1 \text{ km}} = 7,800 \text{ m}$.

8. b. Substitute 113 for F in the given equation. Thus, $F = \frac{9}{5} C + 32$ becomes $113 = \frac{9}{5} C + 32$; $113 - 32 = \frac{9}{5} C$; $81 = \frac{9}{5} C$; $81 \times \frac{5}{9} = C$; $9 \times 5 = C$; C = 45 degrees.

9. a. Recall that *semimonthly* means twice a month. This means he makes $2 \times \$2,300 = \$4,600$ per month. Multiply by 12 months per year: 12 months $\times \$4,600 = \$55,200$ per year.

10. b. First, you should rearrange $D = RT$ into $R = \frac{D}{T}$. Substitute the given values into the formula. Here, $R = 45 \text{ min} = \frac{3}{4}$ hour, and $D = 3$ mi. Thus, $R = \frac{D}{T}$ becomes $R = 3 \text{ mi} \div \frac{3}{4} \text{ hr} = 4 \text{ mph}$.

11. d. The question "What percent of $\frac{1}{8}$ is $\frac{1}{32}$?" can be written mathematically as $\frac{x}{100} \times \frac{1}{8} = \frac{1}{32}$. Recall that *what percent* is $\frac{x}{100}$, *of* means $\times$, and *is* means =. Solving, you get $\frac{x}{800} = \frac{1}{32}$; $x = \frac{800}{32} = 25\%$.

12. c. The Blue Diamond stock rose from \$15 to \$20. This is a difference of $\$20 - \$15 = \$5$. When compared with the original \$15, $\frac{5}{15} = \frac{x}{100}$; $x = \frac{500}{15} = 33\frac{1}{3}\%$.

13. b. If it takes 15 workers 8 days to complete a job, it would take 1 worker $15 \times 8 = 120$ days. It would take 20 workers $120 \div 20 = 6$ days.

14. c. First, line up and add all of the units:

8 yd. 2 ft. 1 in.
6 yd. 1 ft. 9 in.
+ 3 yd. 1 ft. 7 in.
17 yd. 4 ft. 17 in.

Next, note that 12 in. = 1 ft., so 17 yd. 4 ft. 17 in. is the same as 17 yd. 5 ft. 5 in. Next, note that 3 ft. = 1 yd., so you can rewrite the length as 18 yd. 2 ft. 5 in.

15. b. Recall that "What percent" can be expressed as $\frac{x}{100}$. The question "What percent of $\frac{3}{16}$ is

$\frac{1}{64}$?" can be expressed as: $\frac{x}{100} \times \frac{3}{16} = \frac{1}{64}$; $\frac{3 \times x}{1,600} = \frac{1}{64}$; $3 \times x = 25$; $x = \frac{25}{3} = 8\frac{1}{3}\%$.

16. a. 30% (black sector) of the 1,200 nursing students indicated that they would like to pursue pediatrics; $.30 \times 1,200 = 360$ students.

17. b. 20% (darkest gray) of the nursing students chose surgical nursing. Half of these want to transfer to the sister school, so that is 10%. 10% of 1,200 = $.10 \times 1,200 = 120$ students.

18. b. If the same color scheme is used (as stated), then in decreasing size order, the bars should be lightest gray, black, darkest gray, and medium gray. Only choice **b** has bars that match this description.

19. a. You can apply the rules of exponents to the terms that have the same bases. Thus, $(8^5 \times 3^4)$ ÷ $(8^3 \times 3^2)$ is equivalent to $8^{5-3} \times 3^{4-2} = 8^2 \times 3^2 = 64 \times 9 = 576$. Recall that when multiplying and/or dividing exponential numbers, those exponents of numbers with the same base value (e.g., 8^5, 8^3, or 3^4, 3^2) can be either added or subtracted depending on the operation asked to be performed (multiplication → add exponents, division → subtract exponents).

20. c. First, convert the hour into minutes. 1 hour = 60, so Pipe A fills $\frac{1}{60}$ of the tank every minute. Pipe B empties $\frac{1}{45}$ of the tank per minute. This means the net effect—every minute—is $\frac{1}{45} - \frac{1}{60} = \frac{4}{180} - \frac{3}{180} = \frac{1}{180}$ of the tank is drained. If $\frac{1}{2}$ of the tank is initially full, this equals $\frac{90}{180}$ full. It will take 90 minutes for the $\frac{90}{180}$ to drain out (at a rate of $\frac{1}{180}$ per minute). 90 min = $1\frac{1}{2}$ hr.

21. b. Notice that the number grows by 1 and moves to the letter on the right of its current position: B_2CD, BC_3D, BCD_4, B_5CD, BC_6D. Thus, the missing term is BC_3D.

22. d. Note that the number of line segments increases and then decreases by one: 1 → 2 → 3 → 4 → 5 → 4 → 3. Thus the next 2 members of the series will have 2 sides and then 1 side.

23. c. If a 20% deduction was applied, then $1,250 represents 80% of the original cost. This question is really asking: "80% of what is $1,250?" This can be written mathematically as $.80 \times x = 1,250$; $x = \frac{1,250}{.80} = \$1,562.50$.

24. d. The formula for a cylinder is $V = \pi r^2 h$. If you use $\pi \approx \frac{22}{7}$, and substitute the given values into this formula, you have: $V = \frac{22}{7} \times (\sqrt{7})^2 \times 1 = \frac{22}{7} \times 7 = 22$ m³. Three such cylinders will occupy a volume of 3×22 m³ = 66 m³ inside the rectangular crate. The volume of the crate is $lwh = 10 \times 9 \times 1.2 = 108$ m³. The empty space (to be filled with shredded paper) is 108 m³ − 66 m³ = 42 m³.

25. c. Since more than 40 drives are being purchased, use the discounted price. Take 10% ($28) off the cost of each drive. So, instead of costing $280 each, the drives will cost $280 − $28 = $252 each. Next, multiply 40 drives by the price of each drive: $40 \times 252 = \$10,080$.

26. a. The first term progresses from B → C → D → E, so the last triplet will begin with F. Note that the second term is always O. Every other triplet is the inverse of the triplet before it. So, the third letter of the last triplet, like its predecessors, is the next letter of the alphabet after F.

27. a. In order to compare the choices, covert them all into inches:

a. 1 m = 100 cm = 100 cm $\times \frac{39 \text{ in.}}{\text{cm}}$ = 39 in.

b. 1 yd. = 36 in.

c. 32 in.

d. 85 cm is less than 1 m (choice **a**) so you need not waste time converting this choice to inches. Thus, choice **a**, 1 m (39 inches) is the longest.

28. a. This can be solved by equating the percent to its equivalent fractional form(s): $\frac{2}{5}\% = .4\% = .004 = \frac{4}{1,000} = \frac{1}{250}$.

29. a. First, add all the washers together: $23 + 15 + 32 = 70$. There are 15 steel washers, so the chance of pulling a steel washer is 15 out of 70: $\frac{15}{70} = \frac{3}{14}$.

30. d. The volume formula for a cube is $V = s^3$, so here $s^3 = 27$ and $s = 3$ cm. The surface area of one face is $s^2 = 3^2 = 9$ cm^2. Since there are six faces, the total surface area is 6×9 cm$^2 = 54$ cm^2.

31. d. First, list the numbers in order. The middle number will be the median: 5 5 **10** 10 10

32. d. To find the mode, select the number that occurs the most:

10 10 5 5 10

10 occurs three times and is the mode.

33. b. First, add up all the values: $10 + 10 + 5 + 5 + 10 = 40$. Next divide by 5 (the number of values): $40 \div 5 = 8$ inches.

34. d. First, convert $\frac{9}{17}$ to a decimal: $9 \div 17 \approx .529$. Next, to express this value as a percent, move the decimal point over two places to the right $\approx 52.9\%$.

35. b. "The length of a rectangle is equal to 3 inches more than twice the width," can be expressed mathematically as $l = 2w + 3$. You know $w = 2$, so $l = (2)(2) + 3 = 7$. The area is then $A = lw = 7 \times 2 = 14$ square inches.

36. a. First, multiply the number of coins (or bills) by the value of the coin (or bill):

10 20-dollar bills = $10 \times \$20 = \$200$

3 five-dollar bills = $3 \times \$5 = \$15$

98 one-dollar bills = $98 \times \$1 = \$98$

88 quarters = $88 \times \$.25 = \$22$

52 dimes = $52 \times \$.10 = \$5.20$

200 nickels = $200 \times \$.05 = \$10$

125 pennies = $125 \times \$.01 = \$1.25$

Next, add up all the money: $\$200 + \$15 + \$98 + \$22 + \$5.20 + \$10 + \$1.25 = \$351.45$.

37. d. The letters remain the same: DEF. The numbers change as follows (a dash, such as "-" represents no number): - - - → - - 2 → - 2 2 → 2 2 2 → 2 2 3.

38. d. The area of the dark yard is the area of her square yard ($A = s^2$) minus the circle of light around the lamp ($A = \pi r^2$).

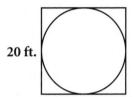

20 ft.

Thus, the dark area = $20^2 - (\pi \times 10^2)$, or $400 - 100\pi$.

39. b. To find the average rate, you must use $D = RT$ with the total distance and the total time as D and T respectively. You are given the total distance of 100 miles. You need the total time. This can be found by using the information in the question. The formula $D = RT$ can be rewritten as $T = \frac{D}{R}$. Making a chart for yourself will help you stay organized:

INFO	TIME
45 mi @ 75 mph	$T = \frac{D}{R} = \frac{45}{75} = \frac{90}{150}$ hr
45 mi @ 50 mph	$T = \frac{D}{R} = \frac{45}{50} = \frac{135}{150}$ hr
10 mi @ 25 mph	$T = \frac{D}{R} = \frac{10}{25} = \frac{60}{150}$ hr

*Note that the least common multiple of 75, 50, and 25 was chosen as the denominator for the times listed.

Total time = $\frac{285}{150}$ hr = 1.9 hr

Now you can use the total time and total distance in the formula $D = RT$. Since you want R, you can rearrange this formula to $R = D \div T$. Thus, you have $R = D \div T = 100 \div 1.9 \approx 53$ mph.

40. **c.** Each little white triangle in the corner is a tiny right triangle with a hypotenuse of $\sqrt{18}$ and a leg of 3. Use $a^2 + b^2 = c^2$ to find the other leg: $3^2 + b^2 = (\sqrt{18})^2$; $9 + b^2 = 18$; $b^2 = 9$; $b = 3$. Thus the width of the rectangle is $3 + 3 = 6$ units. The area of the entire rectangle is $lw = 12 \times 6 = 72$ units^2. To find the area of the shaded region, you must subtract out the area of the 4 tiny triangles. Each triangle has an area equal to $\frac{1}{2}bh = \frac{1}{2} \times 3 \times 3 = 4.5$ units^2, so the four triangles take up $4 \times 4.5 = 18$ units^2. Subtract this amount from the area of the rectangle to find the area of the shaded region: $72 - 18 = 54$ units^2.

41. **d.** To be *recalcitrant* is to be stubbornly resistant.

42. **c.** To have *rapport* is to have mutual trust and emotional affinity.

43. **d.** A *fervent* voice is one that has great emotion or zest.

44. **b.** *Cryptic* means mysterious, hidden, or enigmatic.

45. **a.** *Copious* means plentiful or abundant.

46. **b.** A *deferment* is a delay.

47. **b.** *Exempt* means to be excused from a rule or obligation.

48. **a.** That which is *scintillating* is brilliant or sparkling.

49. **c.** *Frivolous* means not worthy of serious attention; of little importance.

50. **a.** *Subsequent* means following a specified thing in order or succession.

51. **d.** *Accordance* means in agreement or harmony.

52. **b.** *Succulents* are plants that have leaves specifically for storing water.

53. **a.** *Burgeoning* means emerging or new growth.

54. **c.** *Finesse* is skill, tact, and cleverness.

55. **b.** *Judicious* means to use or show good judgment; to be wise or sensible.

56. **b.** The idea that employees will become more valuable if they take courses is stated in the fourth paragraph: "the employer will have had a more sophisticated, more intelligent, and therefore more valuable and productive employee."

57. **c.** This statement describes the many positions that companies can take when considering reimbursement for educational classes. This statement could be verified as fact by surveying companies to find out their tuition reimbursement policies.

58. **d.** The writer of this passage states an opinion: "A company that reimburses employees for all college credit courses—whether job related or not—offers a service not only to the employees but to the entire company." The writer then proceeds to give reasons to persuade the reader of the validity of this statement.

59. **a.** By using a word associated with education, the writer is able to reinforce the importance of education and tuition reimbursement.

60. **c.** The passage is optimistic and describes only positive effects of unconditional reimbursement; there are virtually no negative words.

61. **a.** If employees of companies that offer unconditional tuition reimbursement are more loyal to their companies (see the second and third paragraphs), it follows that other employees will be less loyal because their company is not showing enough dedication to their betterment.

62. **c.** *Expendable* means *replaceable*. The writer uses the word immediately after saying that job security is a thing of the past. This clue tells you that workers do not feel they are important or valuable to a company that can fire them on a moment's notice.

63. b. This main idea is explicitly stated in the last sentence of the first paragraph and again at the end of the passage.

64. a. *Disperse* means to scatter; to *gather* means to collect in one place.

65. c. *Droll* means to have a humorous or odd quality; *sedate* means unruffled or serious.

66. a. Both *commendable* and *admirable* mean worthy, qualified, or desirable.

67. b. *Prevarication* is an evasion of the truth; *veracity* means truthfulness.

68. b. *Mirth* means merriment; *solemnity* means seriousness.

69. d. A *domain* is an area governed by a ruler; a *territory* is an area for which someone is responsible.

70. a. To *orient* means to adjust, become familiar; to *confuse* means to bewilder.

71. b. Every proper noun and adjective in this sentence is correctly capitalized.

72. d. Periods are placed after Dr., Ill., Thurs., and P.M.

73. c. This is a sentence fragment and is missing the helping verb *was* that would make it a complete sentence.

74. a. Choice **a** is the only complete sentence. Choices **b**, **c**, and **d** are run-on sentences.

75. b. This sentence is in the past tense and correctly uses the verb *brought*.

76. d. *Neither* is singular, as is *has been*.

77. d. *Some* is plural, as is *have complained*.

78. a. *Alicia and I* is the subject of the sentence; therefore, the subjective pronoun *I* has to be used to make the sentence correct.

79. d. *Four band members and I* is the subject of the sentence; the subjective pronoun *I* is correct. *Us* is the object of the preposition; the objective pronoun *us* is correct.

80. b. accomodate

81. a. inadvertent

82. c. subpoena

83. d. no mistakes

84. c. circumference

85. d. no mistakes

86. b. council

87. a. fair

88. c. too

89. c. eminent

90. a. It's

5 ▶ Helpful Resources

This book has provided you with focused practice and an essential review of math and vocabulary skills. Now, use these additional helpful resources to drive home some key skills before you sit down to take the civil service exam.

In the math and vocabulary glossaries as well as the commonly tested words appendix, you will find a compiled list of terms you may need to know for the civil service exam. These lists can seem intimidating, but don't let that prevent you from tackling them. If the word list looks intimidating, try this:

1. Figure out how many days there are until you take the civil service exam.
2. Multiply that number by 10.

If you have 30 days until the test day, you can learn 300 new words by learning only ten new words each day! And, remember, some of these words may already be familiar to you. Each night, target ten words that you feel you do not know. Read the definitions and the way each word is used in a sentence. Try to use the words in conversation, in your reports or memos, or even in an e-mail. The more you use a word, the more familiar it will become to you. When words are familiar, you can count on them to help you with all forms of communication—or to pass any kind of test.

One way to manage these word lists is to work with flash cards. Write the vocabulary word on one side and the definition on the other. Or, try writing a sentence that uses the word on one side of the flash card and the definition of the word on the other. Flash cards are easy to handle and they're portable.

In this resource section, you will also find a list of some of the most common Latin and Greek word roots, prefixes, and suffixes. A familiarity with common prefixes, suffixes, and word roots can dramatically improve your ability to determine the meaning of unfamiliar vocabulary words. The tables list common prefixes, suffixes, and word roots; their meanings; an example of a word with that prefix, suffix, or word root; the meaning of that word; and a sentence that demonstrates the meaning of that word. Review the list carefully, taking note of the examples, which are mostly everyday words. Remember to study any roots, prefixes, or suffixes that are unfamiliar to you.

In this section, you will also find a quick math reference sheet with many of the formulas you will need to know for math questions on the civil service exam.

These resources are here to make your math and vocabulary skills stronger before the day of your civil service exam—make the commitment to work with them as you prepare for your exam.

Appendix 1: Glossary of Math Terms

area: a measure of the space inside a two-dimensional figure. Area is expressed in square units.

arithmetic series: a series that progresses by adding (or subtracting) a constant number to each term.

associative law: this property applies to grouping of addition or multiplication equations and expressions. It can be represented as $a + (b + c) = (a + b) + c$ or $a \times (b \times c) = (a \times b) \times c$. For example, $10 + (12 + 14) = (10 + 12) + 14$.

circumference: the distance around a circle.

commutative law: this property applies to addition and multiplication and can be represented as $a + b = b + a$ or $a \times b = b \times a$. For example, $2 + 3 = 3 + 2$ and $4 \times 2 = 2 \times 4$ exhibit the commutative law.

compounded annually: interest is paid each year.

compounded daily: interest is paid every day.

compounded monthly: interest is paid every month.

compounded quarterly: interest is paid four times per year.

compounded semiannually: interest is paid two times per year.

constant rate equation: an equation that is used to relate distance, rate, and time when dealing with a constant velocity: $D = RT$.

denominator: the bottom number in a fraction.

diameter: any line segment that goes through the center of a circle and has both endpoints on the circle.

difference: the answer obtained by subtracting.

distributive law: this property applies to multiplication *over* addition and can be represented as $a(b + c) = ab + ac$. For example, $3(5 + 7) = 3 \times 5 + 3 \times 7$.

geometric series: a series that progresses by multiplying each term by a constant number to get the next term.

improper fraction: a fraction whose numerator is greater than the denominator, such as $\frac{8}{7}$.

least common denominator (LCD): the smallest number that is a multiple of the original denominators present.

mean: the average of a set of values found by adding the values and dividing by the number of values.

median: the middle number in a group of numbers arranged in sequential order. In a set of numbers, half will be greater than the median and half will be less than the median.

mixed number: A number that is expressed as a whole number with a fraction to the right, such as $1\frac{1}{2}$.

mode: the number in a set of numbers that occurs most frequently. To find the mode, look for numbers that occur more than once and find the one that appears *most* often.

numerator: the top number in a fraction.

order of operations: The order in which operations must be performed. An easy way to remember the order of operations is to use the mnemonic **PEMDAS**, where each letter stands for an operation: **P**arentheses: Always calculate the values inside of parentheses first; **E**xponents: Second, calculate exponents (or powers); **M**ultiplication/**D**ivision: Third, multiply or divide in order from left to right; **A**ddition/**S**ubtraction: Last, add or subtract in order from left to right.

percent change: when calculating the percent increase or decrease, equate the ratio of the amount of change to the initial value with the ratio of a new value, x, to 100. The general proportion to use is: $\frac{\text{change}}{\text{initial}} = \frac{x}{100}$

percent error: found by converting the ratio between the calculated value and the actual value to a value out of 100: $\frac{\text{difference in values}}{\text{actual values}} = \frac{x}{100}$

percent: a ratio that expresses a value as per 100 parts. For example, 30% is equivalent to 30 per 100, or $\frac{30}{100}$. You can express a percent as a fraction by placing the number before the percent symbol over the number 100. You can express a percent as a decimal by moving the current decimal point two places to the left.

perimeter: the distance around a two-dimensional geometric figure.

prime number: a number that has only two factors, the number 1 and itself.

product: the answer obtained by multiplying.

proper fraction: a fraction where the numerator is less than the denominator, such as $\frac{1}{2}$.

proportion: a pair of equivalent ratios in the form $\frac{a}{b} = \frac{c}{d}$

quotient: the answer obtained by dividing.

radius: any line that begins at the center of a circle and ends on a point on the circle.

ratio: a comparison of two or more numbers.

reciprocal: the multiplicative inverse of a number; for example, the reciprocal of $\frac{4}{5}$ is $\frac{5}{4}$.

simple interest: interest is calculated with the formula $I = PRT$. The amount of money deposited is called the principal, P. The annual interest rate is represented by R, and T represents the time in years.

sum: the answer obtained by adding.

symbol series: a visual series based on the relationship between images.

volume: a measure of the amount of space inside a three-dimensional shape. Volume is expressed in cubic units.

Appendix 2: Math Formula Sheet

Percent

$$\frac{\text{part}}{\text{whole}} = \frac{\text{percent}}{100} \qquad \frac{\text{is}}{\text{of}} = \frac{\text{percent}}{100} \qquad \frac{\text{change}}{\text{original}} = \frac{\text{percent}}{100}$$

Distance Formula

$D = R \times T$

Simple Interest Formula

$I = P \times R \times T$

Rules of Exponents

$x^0 = 1 \quad x^{-a} = \frac{1}{x^a} \quad x^a \times x^b = x^{a+b} \quad x^a \div x^b = x^{a-b}$

$\frac{x^a}{x^b} = x^{a-b} \qquad (x^a)^b = x^{a \times b} \qquad x^{\frac{1}{a}} = \frac{a}{\sqrt{x}}$

Probability

$P(E) = \frac{\text{\#favorable outcomes}}{\text{\#total outcomes}}$ $P(E_1 \text{ or } E_2) = P(E_1) + P(E_2)$

$P(E_1 \text{ and } E_2) = P(E_1) \times P(E_2)$

Pythagorean theorem:

$a^2 + b^2 = c^2$

Perimeter

Rectangle: $P = 2 \times l + 2 \times w$ \qquad Square: $P = 4 \times s$

Circumference:

$C = \pi \times d$ or $C = 2 \times \pi \times r$

Area

Triangle: $A = \frac{1}{2} \times b \times h$

Rectangle: $A = b \times h$

Trapezoid: $A = \frac{1}{2} \times h \times (b_1 + b_2)$

Volume

$V = B \times h$ (B is the area of the base)

Rectangular Solid: $V = l \times w \times h$

Cylinder: $V = \pi \times r^2 \times h$

Appendix 3: Glossary of Vocabulary Terms

active voice: when the subject is performing the action (as opposed to *passive voice*).

agreement: the state of being balanced in number (e.g., singular subjects and singular verbs; plural antecedents and plural pronouns).

antecedent: the noun that is replaced by a pronoun.

cause: a person or thing that makes something happen.

clause: a group of words containing a subject and predicate.

comparative: the adjective form showing the greater degree in quality or quantity, formed by adding *-er* (e.g., *happier*).

comparison: showing how two ideas or items are similar.

complex sentence: a sentence with at least one dependent and one independent clause.

compound sentence: a sentence with at least two independent clauses.

conjunctive adverb: a word or phrase that often works with a semicolon to connect two independent clauses and show the relationship to one another (e.g., *however, therefore, likewise*).

contraction: a word that uses an apostrophe to show that a letter or letters have been omitted (e.g., *can't*).

contrast: showing how two ideas or items are different.

coordinating conjunction: one of seven words—*and, but, for, nor, or, so, yet*—that serve to connect two independent clauses.

dependent clause: a clause that has a subordinating conjunction and expresses an incomplete thought.

direct object: the person or thing that receives the action of the sentence.

fragment: an incomplete sentence (may or may not have a subject and predicate).

gerund: the noun form of a verb, created by adding *-ing* to the verb base.

helping verb: (auxiliary verb) verbs that help indicate exactly when an action will take place, is taking place, did take place, should take place, might take place, etc.

homophone: a word that sounds exactly like another word but has a different spelling and meaning (e.g., *bare, bear*).

independent clause: a clause that expresses a complete thought and can stand on its own.

indirect object: the person or thing that receives the direct object.

infinitive: the base form of a verb plus the word *to* (e.g., *to go*).

intransitive verb: a verb that does not take an object (the subject performs the action on his/her/itself).

mechanics: the rules governing punctuation, capitalization, and spelling.

modifier: a word or phrase that describes or qualifies a person, place, thing, or action.

parallel structure: a series of words, phrases, or clauses that all follow the same grammatical pattern.

participial phrase: the adjective form of a verb, created by adding *-ing* to the verb base.

passive voice: when the subject of the sentence is being acted upon (passively receives the action).

past participle: the verb form expressing what happened in the past, formed by a past tense helping verb + the simple past tense form of the verb.

phrase: a group of words that do not contain both a subject and a predicate.

predicate: the part of the sentence that tells us what the subject is or does.

present participle: the verb form expressing what is happening now, formed by a present tense helping verb and *-ing*.

proper noun: a noun that identifies a specific person, place, or thing, such as *Elm Street*.

redundancy: the unnecessary repetition of words or ideas.

run-on: a sentence that has two or more independent clauses without the proper punctuation or connecting words (e.g., *subordinating conjunction*) between them.

style: the manner in which something is done; in writing, the combination of a writer's word choice, sentence structure, tone, level of formality, and level of detail.

subject: the person, place, or thing that performs the action of the sentence.

subjunctive: the verb form that indicates something that is wished for or contrary to fact.

subordinating conjunction: a word or phrase that introduces an adverb clause, making the clause dependent and showing its relationship to another (usually independent) clause (e.g., *because, since, while*).

superlative: the adjective form showing the greatest degree in quality or quantity, formed by adding *-est* (e.g., *happiest*).

transition: a word or phrase used to move from one idea to the next and to show the relationship between those ideas (e.g., *however, next, in contrast*).

transitive verb: a verb that takes an object (someone or something receives the action of the verb).

usage: the rules that govern the form of the words you use and how you string words together in sentences.

Appendix 4: Commonly Tested Vocabulary Words ▶

aberration (ăb·ĕ·ˈray·shŏn) *n.* deviation from what is normal, distortion. *His new scientific theory was deemed an aberration by his very conservative colleagues.*

abeyance (ă·ˈbay·ăns) *n.* suspension, being temporarily suspended or set aside. *Construction of the highway is in abeyance until we get agency approval.*

abhor (ab·ˈhohr) *v.* to regard with horror, detest. *I abhor such hypocrisy!*

abjure (ab·ˈjoor) *v.* 1. to repudiate, renounce under oath 2. to give up or reject. *When Joseph became a citizen, he had to abjure his allegiance to his country of origin.*

abrogate (ˈab·rŏ·gayt) *v.* to abolish, do away with, or annul by authority. *It was unclear if the judge would abrogate the lower court's ruling.*

abscond (ab·ˈskond) *v.* to run away secretly and hide, often in order to avoid arrest or prosecution. *Criminals will often head south and abscond with stolen goods to Mexico.*

absolution (ab·sŏ·ˈloo·shŏn) *n.* 1. an absolving or clearing from blame or guilt 2. a formal declaration of forgiveness, redemption. *The jury granted Alan the absolution he deserved.*

abstain (ab·ˈstayn) *v.* to choose to refrain from something, especially to refrain from voting. *I have decided to abstain on this issue.*

abstruse (ab·ˈstroos) *adj.* difficult to comprehend, obscure. *Albert Einstein's abstruse calculations can be understood by only a few people.*

abysmal (ă·ˈbiz·măl) *adj.* 1. extreme, very profound, limitless 2. extremely bad. *Tom's last-place finish in the race was an abysmal turn of events for the team.*

accolade (ˈak·ŏ·layd) *n.* 1. praise or approval 2. a ceremonial embrace in greeting 3. a ceremonious tap on the shoulder with a sword to mark the conferring of knighthood. *He received accolades from his superiors for finding ways to cut costs and increase productivity.*

accretion (ă·ˈkree·shŏn) *n.* 1. growth or increase by gradual, successive addition; building up 2. (in biology) the growing together of parts that are normally separate. *The accretion of sediment in the harbor channel caused boats to run aground.*

acrid (ˈak·rid) *adj.* 1. having an unpleasantly bitter, sharp taste or smell 2. bitter or caustic in language or manner. *The burning tires in the junkyard gave off an acrid odor.*

ad hoc (ad 'hok) *adj.* for a specific, often temporary, purpose; for this case only. *She acted as the ad hoc scout leader while Mr. Davis—the official leader—was ill.*

adamant ('ad·ă·mănt) *adj.* 1. unyielding to requests, appeals, or reason 2. firm, inflexible. *The senator was adamant that no changes would be made to the defense budget.*

addle ('ad·ĕl) *v.* 1. to muddle or confuse 2. to become rotten, as in an egg. *The jury found the defendant addled at the end of the prosecuting attorney's questions.*

ado (ă·'doo) *n.* fuss, trouble, bother. *Without much ado, she completed her book report.*

aficionado (ă·'fish·yo·'nah·doh) *n.* a fan or devotee, especially of a sport or pastime. *The Jeffersons' attendance at every game proved that they were true aficionados of baseball.*

alacrity (ă·'lak·ri·tee) *n.* a cheerful willingness; being happily ready and eager. *The alacrity she brought to her job helped her move up the corporate ladder quickly.*

allay (ă·'lay) *v.* 1. to reduce the intensity of, alleviate 2. to calm, put to rest. *The remarks by the C.E.O did not allay the concerns of the employees.*

altercation (awl·tĕr·'kay·shŏn) *n.* a heated dispute or quarrel. *To prevent an altercation at social functions, one should avoid discussing politics and religion.*

ambivalent (am·'biv·ă·lĕnt) *adj.* having mixed or conflicting feelings about a person, thing, or situation; uncertain. *She was ambivalent about the proposal for the shopping center because she understood the arguments both for and against its construction.*

ameliorate (ă·'meel·yŏ·rayt) *v.* to make or become better, to improve. *The diplomat was able to ameliorate the tense situation between the two nations.*

amorphous (ă·'mor·fŭs) *adj.* having no definite shape or form; shapeless. *The amorphous cloud of steam drifted over her head.*

amulet ('am·yŭ·lit) *n.* something worn around the neck as a charm against evil. *The princess wore an amulet after being cursed by a wizard.*

anachronism (ă·'nak·rŏ·niz·ĕm) *n.* 1. something that is placed into an incorrect historical period 2. a person, custom, or idea that is out of date. *The authenticity and credibility of the 1920s movie were damaged by the many anachronisms that appeared throughout the scenes.*

anarchy ('an·ăr·kee) *n.* 1. the complete absence of government or control resulting in lawlessness 2. political disorder and confusion. *The days immediately following the revolution were marked by anarchy.*

anomaly (ă·'nom·ă·lee) *n.* something that deviates from the general rule or usual form; one that is irregular, peculiar or abnormal. *Winning millions of dollars from a slot machine would be considered an anomaly.*

antipathy (an·'tip·ă·thee) *n.* 1. a strong aversion or dislike 2. an object of aversion. *It is a moment I recall with great antipathy.*

antithesis (an·'tith·ĕ·sis) *n.* the direct or exact opposite, opposition or contrast. *Martin's parenting style is the antithesis of mine.*

apathetic (ap·ă·'thet·ik) *adj.* feeling or showing a lack of interest, concern, or emotion; indifferent, unresponsive. *Ms. Brownstone was distressed by how apathetic her eighth-grade students were.*

aperture ('ap·ĕr·chŭr) *n.* an opening or gap, especially one that lets in light. *The aperture setting on a camera has to be set perfectly to ensure that pictures will have enough light.*

apex ('ay·peks) *n.* 1. the highest point 2. tip, pointed end. *Upon reaching the apex of the mountain, the climbers placed their flag in the snow.*

apocalypse (ă·'pok·ă·lips) *n.* a cataclysmic event bringing about total devastation or the end of the world. *Many people feared an apocalypse would immediately follow the development of nuclear weapons.*

apostate (ă·'pos·tayt) *n.* one who abandons long-held religious or political convictions. *Disillusioned with the religious life, Reverend Gift lost his faith and left the ministry, not caring if he'd be seen as an apostate by colleagues who chose to remain.*

apotheosis (ă·poth·ee·'oh·sis) *n.* deification, an exalted or glorified ideal. *Lancelot was the apotheosis of chivalry until he met Guinevere.*

appease (ă·'peez) *v.* to make calm or quiet, soothe; to still or pacify. *His ability to appease his constituents helped him win the election.*

apprise (ă·'prīz) *v.* to inform, give notice to. *Part of Susan's job as a public defender was to apprise people of their legal rights.*

approbation (ap·rŏ·'bay·shŏn) *n.* approval. *The local authorities issued an approbation to close the street for a festival on St. Patrick's Day.*

appropriate (ă·'prō·prē·ĭt) *v.* to take for one's own use, often without permission; to set aside for a special purpose. *The state legislature will appropriate two million dollars from the annual budget to build a new bridge on the interstate highway.*

apropos (ap·rŏ·'poh) *adj.* appropriate to the situation; suitable to what is being said or done. *The chairman's remarks referring to the founding fathers were apropos since it was the Fourth of July.*

arcane (ahr·'kayn) *adj.* mysterious, secret, beyond comprehension. *A number of college students in the 1980s became involved in the arcane game known as "Dungeons and Dragons."*

archaic (ahr·'kay·ik) *adj.* belonging to former or ancient times; characteristic of the past. *Samantha laughed at her grandfather's archaic views of dating and relationships.*

archetype ('ahr·ki·tīp) *n.* an original model from which others are copied; original pattern or prototype. *Elvis Presley served as the archetype for rock-and-roll performers in the 1950s.*

ardor ('ahr·dŏr) *n.* fiery intensity of feeling; passionate enthusiasm, zeal. *The ardor Larry brought to the campaign made him a natural spokesperson.*

arduous ('ahr·joo·ŭs) *adj.* 1. very difficult, laborious; requiring great effort 2. difficult to traverse or surmount. *Commander Shackleton's arduous journey through the Arctic has become the subject of many books and movies.*

ascetic (ă·'set·ik) *adj.* practicing self-denial, not allowing oneself pleasures or luxuries; austere. *Some religions require their leaders to lead an ascetic lifestyle as an example to their followers.*

askew (ă·'skyoo) *adj. & adv.* crooked, not straight or level; to one side. *Even the pictures on the wall stood askew after my five-year-old son's birthday party.*

asperity ('ă·sper·i·tee) *n.* harshness, severity; roughness of manner, ill temper, irritability. *The asperity that Marvin, the grumpy accountant, brought to the meetings usually resulted in an early adjournment.*

assay ('ă·say) *v.* 1. to try, put to a test 2. to examine 3. to judge critically, evaluate after an analysis. *The chief engineer wanted a laboratory to assay the steel before using it in the construction project.*

assiduous (ă·'sij·oo·ŭs) *adj.* diligent, persevering, unremitting; constant in application or attention. *The nurses in the intensive care unit are known for providing assiduous care to their patients.*

assuage (ă·'swayj) *v.* to make something less severe, to soothe; to satisfy (as hunger or thirst). *The small cups of water offered to the marathon runners helped to assuage their thirst.*

attenuate (ă·'ten·yoo·ayt) *v.* 1. to make thin or slender 2. to weaken, reduce in force, value, or degree. *The Russian army was able to attenuate the strength and number of the German forces by leading them inland during winter.*

audacious (aw·'day·shŭs) *adj.* fearlessly or recklessly daring or bold; unrestrained by convention or propriety. *Detective Malloy's methods were considered bold and audacious by his superiors, and they often achieved results.*

august (aw·'gust) *adj.* majestic, venerable; inspiring admiration or reverence. *Jackie Kennedy's august dignity in the days following her husband's assassination set a tone for the rest of the nation as it mourned.*

auspice ('aw·spis) *n.* 1. protection or support, patronage 2. a forecast or omen. *The children's art museum was able to continue operating through the auspices of an anonymous wealthy benefactor.*

auspicious (aw·'spish·ŭs) *adj.* favorable, showing signs that promise success; propitious. *Valerie believed it an auspicious beginning when it rained on the day that she opened her umbrella store.*

austere (aw·'steer) *adj.* 1. severe or stern in attitude or appearance 2. simple, unadorned, very plain. *With its simple but functional furniture and its obvious lack of decorative elements, the interior of the Shaker meeting hall was considered austere by many people.*

authoritarian (ă·'thor·i·'tair·i·ăn) *adj.* favoring complete, unquestioning obedience to authority as opposed to individual freedom. *The military maintains an authoritarian environment for its officers and enlisted soldiers alike.*

avant-garde (a·vahnt·'gahrd) *adj.* using or favoring an ultramodern or experimental style; innovative, cutting-edge, especially in the arts or literature. *Though it seems very conventional now, in the 1950s, Andy Warhol's art was viewed as avant-garde.*

aversion (ă·'vur·zhŏn) *n.* 1. a strong, intense dislike; repugnance 2. the object of this feeling. *Todd has an aversion to arugula and picks it out of his salads.*

B

baleful ('bayl·fŭl) *adj.* harmful, menacing, destructive, sinister. *Whether it's a man, woman, car, or animal, you can be certain to find at least one baleful character in a Stephen King horror novel.*

banal (bă·'nal) *adj.* commonplace, trite; obvious and uninteresting. *Though Tom and Susan had hoped for an adventure, they found that driving cross-country on the interstate offered mostly banal sites, restaurants, and attractions.*

bane (bayn) *n.* 1. cause of trouble, misery, distress, or harm 2. poison. *The bane of the oak tree is the Asian beetle.*

beguile (bi·'gīl) *v.* to deceive or cheat through cunning; to distract the attention of, divert; to pass time in a pleasant manner, to amuse or charm. *Violet was able to beguile the spy, causing him to miss his secret meeting.*

belie (bi·'lī) *v.* 1. to give a false impression, misrepresent 2. to show to be false, to contradict. *By wearing an expensive suit and watch, Alan hoped to belie his lack of success to everyone at the reunion.*

bellicose ('bel·ĭ·kohs) *adj.* belligerent, quarrelsome, eager to make war. *There was little hope for peace following the election of a candidate known for his bellicose nature.*

belligerent (bi·'lij·ĕr·ĕnt) *adj.* hostile and aggressive, showing an eagerness to fight. *Ms. Rivera always kept an eye on Daniel during recess, as his belligerent attitude often caused problems with other children.*

bevy ('bev·ee) *n.* 1. a large group or assemblage 2. a flock of animals or birds. *There was a lively bevy of eager bingo fans waiting outside the bingo hall for the game to begin.*

bilk (bilk) *v.* to deceive or defraud; to swindle, cheat, especially to evade paying one's debts. *The stockbroker was led away in handcuffs, accused of trying to bilk senior citizens out of their investment dollars.*

blasphemy ('blas·fĕ·mee) *n.* contemptuous or irreverent acts, utterances, attitudes or writings against God or other things considered sacred; disrespect of something sacrosanct. *If you committed blasphemy during the Inquisition, the consequences were severe.*

blatant ('blay·tant) *adj.* completely obvious, not attempting to conceal in any way. *Samuel's blatant disregard of the rules earned him a two-week suspension.*

blight (blīt) *n.* 1. a plant disease that causes the affected parts to wilt and die 2. something that causes this condition, such as air pollution 3. something that impairs or destroys 4. an unsightly object or area.

They still do not know what caused the blight that destroyed half of the trees in the orchard.

blithe (blīth) *adj.* light-hearted, casual, and carefree. *Rachel's blithe attitude toward spending money left her broke and in debt.*

boisterous ('boi·stĕ·rŭs) *adj.* 1. loud, noisy, and lacking restraint or discipline 2. stormy and rough. *The boisterous crowd began throwing cups onto the field during the football game.*

bolster ('bohl·stĕr) *v.* 1. to support or prop up 2. to buoy or hearten. *Coach Edmond's speech bolstered the team's confidence.*

bombastic (bom·'bas·tik) *adj.* speaking pompously, with inflated self-importance. *Ahmed was shocked that a renowned and admired humanitarian could give such a bombastic keynote address.*

boor (boor) *n.* a crude, offensive, ill-mannered person. *Seeing Chuck wipe his mouth with his sleeve, Maribel realized she was attending her senior prom with a classic boor.*

bourgeois (boor·'zhwah) *adj.* typical of the middle class; conforming to the standards and conventions of the middle class. *A house in the suburbs, two children, two cars, and three TVs are key indicators of a bourgeois lifestyle.*

bravado (bră·'vah·doh) *n.* false courage, a show of pretended bravery. *Kyle's bravado often got him in trouble with other kids in the neighborhood.*

broach (brohch) *v.* 1. to bring up, introduce, in order to begin a discussion of 2. to tap or pierce, as in to draw off liquid. *It was hard for Sarah to broach the subject of her mother's weight gain.*

bumptious ('bump·shŭs) *adj.* arrogant, conceited. *The bumptious man couldn't stop talking about himself or looking in the mirror.*

buoyant ('boi·ănt) *adj.* 1. able to float 2. light-hearted, cheerful. *In science class, the children tried to identify which objects on the table would be buoyant.*

burgeon ('bur·jŏn) *v.* to begin to grow and flourish; to begin to sprout, grow new buds, blossom. *The tulip bulbs beneath the soil would burgeon in early spring providing there was no late frost.*

burnish ('bur·nish) *v.* to polish, rub to a shine. *When Kathryn began to burnish the old metal teapot, she realized that it was, in fact, solid silver.*

C

cabal (kă·'bal) *n.* 1. a scheme or conspiracy 2. a small group joined in a secret plot. *With Antonio as their leader, the members of the cabal readied themselves to begin the uprising.*

cadge (kaj) *v.* to beg, to obtain by begging. *Their dog Cleo would cadge at my feet, hoping I would throw him some table scraps.*

capricious (kă·'prish·ŭs) *adj.* impulsive, whimsical and unpredictable. *Robin Williams, the comedian, demonstrates a most capricious nature even when he is not performing.*

careen (kă·'reen) *v.* 1. to lurch from side to side while in motion 2. to rush carelessly or headlong. *Watching the car in front of us careen down the road was very frightening.*

caste (kast) *n.* a distinct social class or system. *While visiting India, Michael was fascinated to learn the particulars of each caste and the way they related to each other.*

castigate ('kas·tĭ·gayt) *v.* to inflict a severe punishment on; to chastise severely. *When she was caught stealing for the second time, Maya knew her mother would castigate her.*

catharsis (kă·'thahr·sis) *n.* the act of ridding or cleansing; relieving emotions via the experiences of others, especially through art. *Survivors of war often experience a catharsis when viewing Picasso's painting* Guernica, *which depicts the bombing of a town during the Spanish civil war.*

censure ('sen·shŭr) *n.* expression of strong criticism or disapproval; a rebuke or condemnation. *After the sen-*

ator was found guilty of taking bribes, Congress unanimously agreed to censure him.

chastise ('chas·tīz) *v.* to punish severely, as with a beating; to criticize harshly, rebuke. *Charles knew that his wife would chastise him after he inadvertently told the room full of guests that she had just had a face lift.*

chauvinist ('shoh·vĭn·ist) *n.* a person who believes in the superiority of his or her own kind; an extreme nationalist. *Though common in the early days of the women's movement, male chauvinists are pretty rare today.*

churlish ('chur·lĭsh) *adj.* ill-mannered, boorish, rude. *Angelo's churlish remarks made everyone at the table uncomfortable and ill at ease.*

circumspect ('sur·kŭm·spekt) *adj.* cautious, wary, watchful. *The captain was circumspect as she guided the boat through the fog.*

coeval (koh·'ee·văl) *adj.* of the same time period, contemporary. *The growth of personal computers and CD players were coeval during the late twentieth century.*

cogent ('koh·jĕnt) *adj.* convincing, persuasive, compelling belief. *Ella's cogent arguments helped the debate team win the state championship.*

collusion (kŏ·'loo·zhŏn) *n.* a secret agreement between two or more people for a deceitful or fraudulent purpose; conspiracy. *The discovery of the e-mail proved that collusion existed between the C.E.O and C.F.O to defraud the shareholders.*

complaisant (kŏm·'play·sănt) *adj.* tending to comply, obliging, willing to do what pleases others. *To preserve family peace and harmony, Lenny became very complaisant when his in-laws came to visit.*

conciliatory (kŏn·'sil·ee·ă·tohr·ee) *adj.* making or willing to make concessions to reconcile, soothe, or comfort; mollifying, appeasing. *Abraham Lincoln made conciliatory gestures toward the South at the end of the Civil War.*

conclave ('kon·klav) *n.* a private or secret meeting. *The double agent had a conclave with the spy she was supposed to be observing.*

consternation (kon·stĕr·'nay·shŏn) *n.* a feeling of deep, incapacitating horror or dismay. *The look of consternation on the faces of the students taking the history exam alarmed the teacher, who thought he had prepared his students for the test.*

contentious (kŏn·'ten·shŭs) *adj.* 1. quarrelsome, competitive, quick to fight 2. controversial, causing contention. *With two contentious candidates on hand, it was sure to be a lively debate.*

conundrum (kŏ·'nun·drŭm) *n.* a hard riddle, enigma; a puzzling question or problem. *Alex's logic professor gave the class a conundrum to work on over the weekend.*

cornucopia (kor·nyŭ·'koh·pi·a) *n.* abundance; a horn of plenty. *The first graders made cornucopias for Thanksgiving by placing papier-mache vegetables into a hollowed-out horn.*

countenance ('kown·tĕ·năns) *n.* the appearance of a person's face, facial features and expression. *As she walked down the aisle, Julia's countenance was absolutely radiant.*

craven ('kray·vĕn) *adj.* cowardly. *"This craven act of violence will not go unpunished," remarked the police chief.*

credulous ('krej·ŭ·lŭs) *adj.* gullible, too willing to believe things. *All the tables, graphs, and charts made the company's assets look too good to the credulous potential investors at the meeting.*

D

daunt (dawnt) *v.* to intimidate, to make afraid or discouraged. *Members of the opposing team were trying to daunt the home team by yelling loudly and beating their chests.*

de facto (dee 'fak·toh) in reality or fact; actual. *Though there was a ceremonial head of government, General Ashtononi was the de facto leader of the country.*

debacle (di·'bah·kĕl) *n.* 1. a disaster or collapse; a total defeat or failure 2. a sudden breaking up or breaking loose; violent flood waters, often caused by the breaking up of ice in a river. *The diplomatic talks became a debacle when the enemy state refused to negotiate.*

decimate ('des·ĭ·mayt) *v.* to destroy a large portion of. *Neglect and time would eventually decimate much of the housing in the inner cities.*

decorum (di·'kohr·ŭm) *n.* appropriateness of behavior, propriety; decency in manners and conduct. *When questions concerning decorum arise, I always refer to Emily Post.*

deign (dayn) *v.* to condescend, to be kind or gracious enough to do something thought to be beneath one's dignity. *Would you deign to spare a dime for a poor old beggar like me?*

delineate (di·'lin·ee·ayt) *v.* to draw or outline, sketch; to portray, depict, describe. *The survey will clearly delineate where their property ends.*

demagogue ('dem·ă·gawg) *n.* a leader who obtains power by appealing to people's feelings and prejudices rather than by reasoning. *Hilter was the most infamous demagogue of the twentieth century.*

demur (di·'mur) *v.* to raise objections, hesitate. *Polly hated to demur, but she didn't think adding ten cloves of garlic to the recipe would taste good.*

demure (di·'myoor) *adj.* modest and shy, or pretending to be so. *When it was to her advantage, Sharon could be very demure, but otherwise she was quite outgoing.*

denigrate ('den·i·grayt) *v.* to blacken the reputation of, disparage, defame. *The movie script reportedly contained scenes that would denigrate the queen, so those scenes were removed.*

denouement (day·noo·'mahn) *n.* the resolution or clearing up of the plot at the end of a narrative; the outcome or solution of an often complex series of events. *The students sat at the edge of their seats as they listened to the denouement of the story.*

deprecate ('dep·rĕ·kayt) *v.* to express disapproval of; to belittle, depreciate. *Grandpa's tendency to deprecate the children's friends was a frequent source of family strife.*

derisive (di·'rī·siv) *adj.* scornful, expressing ridicule; mocking, jeering. *In order to promote productive discussion, derisive comments were forbidden in the classroom.*

derivative (di·'riv·ă·tiv) *adj.* derived from another source, unoriginal. *The word "atomic" is a derivative of the word "atom."*

desecrate ('des·ĕ·krayt) *v.* to violate the sacredness of, to profane. *Someone desecrated the local cemetery by spray-painting graffiti on tombstones.*

desultory (des·'ŭl·tohr·ee) *adj.* aimless, haphazard; moving from one subject to another without logical connection. *The family became concerned listening to Steven's desultory ramblings.*

dichotomy (dī·'kot·ŏ·mee) *n.* division into two usually contradictory parts or kinds. *When the teacher broached the subject of the election, there was a predictable dichotomy among the students.*

diffident ('dif·i·děnt) *adj.* lacking self-confidence, shy and timid. *Alan's diffident nature is often misinterpreted as arrogance.*

dilatory ('dil·ă·tohr·ee) *adj.* slow or late in doing something; intended to delay, especially to gain time. *Resentful for having to work the holiday, Miguel's dilatory approach to getting himself up and dressed was his own small act of passive resistance.*

disabuse (dis·ă·'byooz) *v.* to undeceive, correct a false impression or erroneous belief. *Natalie needed to disabuse Chin of his belief that she was in love with him.*

disconcert (dis·kŏn·'surt) *v.* 1. to upset the composure of, ruffle 2. to frustrate plans by throwing into disorder. *The arrival of Miriam's ex-husband and his new wife managed to disconcert the typically unflappable Miriam.*

disconsolate (dis·'kon·sŏ·lit) *adj.* 1. sad, dejected, disappointed 2. inconsolable, hopelessly unhappy. *The disconsolate look on Peter's face revealed that the letter contained bad news.*

disenfranchise (dis·en·'fran·chīz) *v.* to deprive of the rights of citizenship, especially the right to vote. *The* *independent monitors were at polling locations to ensure neither party tried to disenfranchise incoming voters.*

disingenuous (dis·in·'jen·yoo·ŭs) *adj.* 1. insincere, calculating; not straightforward or frank 2. falsely pretending to be unaware. *Carl's disingenuous comments were not taken seriously by anyone in the room.*

disparage (di·'spar·ij) *v.* to speak of in a slighting or derogatory way, belittle. *Comedians often disparage politicians as part of their comedic routines.*

dissemble (di·'sem·bĕl) *v.* to disguise or conceal one's true feelings or motives behind a false appearance. *Tom needed to dissemble his desire for his boss's job by acting supportive of her planned job change.*

dissuade (di·'swayd) *v.* to discourage from or persuade against a course of action. *I tried to dissuade them from painting their house purple, but they didn't listen.*

dither ('dith·ĕr) *v.* 1. to hesitate, be indecisive and uncertain 2. to shake or quiver. *During a crisis, it is important to have a leader who will not dither.*

dogma ('dawg·mă) *n.* a system of principles or beliefs, a prescribed doctrine. *Some find the dogma inherent in religion a comfort, whereas others find it too restrictive.*

dogmatic (dawg·'ma·tik) *adj.* 1. asserting something in a positive, absolute, arrogant way 2. of or relating to dogma. *His dogmatic style of conversation was not very popular with his young students.*

dross (draws) *n.* 1. waste product, sludge 2. something worthless, commonplace, or trivial. *Work crews immediately began the task of cleaning the dross at the abandoned plastics factory.*

dulcet ('dul·sit) *adj.* melodious, harmonious, sweet-sounding. *The chamber orchestra's dulcet tunes were a perfect ending to a great evening.*

E

ebullient (i·'bul·yĕnt) *adj.* bubbling over with enthusiasm, exuberant. *The ebullient children were waiting to stick their hands into the grab bag and pull out a toy.*

éclat (ay·'klah) *n.* conspicuous success; great acclaim or applause; brilliant performance or achievement. *Even the ruinous deceit of the envious Salieri could not impede the dazzling éclat of the young and gifted Mozart.*

edifying ('ed·ĭ·fī·ing) *adj.* enlightening or uplifting with the aim of improving intellectual or moral development; instructing, improving. *His edifying speech challenged the community to devote more time to charitable causes.*

efficacious (ef·ĭ·'kay·shŭs) *adj.* acting effectively, producing the desired effect or result. *Margaret's efficacious approach to her job in the collections department made her a favorite with the C.F.O.*

effrontery (i·'frun·tĕ·ree) *n.* brazen boldness, impudence, insolence. *The customs officials were infuriated by the effrontery of the illegal alien who nonchalantly carried drugs into the country in his shirt pocket.*

effusive (i·'fyoo·siv) *adj.* expressing emotions in an unrestrained or excessive way; profuse, overflowing, gushy. *Anne's unexpectedly effusive greeting made Tammy uncomfortable.*

egalitarian (i·gal·i·'tair·ee·ăn) *adj.* characterized by or affirming the principle of equal political, social, civil, and economic rights for all persons. *Hannah was moved by the candidate's egalitarian speech.*

eke (eek) *v.* to get or supplement with great effort or strain; to earn or accomplish laboriously. *Working two jobs enabled Quincy to eke out a living wage for his family.*

élan (ay·'lahn) *n.* 1. vivacity, enthusiasm, vigor 2. distinctive style or flair. *The new designer's élan and originality was sure to help him succeed in the highly competitive fashion industry.*

elite (i·'leet) *n.* 1. the best or most skilled members of a social group or class 2. a person or group regarded as superior. *Within the student orchestra, there existed a small group of musical elite who performed around the country.*

eloquent ('el·ŏ·kwĕnt) *adj.* expressing strong emotions or arguments in a powerful, fluent, and persuasive manner. *Abraham Lincoln's Gettysburg Address is considered one of the most eloquent speeches ever given by a U.S. president.*

eminent ('em·ĭ·nĕnt) *adj.* towering above or more prominent than others, lofty; standing above others in quality, character, reputation, etc.; distinguished. *The chairperson proudly announced that the keynote speaker at the animal rights convention would be the eminent primatologist Jane Goodall.*

empirical (em·'pir·i·kal) *adj.* based on observation or experience rather than theory. *Frank's empirical data suggested that mice would climb over the walls of the maze to get to the cheese rather than navigate the maze itself.*

enclave ('en·klayv) *n.* a distinct territory lying wholly within the boundaries of another, larger territory. *The country of Lesotho is an enclave of South Africa.*

endemic (en·'dem·ik) *adj.* 1. prevalent in or characteristic of a specific area or group of people 2. native to a particular region. *Kudzu, a hairy, purple-flowered vine often thought to be endemic to the southeastern United States, was actually imported from Japan.*

enervate ('en·ĕr·vayt) *v.* to weaken, deprive of strength or vitality; to make feeble or impotent. *Stephanie's cutting remarks managed to enervate Hasaan.*

engender (en·'jen·dĕr) *v.* to produce, give rise to, bring into existence. *Professor Sorenson's support worked to engender Samantha's desire to pursue a Ph.D.*

enigma (ĕ·'nig·mă) *n.* 1. something that is puzzling or difficult to understand; a perplexing or inexplicable thing that cannot be explained 2. a baffling problem or difficult riddle. *How Winston came to be the president of this organization is a true enigma.*

enormity (i·'nor·mi·tee) *n.* 1. excessive wickedness 2. a monstrous offense or evil act, atrocity. (*Note:* Enormity is often used to indicate something of great size (e.g., the enormity of the task), but this is considered an incorrect use of the word.) *The enormity of the duo's crimes will never be forgotten.*

ephemeral (i·'fem·ĕ·răl) *adj.* lasting only a very short time, transitory. *Numerous ephemeral ponds and pools can be found in the desert during the rainy season.*

epicurean (ep·i·'kyoor·ee·ăn) *n.* a person devoted to the pursuit of pleasure and luxury, especially the enjoyment of good food and comfort. *While on vacation at a posh resort hotel, Joan became a true epicurean.*

epitome (i·'pit·ŏ·mee) *n.* 1. something or someone that embodies a particular quality or characteristic, a representative example or a typical model 2. a brief summary or abstract. *With his ten-gallon hat, western shirt, and rugged jeans, Alex was the epitome of the American cowboy.*

equanimity (ee·kwă·'nim·i·tee) *n.* calmness of temperament, even-temperedness; patience and composure, especially under stressful circumstances. *The hostage negotiator's equanimity during the standoff was remarkable.*

equivocate (i·'kwiv·ŏ·kayt) *v.* to use unclear or ambiguous language in order to mislead or conceal the truth. *Raj tried to equivocate when explaining why he came home after his curfew.*

eradicate (i·'rad·ĭ·kayt) *v.* to root out and utterly destroy; to annihilate, exterminate. *The exterminator said he would eradicate the vermin from the house.*

erratic (i·'rat·ik) *adj.* 1. moving or behaving in an irregular, uneven, or inconsistent manner 2. deviating from the normal or typical course of action, opinion, etc. *During an earthquake, a seismograph's needle moves in an erratic manner.*

erudite ('er·yŭ·dīt) *adj.* having or showing great learning; profoundly educated, scholarly. *The scholarly work of nonfiction was obviously written by an erudite young author.*

ethos ('ee·thos) *n.* the spirit, attitude, disposition or beliefs characteristic of a community, epoch, region, etc. *The ethos of their group included a commitment to pacifism.*

eulogy ('yoo·lŏ·gee) *n.* a formal speech or piece of writing in praise of someone or something. *Richard was asked to give a eulogy for his fallen comrade.*

euphoria (yoo·'fohr·ee·ă) *n.* a feeling of well-being or high spirits. *When falling in love, it is not uncommon to experience feelings of euphoria.*

evince (i·'vins) *v.* to show or demonstrate clearly; to make evident. *The safety officer tried to evince the dangers of driving under the influence by showing pictures of alcohol-related automobile accidents.*

exacerbate (ig·'zas·ĕr·bayt) *v.* to make worse; to increase the severity, violence, or bitterness of. *You should have known that splashing salt water on Dan's wound would exacerbate his pain.*

exculpate (eks·'kul·payt) *v.* to free from blame, to clear from a charge of guilt. *When Anthony admitted to the crime, it served to exculpate Marcus.*

exigent ('ek·si·jĕnt) *adj.* 1. urgent, requiring immediate action or attention, critical 2. requiring much effort or precision, demanding. *The late-night call on Paul's cell phone concerned matters of an exigent nature.*

exorbitant (ig·'zor·bi·tănt) *adj.* greatly exceeding the bounds of what is normal or reasonable; inordinate and excessive. *Three thousand dollars is an exorbitant amount to pay for a scarf.*

expedient (ik·'spee·dee·ĕnt) *adj.* (1) appropriate for a purpose, a suitable means to an end (2) serving to promote one's own interests rather than principle. *A quick divorce was an expedient end to the couple's two-month marriage.*

expunge (ik·'spunj) *v.* to wipe or rub out, delete; to eliminate completely, annihilate. *After finishing probation, juveniles can petition the courts to expunge their criminal records.*

extenuate (ik·'sten·yoo·ayt) *v.* to reduce the strength or lessen the seriousness of, to try to partially excuse. *Fred claimed that extenuating circumstances forced him to commit forgery.*

F

facetious (fă·'see·shŭs) *adj.* humorous and witty, cleverly amusing; jocular, sportive. *Ms. Weston's facetious remarks always made people laugh.*

fatuous ('fach·oo·ŭs) *adj.* complacently stupid; feeble-minded and silly. *Since Sam was such an intellectually accomplished student, Mr. Britt was surprised to discover that Sam's well-meaning but fatuous parents were not at all like him.*

feckless ('fek·lis) *adj.* 1. lacking purpose or vitality; feeble, weak 2. incompetent and ineffective, careless. *Jake's feckless performance led to his termination from the team.*

fecund ('fek·ŭnd) *adj.* fertile. *The fecund soil in the valley was able to sustain the growing community.*

feign (fayn) *v.* to pretend, to give the false appearance of. *Walter feigned illness to avoid attending the meeting.*

felicitous (fi·'lis·i·tŭs) *adj.* 1. apt, suitably expressed, apropos 2. marked by good fortune. *The felicitous turn of events during her promotional tour propelled Susan's book to the bestseller list.*

fervent ('fur·ĕnt) *adj.* 1. having or showing great emotion; ardent, zealous 2. extremely hot, burning. *Norman had a fervent belief that aliens had already landed on earth.*

fervor ('fur·vŏr) *n.* zeal, ardor, intense emotion. *The fervor of the fans in the stands helped propel the team to victory.*

fetter ('fet·ĕr) *v.* 1. to shackle, put in chains 2. to impede or restrict. *The presence of two security guards fettered their plans to get backstage.*

flaccid ('fla-sid) *adj.* hanging loose or wrinkled; weak, flabby, not firm. *The skin of cadavers becomes flaccid in a matter of hours.*

flippant ('flip·ănt) *adj.* not showing proper seriousness; disrespectful, saucy. *Ursula's flippant remarks in front of her fiancé's parents were an embarrassment to us all.*

florid ('flor·id) *adj.* 1. elaborate, ornate 2. (of complexion) ruddy, rosy. *The florid architecture in Venice did* *not appeal to me; I prefer buildings without so much ornamentation.*

flout (flowt) *v.* to disobey openly and scornfully; to reject, mock, go against (as in a tradition or convention). *Flappers in the early 20th century would flout convention by bobbing their hair and wearing very short skirts.*

forbearance (for·'bair·ăns) *n.* patience, willingness to wait, tolerance. *Gustaf dreaded the security check in the airport, but he faced it with great forbearance because he knew it was for his own safety.*

forestall (fohr·'stawl) *v.* to prevent by taking action first, preempt. *The diplomat was able to forestall a conflict by holding secret meetings with both parties.*

forswear (for·'swair) *v.* 1. to give up, renounce 2. to deny under oath. *Natasha had to forswear her allegiance to her homeland in order to become a citizen of the new country.*

frugal ('froo·găl) *adj.* 1. careful and economical, sparing, thrifty 2. costing little. *My grandparents survived the Great Depression by being very frugal.*

fulminate ('ful·mĭ·nayt) *v.* 1. to issue a thunderous verbal attack, berate 2. to explode or detonate. *The senator was prone to fulminating when other legislators questioned her ideology.*

fulsome ('ful·sŏm) *adj.* offensive due to excessiveness, especially excess flattery or praise. *Her new coworker's fulsome attention bothered Kathryn.*

G

gainsay ('gayn·say) *v.* to deny, contradict, or declare false; to oppose. *Petra would gainsay all accusations made against her.*

gargantuan (gahr·'gan·choo·ăn) *adj.* gigantic, huge. *It was a gargantuan supermarket for such a small town.*

garish ('gair·ish) *adj.* excessively bright or overdecorated, gaudy; tastelessly showy. *Though Susan thought Las Vegas was garish, Emily thought it was perfectly beautiful.*

garrulous ('gar·ŭ·lŭs) *adj.* talkative. *Andrew had the unfortunate luck of being seated next to a garrulous young woman for his 12-hour flight.*

genteel (jen·'teel) *adj.* elegantly polite, well-bred, refined. *The genteel host made sure that the entrées were cooked to each guest's specifications.*

gregarious (grĕ·'gair·ee·ŭs) *adj.* 1. seeking and enjoying the company of others, sociable 2. tending to form a group with others of the same kind. *John was a gregarious fellow who always had fun at social events.*

guffaw (gu·'faw) *n.* a noisy, coarse burst of laughter. *Michael let out quite a guffaw when Jamal told him the outlandish joke.*

guile (gīl) *n.* treacherous cunning; shrewd, crafty deceit. *The most infamous pirates displayed tremendous guile.*

H

hallow ('hal·oh) *v.* to make holy, consecrate. *The religious leader proclaimed the new worship hall a hallowed space.*

hapless ('hap·lis) *adj.* unlucky, unfortunate. *The hapless circumstances of her journey resulted in lost luggage, missed connections, and a very late arrival.*

harangue (hă·'rang) *n.* a long, often scolding or bombastic speech; a tirade. *Members of the audience began to get restless during the senator's political harangue.*

harbinger ('hahr·bin·jĕr) *n.* a person, thing, or event that foreshadows or indicates what is to come; a forerunner or precursor. *The arrival of the robins is a harbinger of spring.*

harrowing ('har·oh·ing) *adj.* distressing, creating great stress or torment. *The turbulent flight proved to be a harrowing experience for Jane.*

haughty ('haw·tee) *adj.* scornfully arrogant and condescending; acting as though one is superior and others unworthy, disdainful. *Stanley is so haughty that he has very few friends.*

hegemony (hi·'jem·ŏ·nee) *n.* predominant influence or leadership, especially of one government over others.

A military takeover in the impoverished country secured the hegemony of the Centrist Party in its bid for power.

hermetic (hur·'met·ik) *adj.* having an airtight closure; protected from outside influences. *Astronauts go for space walks only when wearing hermetic space suits.*

I

iconoclast (ī·'kon·oh·klast) *n.* 1. a person who attacks and seeks to overthrow traditional ideas, beliefs, or institutions 2. someone who opposes and destroys idols used in worship. *Using words as weapons, the well-spoken iconoclast challenged religious hypocrisy and fanaticism wherever she found it.*

ignoble (ig·'noh·bĕl) *adj.* 1. lacking nobility in character or purpose, dishonorable 2. not of the nobility, common. *Mark was an ignoble successor to such a well-respected leader, and many members of the organization resigned.*

ignominious (ig·nŏ·'min·ee·ŭs) *adj.* 1. marked by shame or disgrace 2. deserving disgrace or shame; despicable. *The evidence of plagiarism brought an ignominious end to what had been a notable career for the talented young author.*

imbroglio (im·'brohl·yoh) *n.* a confused or difficult situation, usually involving disagreement. *An imbroglio developed when the bus drivers went on strike, leaving thousands of commuters stranded at the bus station with no way to get home.*

immolate ('im·ŏ·layt) *v.* 1. to kill, as a sacrifice 2. to kill or destroy by fire. *After the relationship ended, she chose to immolate the letters they had exchanged.*

impasse ('im·pas) *n.* a deadlock, stalemate; a difficulty without a solution. *The labor negotiations with management reached an impasse, and a strike seemed imminent.*

impassive (im·'pas·iv) *adj.* not showing or feeling emotion or pain. *It was hard to know what she was feeling by looking at the impassive expression on her face.*

impecunious (im·pĕ·'kyoo·nee·ŭs) *adj.* having little or no money; poor, penniless. *Many impecunious immigrants to the United States eventually were able to make comfortable lives for themselves.*

imperialism (im·'peer·ee·ă·liz·ĕm) *n.* the policy of extending the rule or authority of a nation or empire by acquiring other territories or dependencies. *Great Britain embraced imperialism, acquiring so many territories that the sun never set on the British Empire.*

imperious (im·'peer·ee·ŭs) *adj.* overbearing, bossy, domineering. *Stella was relieved with her new job transfer because she would no longer be under the control of such an imperious boss.*

impetuous (im·'pech·oo·ŭs) *adj.* 1. characterized by sudden, forceful energy or emotion; impulsive, unduly hasty and without thought 2. marked by violent force. *It was an impetuous decision to run off to Las Vegas and get married after a one-week courtship.*

implacable (im·'plak·ă·bĕl) *adj.* incapable of being placated or appeased; inexorable. *Some of the people who call the customer service desk for assistance are implacable, but most are relatively easy to serve.*

importune (im·por·'toon) *v.* 1. to ask incessantly, make incessant requests 2. to beg persistently and urgently. *Children can't help but importune during the holidays, constantly nagging for the irresistible toys they see advertised on television.*

imprecation (im·prĕ·'kay·shŏn) *n.* an invocation of evil, a curse. *In the book I'm reading, the gypsy queen levies an imprecation on the lead character.*

impudent ('im·pyŭ·dĕnt) *adj.* 1. boldly showing a lack of respect, insolent 2. shamelessly forward, immodest. *Thumbing his nose at the principal was an impudent act.*

impute (im·'pyoot) *v.* to attribute to a cause or source, ascribe, credit. *Doctors impute the reduction in cancer deaths to the nationwide decrease in cigarette smoking.*

incendiary (in·'sen·dee·er·ee) *adj.* 1. causing or capable of causing fire; burning readily 2. of or involving arson 3. tending to incite or inflame, inflammatory. *Fire marshals checked for incendiary devices in the theater after they received an anonymous warning.*

inchoate (in·'koh·it) *adj.* 1. just begun; in an initial or early stage of development, incipient 2. not yet fully formed, undeveloped, incomplete. *During the inchoate stage of fetal growth, it is difficult to distinguish between a cow, a frog, or a human; as they mature, the developing embryos take on the characteristics of their own particular species.*

incredulous (in·'krej·ŭ·lŭs) *adj.* skeptical, unwilling to believe. (*Note:* Do not confuse with *incredible,* meaning "implausible or beyond belief.") *The members of the jury were incredulous when they heard the defendant's far-fetched explanation of the crime.*

incursion (in·'kur·zhŏn) *n.* a raid or temporary invasion of someone else's territory; the act of entering or running into a territory or domain. *There was an incursion on the western border of their country.*

indefatigable (in·di·'fat·ĭ·gă·bĕl) *adj.* not easily exhausted or fatigued; tireless. *The indefatigability of the suffragette movement led to the passage of the 19th Amendment, guaranteeing women the right to vote.*

indolent ('in·dŏ·lĕnt) *adj.* 1. lazy, lethargic, inclined to avoid labor 2. causing little or no pain; slow to grow or heal. *Iris's indolent attitude did not bode well for her professional future.*

indomitable (in·'dom·i·tă·bĕl) *adj.* not able to be vanquished or overcome, unconquerable; not easily discouraged or subdued. *The indomitable spirit of the Olympic athletes was inspirational.*

ineluctable (in·i·'luk·tă·bĕl) *adj.* certain, inevitable; not to be avoided or overcome. *The ineluctable outcome of the two-person race was that there would be one winner and one loser.*

infidel ('in·fi·dĕl) *n.* 1. a person with no religious beliefs 2. a non-believer, one who does not accept a particular religion, doctrine, or system of beliefs. *Because Tom had been raised with strict religious beliefs, it was no surprise that he was viewed as a heathen and an infidel by his family when he refused to be married in the church.*

ingenuous (in·'jen·yoo·ŭs) *adj.* 1. not cunning or deceitful, unable to mask feelings; artless, frank, sincere 2. lacking sophistication or worldliness. (*Note:* Do not confuse with *ingenious,* meaning "remarkably clever.") *Don's expression of regret was ingenuous, for even though he didn't know her well, he felt a deep sadness when Mary died.*

inimitable (i·'nim·i·tă·bĕl) *adj.* defying imitation, unmatchable. *His performance on the tennis court was inimitable, and he won three championships.*

inscrutable (in·'scroo·tă·bĕl) *adj.* baffling, unfathomable, incapable of being understood. *It was completely inscrutable how the escape artist got out of the trunk.*

insolent ('in·sŏ·lĕnt) *adj.* haughty and contemptuous; brazen, disrespectful, impertinent. *Parents of teenagers often observe the insolent behavior that typically accompanies adolescence.*

insouciant (in·'soo·see·ănt) *adj.* unconcerned, carefree, indifferent. *Wendy's insouciant attitude toward her future concerned her father, who expected her to go to college.*

interdict (in·tĕr·'dikt) *v.* to prohibit, forbid. *Carlos argued that the agriculture department should interdict plans to produce genetically modified foods.*

intractable (in·'trak·tă·bĕl) *adj.* unmanageable, unruly, stubborn. *The young colt was intractable, and training had to be cancelled temporarily.*

intransigent (in·'tran·si·jĕnt) *adj.* unwilling to compromise, stubborn. *Young children can be intransigent when it comes to what foods they will eat, insisting on familiar favorites and rejecting anything new.*

intrepid (in·'trep·id) *adj.* fearless, brave, undaunted. *The intrepid nature and fortitude of the U.S. Marines is legendary.*

inured (in·'yoord) *adj.* accustomed to, adapted. *Trisha had become inured to her boss's criticism, and it no longer bothered her.*

inveigle (in·'vay·gĕl) *v.* 1. to influence or persuade through gentle coaxing or flattery; to entice. *Vanessa inveigled her way into a promotion that should have gone to Marie.*

inveterate (in·'vet·ĕ·rit) *adj.* habitual; deep rooted, firmly established. *I am an inveterate pacifist and am unlikely to change my mind.*

involute ('in·vŏ·loot) *adj.* intricate, complex. *The tax reform committee faces an extremely involute problem if it wants to distribute the tax burden equally.*

iota (ī·'oh·tă) *n.* a very small amount; the smallest possible quantity. *Professor Carlton is so unpopular because he doesn't have one iota of respect for his students.*

irascible (i·'ras·ĭ·bĕl) *adj.* irritable, easily aroused to anger, hot tempered. *Her irascible temperament caused many problems with the staff at the office.*

ire (īr) *n.* anger, wrath. *I was filled with ire when Vladimir tried to take credit for my work.*

irk (urk) *v.* to annoy, irritate, vex. *Being a teenager means being continually irked by your parents—and vice versa.*

irresolute (i·'rez·ŏ·loot) *adj.* feeling or showing uncertainty; hesitant, indecisive. *Sandra is still irresolute, so if you talk to her, you might help her make up her mind.*

J

jocund ('jok·ŭnd) *adj.* merry, cheerful; sprightly and lighthearted. *Alexi's jocund nature makes it a pleasure to be near her.*

L

laconic (lă·'kon·ik) *adj.* brief, to the point, terse. *Morrison's ten-minute commencement address was everything you could have asked for: laconic, powerful, and inspirational.*

laissez-faire (les·ay·'fair) *adj.* hands-off policy; noninterference by the government in business and economic affairs. *I believe a more laissez-faire approach by management would make everyone more cooperative and productive.*

libertine ('lib·ĕr·teen) *n.* one who lives or acts in an immoral or irresponsible way; one who acts according to his or her own impulses and desires and is unrestrained by conventions or morals. *They claim to be avant-garde, but in my opinion, they're just a bunch of libertines.*

lilliputian (lil·i·'pyoo·shăn) *adj.* 1. very small, tiny 2. trivial or petty. *My troubles are lilliputian compared to hers, and I am thankful that I do not have such major issues in my life.*

loquacious (loh·'kway·shŭs) *adj.* talkative, garrulous. *The loquacious woman sitting next to me on the six-hour bus ride talked the entire time.*

lucid ('loo·sid) *adj.* 1. very clear, easy to understand, intelligible 2. sane or rational. *Andrea presented a very lucid argument that proved her point beyond a shadow of a doubt.*

lucrative ('loo·kră·tiv) *adj.* profitable, producing much money. *Teaching is a very rewarding career, but unfortunately it is not very lucrative.*

lugubrious (luu·'goo·bree·ŭs) *adj.* excessively dismal or mournful, often exaggeratedly or ridiculously so. *Billy looks like a fool, acting so lugubrious over losing a silly bet.*

M

maladroit (mal·ă·'droit) *adj.* clumsy, bungling, inept. *The maladroit waiter broke a dozen plates and spilled coffee on two customers.*

malaise (mă·'layz) *n.* a feeling of illness or unease. *After his malaise persisted for more than a week, Nicholas went to see a doctor.*

malapropism ('mal·ă·prop·iz·ĕm) *n.* comical misuse of words, especially those that are similar in sound. *His malapropisms may make us laugh, but they won't win our vote.*

malfeasance (măl·'fee·zăns) *n.* misconduct or wrongdoing, especially by a public official; improper professional conduct. *The city comptroller was found guilty of malfeasance and removed from office.*

malinger (mă·'ling·gĕr) *v.* to pretend to be injured or ill in order to avoid work. *Stop malingering and give me a hand with this job.*

malleable ('mal·ee·ă·bĕl) *adj.* 1. easily molded or pressed into shape 2. easily controlled or influenced 3. easily adapting to changing circumstances. *You should be able to convince Xiu quickly; she's quite a malleable person.*

maverick ('mav·ĕr·ik) *n.* rebel, nonconformist, one who acts independently. *Madonna has always been a maverick in the music industry.*

mélange (may·'lahnzh) *n.* a mixture or assortment. *There was a very interesting mélange of people at the party.*

mellifluous (me·'lif·loo·ŭs) *adj.* sounding sweet and flowing; honeyed. *Her mellifluous voice floated in through the windows and made everyone smile.*

mendacity (men·'das·i·tee) *n.* 1. the tendency to be dishonest or untruthful 2. a falsehood or lie. *Carlos's mendacity has made him very unpopular with his classmates, who don't feel they can trust him.*

mercurial (mĕr·'kyoor·ee·ăl) *adj.* 1. liable to change moods suddenly 2. lively, changeable, volatile. *Fiona is so mercurial that you never know what kind of reaction to expect.*

meretricious (mer·ĕ·'trish·ŭs) *adj.* gaudy, tawdry; showily attractive but false or insincere. *With its casinos and attractions, some people consider Las Vegas the most meretricious city in the country.*

mete (meet) *v.* to distribute, allot, apportion. *The punishments were meted out fairly to everyone involved in the plot.*

mettlesome ('met·ĕl·sŏm) *adj.* courageous, high-spirited. (*Note:* Do not confuse with *meddlesome*, meaning *inclined to interfere*.) *Alice's mettlesome attitude was infectious and inspired us all to press on.*

mince (mins) *v.* 1. to cut into very small pieces 2. to walk or speak affectedly, as with studied refinement 3. to say something more delicately or indirectly for the sake of politeness or decorum. *Please don't mince your words—just tell me what you want to say.*

minutiae (mĭ·nōō'shē·a) *n., pl.* very small details; trivial or trifling matters. *His attention to the minutiae of the process enabled him to make his great discovery.*

mirth (murth) *n.* great merriment, joyous laughter. *The joyous wedding celebration filled the reception hall with mirth throughout the evening.*

misanthrope ('mis·an·throhp) *n.* one who hates or distrusts humankind. *Pay no mind to his criticism; he's a real misanthrope, and no one can do anything right in his eyes.*

miscreant ('mis·kree·ănt) *n.* a villain, criminal; evil person. *The miscreant had eluded the police for months, but today he was finally captured.*

mitigate ('mit·ĭ·gayt) *v.* 1. to make less intense or severe 2. to moderate the force or intensity of, soften, diminish, alleviate. *The unusual extenuating circumstances mitigated her punishment.*

mollify ('mol·ĭ·fī) *v.* 1. to soothe the anger of, calm 2. to lessen in intensity 3. to soften, make less rigid. *The crying child was quickly mollified by her mother.*

moot (moot) *adj.* debatable, undecided. *Although this is a moot issue, it is one that is often debated among certain circles.*

morose (mŏ·'rohs) *adj.* gloomy, sullen, melancholy. *My daughter has been morose ever since our dog ran away.*

multifarious (mul·ti·'fair·ee·ŭs) *adj.* very varied, greatly diversified; having many aspects. *The job requires the ability to handle multifarious tasks.*

mundane (mun·'dayn) *adj.* 1. dull, routine; commonplace, ordinary 2. worldly as opposed to spiritual. *My job may be mundane, but it is secure and it pays well.*

N

nadir ('nay·dĭr) *n.* the very bottom, the lowest point. *When he felt he was at the nadir of his life, Robert began to practice mediation to elevate his spirits.*

narcissism ('narh·si·siz·ĕm) *n.* admiration or worship of oneself; excessive interest in one's own personal features. *Some critics say that movie stars are guilty of narcissism.*

nascent ('nas·ĕnt) *adj.* coming into existence, emerging. *The nascent movement gathered strength quickly and soon became a nationwide call to action.*

nemesis ('nem·ĕ·sis) *n.* 1. source of harm or ruin, the cause of one's misery or downfall; bane 2. agent of retribution or vengeance. *In* Frankenstein, *the monster Victor creates becomes his nemesis.*

nexus ('nek·sŭs) *n.* 1. a means of connection, a link or tie between a series of things 2. a connected series or group 3. the core or center. *The nexus between the lobbyists and the recent policy changes is clear.*

noisome ('noi·sŏm) *adj.* 1. offensive, foul, especially in odor; putrid 2. harmful, noxious. *What a noisome odor is coming from that garbage can!*

non sequitur (non 'sek·wi·tŭr) *n.* a conclusion that does not logically follow from the evidence. *Marcus's argument started off strong, but it degenerated into a series of non sequiturs.*

nonchalant (non·shă·'lahnt) *adj.* indifferent or cool, not showing anxiety or excitement. *Victoria tried to be nonchalant, but I could tell she was nervous.*

noxious ('nok·shŭs) *adj.* unpleasant and harmful, unwholesome. *The noxious smell drove everyone from the room.*

nullify ('nul·ĭ·fī) *v.* 1. to make null (without legal force), invalidate 2. to counteract or neutralize the effect of. *The opponents wanted to nullify the bill before it became a law.*

O

obdurate ('ob·dŭ·rit) *adj.* stubborn and inflexible; hard-hearted, not easily moved to pity. *I doubt he'll change his mind; he's the most obdurate person I know.*

obfuscate ('ob·fus·kayt) *v.* 1. to make obscure or unclear, to muddle or make difficult to understand 2. to dim or darken. *Instead of clarifying the matter, Walter only obfuscated it further.*

obstreperous (ob·'strep·ĕ·rŭs) *adj.* noisily and stubbornly defiant; aggressively boisterous, unruly. *The obstreperous child refused to go to bed.*

obtrusive (ŏb·'troo·siv) *adj.* 1. prominent, undesirably noticeable 2. projecting, thrusting out 3. tending to push one's self or one's ideas upon others, forward, intrusive. *Thankfully, Minsun survived the accident, but she was left with several obtrusive scars.*

obtuse (ŏb·'toos) *adj.* 1. stupid and slow to understand 2. blunt, not sharp or pointed. *Please don't be so obtuse; you know what I mean.*

obviate ('ob·vee·ayt) *v.* to make unnecessary, get rid of. *Hiring Magdalena would obviate the need to hire a music tutor, for she is also a classical pianist.*

occult (ŏ·'kult) *adj.* 1. secret, hidden, concealed 2. involving the realm of the supernatural 3. beyond ordinary understanding, incomprehensible. *The rites and beliefs of the occult organization were finally made a matter of public record after a long investigation.*

odious ('oh·di·ŭs) *adj.* contemptible, hateful, detestable. *This is an odious policy that will only damage the environment more.*

officious (ŏ·'fish·ŭs) *adj.* meddlesome, bossy; eagerly offering unnecessary or unwanted advice. *My officious Aunt Midge is coming to the party, so be prepared for lots of questions and advice.*

oligarchy ('ol·ĭ·gahr·kee) *n.* form of government in which the power is in the hands of a select few. *The small governing body calls itself a democracy, but it is clearly an oligarchy.*

omnipotent (om·'nip·ŏ·tĕnt) *adj.* having unlimited or universal power or force. *In Greek mythology, Zeus was the most powerful god, but he was not omnipotent, since even his rule was often held in check by the unchangeable laws of the Three Fates.*

omniscient (om·'nish·ĕnt) *adj.* having infinite knowledge; knowing all things. *In a story with an omniscient narrator, you can hear the thoughts and feelings of all of the characters.*

onus ('oh·nŭs) *n.* duty or responsibility of doing something; task, burden. *It was Clark's idea, so the onus is on him to show us that it will work.*

opprobrious (ŏ·'proh·bree·ŭs) *adj.* 1. expressing contempt or reproach; scornful, abusive 2. bringing shame or disgrace. *It was inappropriate to make such opprobrious remarks in front of everybody.*

opulent ('op·yŭ·lĕnt) *adj.* 1. possessing great wealth, affluent 2. abundant, luxurious. *Lee is very wealthy, but he does not live an opulent lifestyle.*

ostensible (o·'sten·sĭ·bĕl) *adj.* seeming, appearing as such, put forward (as of a reason) but not necessarily so; pretended. *The ostensible reason for the meeting is to discuss the candidates, but I believe they have already made their decision.*

ostracize ('os·tră·sīz) *v.* to reject, cast out from a group or from society. *Kendall was ostracized after he repeatedly stole from his friends.*

overweening (oh·vĕr·'wee·ning) *adj.* 1. presumptuously arrogant, overbearing 2. excessive, immoderate. *I quit because I couldn't stand to work for such an overweening boss.*

oxymoron (oks·ee·'moh·rŏn) *n.* a figure of speech containing a seemingly contradictory combination of expressions. *The term "non-working mother" is a contemptible oxymoron.*

P

palliate ('pal·ee·ayt) *v.* 1. to make something less intense or severe, mitigate, alleviate; to gloss over, put a positive spin on 2. to provide relief from pain, relieve the symptoms of a disease or disorder. *The governor tried to palliate his malfeasance, but it soon became clear that he would not be able to prevent a scandal.*

pallor ('pal·ŏr) *n.* paleness, lack of color. *The fever subsided, but her pallor remained for several weeks.*

paradigm ('par·ă·dīm) *n.* 1. something that serves as a model or example 2. set of assumptions, beliefs, values or practices that constitutes a way of understanding or doing things. *Elected "Employee of the Month," Winona is a paradigm of efficiency.*

pariah (pă·'rī·ă) *n.* an outcast, a rejected and despised person. *After he told a sexist joke, Jason was treated like a pariah by all of the women in the office.*

partisan ('pahr·ti·zăn) *n.* 1. a person fervently and often uncritically supporting a group or cause 2. a guerilla, a member of an organized body of fighters who attack or harass an enemy. *The partisan lobby could not see the logic of the opposing senator's argument and did not understand how the proposed legislation would infringe upon basic constitutional rights.*

paucity ('paw·si·tee) *n.* scarcity, smallness of supply or quantity. *The paucity of food in the area drove the herd farther and farther to the south.*

peccadillo (pek·ă·'dil·oh) *n.* a trivial offense, a small sin or fault. *Don't make such a big deal out of a little peccadillo.*

pedantic (pi·'dăn·tik) *adj.* marked by a narrow, tiresome focus on or display of learning, especially of rules or trivial matters. *Her lessons were so pedantic that I found I was easily bored.*

pedestrian (pĕ·'des·tri·ăn) *adj.* commonplace, trite; unremarkable, unimaginative, dull. *Although the film received critical acclaim, its pedestrian plot has been overused by screenwriters for decades.*

pellucid (pĕ·'loo·sid) *adj.* 1. translucent, able to be seen through with clarity 2. (e.g., of writing) very clear, easy to understand. *Senator Waterson's pellucid argument made me change my vote.*

penchant ('pen·chănt) *n.* a strong inclination or liking. *I have a real penchant for science fiction and spend hours reading my favorite authors every night.*

penultimate (pi·'nul·tĭ·mit) *adj.* next to last. *There's a real surprise for the audience in the penultimate scene.*

penury ('pen·yŭ·ree) *n.* extreme poverty, destitution. *After ten years of penury, it's good to be financially secure again.*

peremptory (pĕ·'remp·tŏ·ree) *adj.* 1. offensively self-assured, dictatorial 2. commanding, imperative, not allowing contradiction or refusal 3. putting an end to debate or action. *The father's peremptory tone ended the children's bickering.*

perfidious (pĕr·'fid·ee·ŭs) *adj.* treacherous, dishonest; violating good faith, disloyal. *The perfidious knight betrayed his king.*

perfunctory (pĕr·'fungk·tŏ·ree) *adj.* done out of a sense of duty or routine but without much care or interest; superficial, not thorough. *We were not satisfied with his perfunctory work; we felt a more thorough job could have been done.*

perjury ('pur·jŭ·ree) *n.* the deliberate willful giving of false, misleading, or incomplete testimony while under oath. *William was convicted of perjury for lying about his whereabouts on the night of the crime.*

pernicious (pĕr·'nish·ŭs) *adj.* deadly, harmful, very destructive. *Nancy's opponent started a pernicious rumor that destroyed her chances of winning.*

personable ('pur·sŏ·nă·bĕl) *adj.* pleasing in appearance or manner, attractive. *Sandra is personable and well-liked by her peers.*

pertinacious (pur·tĭ·'nay·shŭs) *adj.* extremely stubborn or persistent; holding firmly to a belief, purpose, or course of action. *The pertinacious journalist finally uncovered the truth about the factory's illegal disposal of toxins.*

petrify ('pet·rĭ·fī) *v.* 1. to make hard or stiff like a stone 2. to stun or paralyze with fear, astonishment, or dread. *I was petrified when I heard the door open in the middle of the night.*

petulant ('pech·ŭ·lănt) *adj.* peevish; unreasonably or easily irritated or annoyed. *The pouting and sulking child could only be described as petulant!*

philistine ('fil·i·steen) *n.* a smug, ignorant person; someone who is uncultured and commonplace. *Richards thinks he is cosmopolitan, but he's really just a philistine.*

phoenix ('fee·niks) *n.* 1. a person or thing of unmatched beauty or excellence 2. a person or thing that has become renewed or restored after suffering calamity or apparent annihilation (after the mythological bird that periodically immolated itself and rose from the ashes as a new phoenix). *The phoenix is often used to symbolize something that is indomitable or immortal.*

pillage ('pil·ij) *v.* to forcibly rob of goods, especially in time of war; to plunder. *The barbarians pillaged the village before destroying it with fire.*

piquant ('pee·kănt) *adj.* 1. agreeably pungent, sharp or tart in taste 2. pleasantly stimulating or provocative. *The spicy shrimp salad is wonderfully piquant.*

pique (peek) *v.* to wound (someone's) pride, to offend; to arouse or provoke. *The article really piqued my interest in wildlife preservation.*

pith (pith) *n.* 1. the essential or central part; the heart or essence (of the matter, idea, experience, etc.) 2. (in biology) the soft, sponge-like central cylinder of the stems of most flowering plants. *Her brief, but concise, statement went right to the pith of the argument and covered the most important issues.*

placid ('plas·id) *adj.* calm and peaceful; free from disturbance or tumult. *Lake Placid is as calm and peaceful as its name suggests.*

plaintive ('playn·tiv) *adj.* expressing sorrow; mournful, melancholy. *Janice's plaintive voice made me decide to stay and comfort her longer.*

platitude ('plat·i·tood) *n.* a trite or banal statement, especially one uttered as if it were new. *Matthew offered me several platitudes but no real advice.*

plethora ('pleth·ŏ·ra) *n.* an overabundance, extreme excess. *There was a plethora of food at the reception.*

poignant ('poin·yănt) *adj.* 1. arousing emotion, deeply moving, touching 2. keenly distressing; piercing or incisive. *They captured the poignant reunion on film.*

polemical (pŏ·'lem·ik·ăl) *adj.* controversial, argumentative. *The analyst presented a highly polemical view of the economic situation.*

poseur (poh·'zur) *n.* someone who takes on airs to impress others; a phony. *My first impression of the arrogant newcomer told me that he was a poseur; I just had a hunch that he wasn't what he seemed to be.*

pragmatic (prag·'mat·ik) *adj.* practical, matter-of-fact; favoring utility. *Since you don't have money or time to waste, I think you should take the most pragmatic approach.*

precarious (pri·'kair·ee·ŭs) *adj.* 1. fraught with danger 2. dangerously unsteady or insecure. *Between hang-gliding and rock-climbing, Abram is constantly placing himself in very precarious positions.*

precept ('pree·sept) *n.* a rule establishing standards of conduct. *The headmaster reviewed the precepts of the school with the students.*

precipitous (pri·'sip·i·tŭs) *adj.* 1. extremely steep, dropping sharply 2. hasty, rash, foolhardy. *Driving through the state park, you spotted a grizzly bear on a precipitous cliff and wondered if he would fall.*

pretentious (pri·'ten·shŭs) *adj.* showy, pompous, putting on airs. *Hannah thinks that being pretentious will make people like her, but she is sorely mistaken.*

prevaricate (pri·'var·i·kayt) *v.* to tell lies, to stray from or evade the truth. *Quit prevaricating and tell me what really happened.*

primeval (prī·'mee·văl) *adj.* ancient, original, belonging to the earliest ages. *The primeval art found in the caves was discovered by accident.*

pristine (pris·'teen) *adj.* 1. in its original and unspoiled condition, unadulterated 2. clean, pure, free from contamination. *We were awed by the beauty of the pristine forest in northern Canada.*

prodigal ('prod·ĭ·găl) *adj.* 1. recklessly wasteful or extravagant, especially with money 2. given in great abundance, lavish or profuse. *The parable of the prodigal son shows what can happen when money is wasted.*

profligate ('prof·lĭ·git) *adj.* 1. recklessly wasteful or extravagant, prodigal 2. lacking moral restraint, dissolute. *The profligate man quickly depleted his fortune.*

proletariat (proh·lĕ·'tair·ee·ăt) *n.* the working class, those who do manual labor to earn a living. *The proletariats demanded fewer hours and better wages.*

propinquity (proh·'ping·kwi·tee) *n.* 1. proximity, nearness 2. affinity, similarity in nature. *The two scientific elements demonstrate a remarkable propinquity.*

propitious (proh·'pish·ŭs) *adj.* auspicious, presenting favorable circumstances. *These are propitious omens indeed and foretell a good journey.*

prosaic (proh·'zay·ik) *adj.* unimaginative, ordinary, dull. *The prosaic novel was rejected by the publisher.*

proscribe (proh·'skrīb) *v.* 1. to prohibit, forbid; to banish or outlaw 2. to denounce or condemn. *The king proscribed the worship of idols in his kingdom.*

protean ('proh·tee·ăn) *adj.* taking many forms, changeable; variable, versatile. *In Native American mythology, the coyote is often called the "shape shifter" because he is such a protean character.*

protocol ('proh·tŏ·kawl) *n.* 1. etiquette, ceremony, or procedure with regard to people's rank or status 2. a first copy of a treaty or document. *Jackson was fired for repeatedly refusing to follow protocol.*

provident ('prov·i·dĕnt) *adj.* wisely providing for future needs; frugal, economical. *Because my parents were so provident, I didn't have to struggle to pay for college.*

proxy ('prok·see) *n.* 1. a person or agent authorized to represent or act for another 2. a document authorizing this substitution. *The president appointed a proxy to handle business matters during his absence.*

puerile ('pyoŏ·rĭl) *adj.* 1. childish, immature 2. suitable only for children, belonging to or of childhood.

Andrew is a remarkably successful businessman for someone so puerile.

pugnacious (pug·'nay·shŭs) *adj.* contentious, quarrelsome, eager to fight, belligerent. *Don't be so pugnacious—I don't want to fight.*

punctilious (pungk·'til·i·ŭs) *adj.* very conscientious and precise, paying great attention to details or trivialities, especially in regard to etiquette. *Kira is as punctilious in her personal affairs as she is in the workplace.*

pundit ('pun·dit) *n.* a learned person or scholar; one who is an authority on a subject. *The journalist consulted several legal pundits before drafting the article.*

pungent ('pun·jĕnt) *adj.* 1. having a strong, sharp taste or smell 2. penetrating, caustic, stinging. *I love the pungent taste of a good, strong curry.*

purloin (pŭr·'loin) *v.* to steal. *The thief purloined a sculpture worth thousands of dollars.*

purport (pur·'pohrt) *v.* 1. to be intended to seem, to have the appearance of being 2. propose or intend. *The letter purports to express your opinion on the matter.*

Q

quaff (kwahf) *v.* to drink hurriedly or heartily; to swallow in large draughts. *He quickly quaffed three glasses of water.*

quail (kwayl) *v.* to draw back in fear, flinch, cower. *Mona quailed as soon as Otto entered the room.*

querulous ('kwer·ŭ·lŭs) *adj.* complaining, peevish, discontented. *He's a cantankerous and querulous old man, but I love him.*

queue (kyoo) *n.* 1. a line of people or vehicles waiting their turn 2. a pigtail. *Look how long the queue is! We'll be waiting for hours.*

quid pro quo (kwid proh 'kwoh) *n.* a thing given in return for something; an equal exchange or substitution. *Let's come up with a quid pro quo arrangement that will create a win–win situation for both sides.*

quiescent (kwi·'es·ĕnt) *adj.* inactive, quiet, at rest; dormant, latent. *The volcano is quiescent at the moment, but who knows when it will erupt again.*

quintessence (kwin·'tes·ĕns) *n.* 1. the essence of a substance 2. the perfect example or embodiment of something. *Maura is the quintessence of kindness.*

quixotic (kwik·'sot·ik) *adj.* extravagantly chivalrous and unselfish; romantically idealistic, impractical. *His quixotic ways charmed all the women at the dance.*

quotidian (kwoh·'tid·ee·ăn) *adj.* 1. daily 2. commonplace, pedestrian. *Prudence took her quotidian dose of medicine.*

R

rakish ('ray·kish) *adj.* 1. debonair, smartly dressed or mannered, jaunty in appearance or manner 2. unconventional and disreputable; dissolute or debauched. *The rakish young woman charmed everyone at the table.*

rancor ('rang·kŏr) *n.* a bitter feeling of ill will, long-lasting resentment. *Greg is full of rancor toward his brother, and this causes tension at family gatherings.*

rapacious (ră·'pay·shŭs) *adj.* excessively greedy and grasping (especially for money); voracious, plundering. *The rapacious general ordered his soldiers to pillage the town.*

raucous (raw-kŭs) *adj.* 1. unpleasantly loud and harsh 2. boisterous, disorderly, disturbing the peace. *The raucous music kept us awake all night.*

reactionary (ree·'ak·shŏ·ner·ee) *n.* a person who favors political conservativism; one who is opposed to progress or liberalism. *It should be an interesting marriage: he's a reactionary and she's as liberal as they come.*

recalcitrant (ri·'kal·si·trănt) *adj.* disobedient, unruly, refusing to obey authority. *The recalcitrant child was sent to the principal's office for the third time in a week.*

recidivism (ri·'sid·ĭ·vizm) *n.* a relapse or backslide, especially into antisocial or criminal behavior after conviction and punishment. *Allowing prisoners to earn their GED or a college degree has been shown to greatly reduce recidivism.*

recondite ('rek·ŏn·dīt) *adj.* 1. not easily understood, obscure, and abstruse 2. dealing with abstruse or profound matters. *He loves the challenge of grasping a recondite subject.*

refractory (ri·'frak·tŏ·ree) *adj.* stubborn, unmanageable, resisting control or discipline. *Elena is a counselor for refractory children in an alternative school setting.*

regale (ri·'gayl) *v.* to delight or entertain with a splendid feast or pleasant amusement. *The king regaled his guests until the early morning hours.*

remonstrate (ri·'mon·strayt) *v.* 1. to say or plead in protest, objection, or opposition 2. to scold or reprove. *The children remonstrated loudly when their babysitter told them they couldn't watch that movie.*

renegade ('ren·ĕ·gayd) *n.* 1. a deserter; one who rejects a cause, group, etc. 2. a person who rebels and becomes an outlaw. *The renegade soldier decided to join the guerilla fighters.*

renowned (ri·'nownd) *adj.* famous; widely known and esteemed. *The renowned historian Stephen Ambrose wrote many books that were popular with both scholars and the general public.*

repartee (rep·ăr·'tee) *n.* 1. a quick, witty reply 2. the ability to make witty replies. *He wasn't expecting such a sharp repartee from someone who was normally so quiet.*

replete (ri·'pleet) *adj.* 1. well-stocked or abundantly supplied 2. full, gorged. *The house was replete with expensive antiques.*

repose (ri·'pohz) *n.* 1. resting or being at rest 2. calmness, tranquility, peace of mind. *The wail of a police siren disturbed my repose.*

reprehensible (rep·ri·'hen·sĭ·bĕl) *adj.* deserving rebuke or censure. *The reprehensible behavior of the neighborhood bully angered everyone on the block.*

reprieve (ri·'preev) *n.* 1. postponement or cancellation of punishment, especially of the death sentence 2. temporary relief from danger or discomfort. *The court granted him a reprieve at the last moment because of DNA evidence that absolved him.*

reprisal (ri·'prī·zăl) *n.* 1. an act of retaliation for an injury with the intent of inflicting at least as much harm in return 2. the practice of using political or military force without actually resorting to war. *The president promised a swift reprisal for the attack.*

reprobate ('rep·rŏ·bayt) *n.* an immoral or unprincipled person; one without scruples. *Edgar deemed himself a reprobate, a criminal, and a traitor in his written confession.*

repudiate (ri·'pyoo·di·ayt) *v.* to disown, disavow, reject completely. *Ms. Tallon has repeatedly repudiated your accusations.*

rescind (ri·'sind) *v.* to repeal or cancel; to void or annul. *They have rescinded their offer, so you must find another buyer.*

resonant ('rez·ŏ·nănt) *adj.* echoing, resounding. *The new announcer at the stadium has a wonderfully resonant voice.*

reticent ('ret·i·sĕnt) *adj.* tending to keep one's thoughts and feelings to oneself; reserved, untalkative, silent. *Annette is very reticent, so don't expect her to tell you much about herself.*

rigmarole ('rig·mă·rohl) (also *rigamarole*) *n.* 1. rambling, confusing, incoherent talk 2. a complicated, petty procedure. *You had to go through a great deal of rigmarole to get this approved.*

rogue (rohg) *n.* 1. a dishonest, unprincipled person 2. a pleasantly mischievous person 3. a vicious and solitary animal living apart from the herd. *Yesterday, that rogue hid all of my cooking utensils; today he's switched everything around in the cupboards!*

roil (roil) *v.* 1. to make a liquid cloudy or muddy 2. to stir up or agitate 3. to anger or annoy. *That you could even think such a thing really roils me.*

rubric ('roo·brik) *n.* 1. a class or category 2. a heading, title, or note of explanation or direction. *I would put this under the rubric of "quackery," not "alternative medicine."*

S

sacrilegious (sak·rĭ·'lij·ŭs) *adj.* disrespectful or irreverent towards something regarded as sacred. *Her book was criticized by the church for being sacrilegious.*

sagacious (să·'gay·shŭs) *adj.* having or showing sound judgment; perceptive, wise. *My sagacious uncle always gives me good, sound advice.*

salient ('say·lee·ĕnt) *adj.* 1. conspicuous, prominent, highly noticeable; drawing attention through a striking quality 2. spring up or jutting out. *Jill's most salient feature is her stunning auburn hair.*

salutary ('sal·yŭ·ter·ee) *adj.* producing a beneficial or wholesome effect; remedial. *To promote better health, I've decided to move to a more salutary climate.*

sanctimonious (sangk·tĭ·'moh·nee·ŭs) *adj.* hypocritically pious or devout; excessively self-righteous. *The thief's sanctimonious remark that "a fool and his money are soon parted" only made the jury more eager to convict him.*

sangfroid (sahn·'frwah) *n.* composure, especially in dangerous or difficult circumstances. *I wish I had Jane's sangfroid when I find myself in a confrontational situation.*

sanguine ('sang·gwin) *adj.* 1. confidently cheerful, optimistic 2. of the color of blood; red. *People are drawn to her because of her sanguine and pleasant nature.*

sardonic (sahr·'don·ik) *adj.* sarcastic, mocking scornfully. *I was hurt by his sardonic reply.*

saturnine ('sat·ŭr·nīn) *adj.* gloomy, dark, sullen. *The saturnine child sulked for hours.*

savoir faire ('sav·wahr 'fair) *n.* knowledge of the right thing to do or say in a social situation; graceful tact. *Savoir faire is essential if you want to be a successful diplomat.*

schism ('skiz·ĕm) *n.* a separation or division into factions because of a difference in belief or opinion. *The schism between the two parties was forgotten as they united around a common cause.*

scintilla (sin·'til·ă) *n.* a trace or particle; minute amount, iota. *She has not one scintilla of doubt about his guilt.*

scurvy ('skur·vee) *adj.* contemptible, mean. *That scurvy knave has ruined my plans again.*

sedulous ('sej·ŭ·lŭs) *adj.* diligent, persevering, hard working. *After years of sedulous research, the researchers discovered a cure.*

semantics (si·'man·tiks) *n.* 1. the study of meaning in language 2. the meaning, connotation, or interpretation of words, symbols, or other forms 3. the study of relationships between signs or symbols and their meanings. *He claims it's a matter of semantics, but the issue is not open to interpretation.*

sententious (sen·'ten·shŭs) *adj.* 1. expressing oneself tersely, pithy 2. full of maxims and proverbs offered in a self-righteous manner. *I was looking for your honest opinion, not a sententious reply.*

shiftless ('shift·lis) *adj.* lazy and inefficient; lacking ambition, initiative, or purpose. *My shiftless roommate has failed all of his classes.*

simian ('sim·ee·ăn) *adj.* of or like an ape or monkey. *Creationists do not believe that humans have simian ancestors.*

sinuous ('sin·yoo·ŭs) *adj.* winding, undulating, serpentine. *It is dangerous to drive fast on such a sinuous road.*

slake (slayk) *v.* 1. to satisfy, quench 2. to reduce the intensity of, moderate, allay. *The deer slaked its thirst at the river.*

sodden ('sod·ĕn) *adj.* 1. thoroughly saturated, soaked 2. expressionless or dull, unimaginative. *Caught in an unexpected rainstorm, I was sodden by the time I reached the bus stop.*

solecism ('sol·ĕ·siz·ĕm) *n.* 1. a mistake in the use of language 2. violation of good manners or etiquette, impropriety. *Frank's solecism caused his debate team much embarrassment.*

sophistry ('sof·i·stree) *n.* clever but faulty reasoning; a plausible but invalid argument intended to deceive by appearing sound. *I was amused by his sophistry, but knew he had a little more research to do before he presented his argument to the distinguished scholars in his field.*

sordid ('sor·did) *adj.* 1. dirty, wretched, squalid 2. morally degraded. *This sordid establishment should be shut down immediately.*

specious ('spee·shŭs) *adj.* 1. seemingly plausible but false 2. deceptively pleasing in appearance. *Vinnie did not fool me with his specious argument.*

spurious ('spyoor·ee·ŭs) *adj.* false, counterfeit, not genuine or authentic. *The expert confirmed that the Willie Mays autograph was spurious.*

squalid ('skwol·id) *adj.* 1. filthy and wretched 2. morally repulsive, sordid. *The housing inspectors noted such deplorable and squalid living conditions in the building on Water Street that they were forced to evacuate the tenants.*

stoical ('stoh·i·kăl) *adj.* seemingly unaffected by pleasure or pain; indifferent, impassive. *He remained stoical while his wife told him she was leaving.*

stolid ('stohl·id) *adj.* not feeling or showing emotion, impassive; not easily aroused or excited. *Maxine is a very stolid person, so it will be difficult to tell how she feels.*

stringent ('strī·dĕnt) *adj.* very strict, according to very rigorous rules, requirements or standards. *The stringent eligibility requirements greatly limited the number of candidates for the scholarship.*

stultify ('stul·tĭ·fī) *v.* 1. to impair or make ineffective, cripple 2. to make (someone) look foolish or incompetent. *Of course I'm angry! You stultified me at that meeting!*

stymie ('stī·mee) *v.* to hinder, obstruct, thwart; to prevent the accomplishment of something. *The negotiations were stymied by yet another attack.*

sublime (sŭ·'blīm) *adj.* having noble or majestic qualities; inspiring awe, adoration, or reverence; lofty, supreme. *Beethoven's music is simply sublime.*

subliminal (sub·'lim·ĭ·năl) *adj.* below the threshold of consciousness. *Subliminal advertising is devious but effective.*

subvert (sub·'vurt) *v.* 1. to overthrow 2. to ruin, destroy completely 3. to undermine. *She quietly subverted his authority by sharing internal information with outside agents.*

sundry ('sun·dree) *adj.* various, miscellaneous. *The sundry items in her backpack reveal a great deal about her personality.*

supercilious (soo·pĕr·'sil·ee·ŭs) *adj.* haughty, scornful, disdainful. *Sunil's supercilious attitude and sarcastic remarks annoy me greatly.*

supplicant ('sup·lĭ·kănt) *n.* a person who asks humbly for something; one who beseeches or entreats. *The supplicants begged for forgiveness.*

surly ('sur·lee) *adj.* bad-tempered, gruff, or unfriendly in a way that suggests menace. *Emily received a surly greeting from the normally cheerful receptionist.*

surrogate ('sur·ŏ·git) *n.* a substitute; one who takes the place of another. *Martha agreed to be a surrogate mother for her sister.*

svelte (svelt) *adj.* slender and graceful, suave. *The svelte actress offered a toast to her guests.*

sycophant ('sik·ŏ·fănt) *n.* a person who tries to win the favor of influential or powerful people through flattery; a fawning parasite. *The president is surrounded by sycophants, so how will he really know if his ideas have merit?*

T

taciturn ('tas·i·turn) *adj.* habitually untalkative, reserved. *I've always known him to be taciturn, but yesterday he regaled me with tales of his hiking adventures.*

tangible ('tan·jĭ·bĕl) *adj.* able to be perceived by touch, palpable; real or concrete. *There is no tangible evidence of misconduct; it's all hearsay.*

tawdry ('taw·dree) *adj.* gaudy or showy but without any real value; flashy and tasteless. *I've never seen such a tawdry outfit as the three-tiered taffeta gown that the music singer wore to the awards ceremony!*

teem (teem) *v.* to be full of; to be present in large numbers. *This city is teeming with tourists during the summer months.*

temerity (tĕ·'mer·i·tee) *n.* foolish disregard of danger; brashness, audacity. *This is no time for temerity; you must move cautiously to avoid any further damage.*

tenacious (tĕ·'nay·shŭs) *adj.* 1. holding firmly to something, such as a right or principle; persistent, stubbornly unyielding 2. holding firmly, cohesive 3. sticking firmly, adhesive 4. (of memory) retentive. *When it comes to fighting for equality, she is the most tenacious person I know.*

tendentious (ten·'den·shŭs) *adj.* biased, not impartial, partisan; supporting a particular cause or position. *The tendentious proposal caused an uproar on the Senate floor.*

tenet ('ten·it) *n.* a belief, opinion, doctrine or principle held to be true by a person, group, or organization. *This pamphlet describes the tenets of Amnesty International.*

tenuous ('ten·yoo·ŭs) *adj.* 1. unsubstantial, flimsy 2. having little substance or validity. *Though the connection between the two crimes seemed tenuous at first, a thorough investigation showed they were committed by the same person.*

timorous ('tim·ŏ·rŭs) *adj.* fearful, timid, afraid. *The stray dog was timorous, and it took a great deal of coaxing to get him to come near the car.*

toil (toil) *n.* exhausting labor or effort; difficult or laborious work. *v.* to work laboriously, labor strenuously. *Evan toiled for hours before solving the problem.*

totalitarian (toh·'tal·i·'tair·ee·ăn) *adj.* of a form of government in which those in control neither recognize nor tolerate rival parties or loyalties, demanding total submission of the individual to the needs of the state. *The totalitarian regime fell quickly when the people revolted.*

tractable ('trak·tă·bĕl) *adj.* easily managed or controlled; obedient, docile. *In the novel* Brave New World, *the World Controllers use hypnosis and a "happiness drug" to make everyone tractable.*

transient ('tran·zhĕnt) *adj.* lasting only a very short time; fleeting, transitory, brief. *Their relationship was transient but profound.*

trenchant ('tren·chănt) *adj.* 1. penetrating, forceful, effective 2. extremely perceptive, incisive 3. clear-cut, sharply defined. *It was a trenchant argument, and it forced me to change my mind about the issue.*

tribunal (trī·'byoo·năl) *n.* a court of justice. *He will be sentenced for his war crimes by an international tribunal.*

truculent ('truk·yŭ·lĕnt) *adj.* 1. defiantly aggressive 2. fierce, violent 3. bitterly expressing opposition. *The outspoken council president gave a truculent speech arguing against the proposal.*

truncate ('trung·kayt) *v.* to shorten or terminate by (or as if by) cutting the top or end off. *The glitch in the software program truncated the lines of a very important document I was typing.*

tumultuous (too·'mul·choo·ŭs) *adj.* 1. creating an uproar, disorderly, noisy 2. a state of confusion, turbulence, or agitation, tumult. *It was another tumultuous day for the stock market, and fluctuating prices were wreaking havoc for investors.*

turpitude ('tur·pi·tood) *n.* 1. wickedness 2. a corrupt or depraved act. *Such turpitude deserves the most severe punishment.*

U

umbrage ('um·brij) *n.* offense, resentment. *I took great umbrage at your suggestion that I twisted the truth.*

undulate ('un·jŭ·layt) *v.* to move in waves or in a wavelike fashion, fluctuate. *The curtains undulated in the breeze.*

untoward (un·'tohrd) *adj.* 1. contrary to one's best interest or welfare; inconvenient, troublesome, adverse 2. improper, unseemly, perverse. *Jackson's untoward remarks made Amelia very uncomfortable.*

upbraid (up·'brayd) *v.* to reprove, reproach sharply, condemn; admonish. *The child was upbraided for misbehaving during the ceremony.*

urbane (ur·'bayn) *adj.* elegant, highly refined in manners, extremely tactful and polite. *Christopher thinks he's so urbane, but he's really quite pedestrian.*

V

vacuous ('vak·yoo·ŭs) *adj.* empty, purposeless; senseless, stupid, inane. *This TV show is yet another vacuous sitcom.*

venal ('vee·năl) *adj.* easily bribed or corrupted; unprincipled. *The venal judge was removed and disbarred.*

venerable ('ven·ĕ·ră·bĕl) *adj.* worthy of reverence or respect because of age, dignity, character or position. *The venerable Jimmy Carter won the Nobel Peace Prize.*

verbose (vĕr·'bohs) *adj.* using more words than necessary; wordy, long-winded. *Her verbose letter rambled so much that it didn't seem to have a point.*

verisimilitude (ver·'i·si·'mil·i·tood) *n.* the appearance of being true or real. *The movie aims for complete verisimilitude and has painstakingly recreated the details of everyday life in the 1920s.*

veritable ('ver·i·tă·bĕl) *adj.* real, true, genuine. *Einstein was a veritable genius.*

vex (veks) *v.* 1. to annoy, irritate 2. to cause worry to. *I was completely vexed by his puerile behavior.*

vitriolic (vit·ri·'ol·ik) *adj.* savagely hostile or bitter, caustic. *Her vitriolic attack on her opponent was so hostile that it may cost her the election.*

volatile ('vol·ă·til) *adj.* 1. varying widely, inconstant, changeable, fickle 2. unstable, explosive, likely to change suddenly or violently 3. (in chemistry) evaporating readily. *Dan's volatile personality has been compared to that of Dr. Jekyll and Mr. Hyde.*

voluble ('vol·yŭ·bĕl) *adj.* 1. talking a great deal and with great ease; language marked by great fluency; rapid, nimble speech 2. turning or rotating easily on an axis. *Your new spokesperson is very voluble and clearly comfortable speaking in front of large audiences.*

voracious (voh·'ray·shŭs) *adj.* excessively greedy, rapacious; having a great appetite for something, devouring greedily. *I have always been a voracious reader and consume dozens of books every month.*

X

xenophobia (zen·ŏ·'foh·bee·ă) *n.* a strong dislike, distrust, or fear of foreigners. *Many atrocities have been committed because of xenophobia.*

Z

zenith ('zee·nith) *n.* 1. the highest point, top, peak 2. the point in the sky directly above the observer. *She is at the zenith of her career and has won every case this year.*

Appendix 5: Prefixes, Suffixes, and Word Roots ▶

▶ Prefixes

Prefixes are syllables added to the beginnings of words to change or add to their meaning. This table lists some of the most common prefixes in the English language. They are grouped together by similar meanings.

PREFIX	MEANING	EXAMPLE	DEFINITION	SENTENCE
uni-	one	unify *v.*	to form into a single unit, to unite	The new leader was able to **unify** the three factions into one strong political party.
mono-	one	monologue *n.*	a long speech by one person or performer	I was very moved by the **monologue** in Scene III.
bi-	two	bisect *v.*	to divide into two equal parts	If you **bisect** a square, you will get two rectangles of equal size.
duo-	two	duality *n.*	having two sides or parts	The novel explores the **duality** of good and evil in humans.
tri-	three	triangle *n.*	a figure having three angles	In an isosceles **triangle**, two of the three angles are the same size.
quadri-	four	quadruped *n.*	an animal with four feet	Some **quadrupeds** evolved into bipeds.

PREFIX	MEANING	EXAMPLE	DEFINITION	SENTENCE
tetra-	four	tetralogy *n.*	series of four related artistic works	"Time Zone" was the fourth and final work in Classman's **tetralogy**.
quint-	five	quintuplets *n.*	five offspring born at one time	Each **quintuplet** weighed less than four pounds at birth.
pent-	five	pentameter *n.*	a line of verse (poetry) with five metrical feet	Most of Shakespeare's sonnets are written in iambic **pentameter**.
multi-	many	multifaceted *adj.*	having many sides	This is a **multifaceted** issue, and you must examine each side carefully.
poly-	many	polyglot *n.*	one who speaks or understands several language	It's no wonder she's a **polyglot**; she's lived in eight different countries.
omni-	all	omniscient *adj.*	knowing all	Dr. Perez seems **omniscient**; she knows what all of us are thinking in class.
micro-	small	microcosm *n.*	little or miniature world; something representing something else on a very small scale	Some people say that Brooklyn Heights, the Brooklyn district across the river from the Wall Street area, is a **microcosm** of Manhattan.
mini-	small	minority *n.*	small group within a larger group	John voted for Bridget, but he was in the **minority**; most people voted for Elaine.
macro-	large	macrocosm *n.*	the large scale world or universe; any great whole	Any change to the **macrocosm** will eventually effect the microcosm.
ante-	before	anticipate *v.*	to give advance thought; to foresee; expect	His decades of experience enabled him to **anticipate** the problem.
pre-	before	precede *v.*	to come before in time or order	The appetizers **preceded** the main course.
post-	after	postscript *n.*	message added after the close of a letter	His **postscript** was almost as long as his letter!

PREFIX	MEANING	EXAMPLE	DEFINITION	SENTENCE
inter-	between	intervene *v.*	to come between	Romeo, trying to make peace, **intervened** in the fight between Tybalt and Mercutio.
inter-	together	interact *v.*	to act upon or influence each other	The psychologist took notes as she watched the children **interact**.
intra-	within	intravenous *adj.*	within or into a vein	She couldn't eat and had to be fed **intravenously** for three days.
intro-	into, within	introvert *n.*	a person whose attention is largely directed inward, toward himself or herself; a shy or withdrawn person	Unlike his flamboyant sister, quiet Zeke was a real **introvert**.
in-	in, into	induct *v.*	to bring in (to a group)	She was **inducted** into the honor society.
ex-	out, from	expel *v.*	to drive out or away	Let's **expel** the invaders!
circum-	around	circumscribe *v.*	to draw a line around; to mark the limits of	She carefully **circumscribed** the space that would become her office.
sub-	under	subvert *v.*	to bring about the destruction of, overthrow; to undermine	His attempt to **subvert** my authority will cost him his job.
super-	above, over	supervisor *n.*	one who watches over	Alex refused the promotion to **supervisor** because he didn't feel comfortable being his friends' boss.
con-	with, together	consensus *n.*	general agreement	After hours of debate, the group finally reached a **consensus** and selected a candidate.
non-	not	nonviable *adj.*	not able to live or survive	The farmer explained that the seedling was **nonviable**.
in-	not	invariable *adj.*	not changing	The weather here is **invariable**—always sunny and warm.
un-	not, against	unmindful *adj.*	not conscious or aware of; forgetful	For better or worse, he is **unmindful** of office politics.

PREFIX	MEANING	EXAMPLE	DEFINITION	SENTENCE
contra-	against	contradict *v.*	to state that (what is said) is untrue; to state the opposite of	I know we don't have to agree on everything, but she **contradicts** *everything* I say.
anti-	against, opposite	antipode *n.*	exact or direct opposite	North is the **antipode** of south.
counter-	against, opposing	counterproductive *adj.*	working against production	Complaining is **counterproductive**.
dis-	away,	dispel *v.*	to drive away	To **dispel** rumors that I was quitting, I scheduled a series of meetings for the next three months.
dis-	not,	opposite of disorderly *adj.*	not having order; messy, untidy, uncontrolled or unruly	Two people were hurt when the crowd became **disorderly** during the protest.
mis-	wrong, ill	misuse *v.*	to use wrongly	She **misused** her authority when she reassigned Charlie to a new team.
mal-	bad, wrong,	maltreat *v.*	to treat badly or wrongly	After the dog saved his life, he swore he would never **maltreat** another animal.
mal-	ill	malaise *n.*	feeling of discomfort or illness	The **malaise** many women feel during the first few months of pregnancy is called "morning sickness."
pseudo-	false, fake	pseudonym *n.*	false or fake name	Mark Twain is a **pseudonym** for Samuel Clemens.
auto-	by oneself or by itself	automaton *n.*	a robot; a person who seems to act mechanically and without thinking	The workers on the assembly line looked like **automatons**.
co-	together with; jointly	cohesive *adj.*	having a tendency to bond or stick together; united	Though they came from different backgrounds, they have formed a remarkably **cohesive** team.

▶ Suffixes

Suffixes are syllables added to the *ends* of words to change or add to their meaning. This table lists some of the most common suffixes in the English language. They are grouped together by similar meanings.

SUFFIX	MEANING	EXAMPLE	DEFINITION	SENTENCE
-en	to cause to become	broaden *v.*	to make more broad, widen	Traveling around the world will **broaden** your understanding of other cultures.
-ate	to cause to be	resuscitate *v.*	to bring or come back to life or consciousness; to revive	Thanks to a generous gift from an alumnus, we were able to **resuscitate** the study-abroad program.
-ify/-fy	to make or cause to be	electrify *v.*	to charge with electricity	The singer **electrified** the audience with her performance.
-ize	to make, to give	alphabetize *v.*	to put in alphabetical order	Please **alphabetize** these files for me.
-al	capable of, suitable for	practical *adj.*	suitable for use; involving activity, as distinct from study or theory	He has years of **practical**, on-the-job experience.
-ial	pertaining to	commercial *adj.*	of or engaged in commerce	**Commercial** vehicles must have special license plates.
-ic	pertaining to	aristocratic *adj.*	of or pertaining to the aristocracy	Though he was never rich or powerful, he has very **aristocratic** manners.
-ly	resembling, having the qualities of	tenderly *adv.*	done with tenderness; gently, delicately, lovingly	He held the newborn baby **tenderly** in his arms.
-ly	in the manner of	boldly *adv.*	in a bold manner	Despite his fear, he stepped **boldly** onto the stage.
-ful	full of	meaningful *adj.*	significant, full of meaning	When Robert walked into the room with Annette, she cast me a **meaningful** glance.
-ous, -ose	full of	humorous *adj.*	full of humor, funny	His **humorous** speech made the evening go by quickly.

SUFFIX	MEANING	EXAMPLE	DEFINITION	SENTENCE
-ive	having the quality of	descriptive *adj.*	giving a description	The letter was so **descriptive** that I could picture every place he'd been.
-less	lacking, free of	painless *adj.*	without pain, not causing pain	The doctor assured me that it is a **painless** procedure.
-ish	having the quality of	childish *adj.*	like a child; unsuitable for a grown person	He didn't get the job because of his **childish** behavior during the interview.
-ance/ -ence	quality or state of	tolerance *n.*	willingness or ability to tolerate a person or thing	He has a high level of **tolerance** for rudeness.
-acy	quality or state of	indeterminacy *n.*	state or quality of being undetermined (without defined limits) or vague	The **indeterminacy** of his statement made it impossible to tell which side he was on.
-tion	act, state or condition of	completion *n.*	the act of completing; the state of being completed or finished	The second siren signaled the **completion** of the fire drill.
-or/-er	one who does or performs the action of	narrator *n.*	one who tells the story, gives an account of	A first-person **narrator** is usually not objective.
-atrium -orium -etum	place for	arboretum *n.*	a garden devoted primarily to trees and shrubs	They built a deck with an **arboretum** for their bonsai tree collection.
-ary	place for, pertaining to	sanctuary *n.*	a sacred place, refuge	With three noisy roommates, Ellen frequently sought the quiet **sanctuary** of the library.
-cide	kill	pesticide *n.*	substance for killing insects	This **pesticide** is also dangerous for humans.
-ism	quality, state or condition of; doctrine of	optimism *n.*	belief that things will turn out for the best; tendency to take a hopeful view of things	Her **optimism** makes people want to be around her.
-ity	quality or state of	morality *n.*	state or quality of being moral	He argued that the basic **morality** of civilized societies hasn't changed much over the centuries.

SUFFIX	MEANING	EXAMPLE	DEFINITION	SENTENCE
-itis	inflammation of	tonsillitis *n.*	inflammation and infection of the tonsils	Her **tonsillitis** was so severe that doctors had to remove her tonsils immediately.
-ment	act or condition of	judgment *n.*	ability to judge or make decisions wisely; act of judging	He exercised good **judgment** by keeping his mouth shut during the meeting.
-ology	the study of	zoology *n.*	the scientific study of animal life	She took a summer job at the zoo because of her strong interest in **zoology**.

▶ Common Latin Word Roots

Many words in the English language have their origins in Latin. The following table shows the original Latin words that you have used (whether you know it or not) to create various English words. The Latin words serve as **roots,** providing the core meaning of the words; prefixes, suffixes, and other alterations give each word its distinct meaning. The word roots are listed in alphabetical order.

ROOT	MEANING	EXAMPLE	DEFINITION	SENTENCE
amare	to love	amorous *adj.*	readily showing or feeling love	She told him to stop his **amorous** advances, as she was already engaged.
audire	to hear	audience *n.*	assembled group of listeners or spectators; people within hearing	The **audience** was stunned when the game show host slapped the contestant.
bellum	war	belligerent *adj.*	inclined to fight; hostile, aggressive	The citizens feared that their **belligerent** leader would start an unjust war.
capere	to take	captivate *v.*	to capture the fancy of	The story **captivated** me from the beginning; I couldn't put the book down.
dicere	to say, speak	dictate *v.*	to state or order; to say what needs to be written down	She began to **dictate** her notes into the microphone.

ROOT	MEANING	EXAMPLE	DEFINITION	SENTENCE
duco	to lead	conduct *v.*	to lead or guide (thorough)	He **conducted** a detailed tour of the building.
equus	equal	equilibrium *n.*	a state of balance	I have finally achieved an **equilibrium** between work and leisure.
facere	to make or do	manufacture *v.*	to make or produce	The clothes are **manufactured** here in this factory.
lucere	to light	lucid *adj.*	very clear	No one could possibly have misunderstood such a **lucid** explanation.
manus	hand	manicure *n.*	cosmetic treatment of the fingernails	To maintain her long fingernails, she gets a **manicure** every week.
medius	middle	median *adj.*	middle point; middle in a set of numbers	The **median** household income in this wealthy neighborhood is $89,000.
mittere	to send	transmit *v.*	to send across	The message was **transmitted** over the intercom.
omnis	all, every	omnipresent *adj.*	present everywhere	That top-40 song is **omnipresent**; everywhere I go, I hear it playing.
plicare	to fold	application *n.*	putting one thing on another; making a formal request	His loan **application** was denied because of his poor credit history.
ponere/ positum	to place	position *n.*	the place a person or thing occupies	Although he is only 22, he holds a very powerful **position** in the company.
protare	to carry	transport *v.*	to carry across	The goods will be **transported** by boat.
quarere	to ask, question	inquiry *n.*	act of inquiry, investigation, or questioning	The **inquiry** lasted several months but yielded no new information.
scribere	to write	scribe *n.*	person who makes copies of writings	The **scribe** had developed thick calluses on his fingers from years of writing.

ROOT	MEANING	EXAMPLE	DEFINITION	SENTENCE
sentire	to feel	sentient *adj.*	capable of feeling	No **sentient** beings should be used for medical research.
specere	to look at	spectacle *n.*	striking or impressive sight	The debate was quite a **spectacle**—you should have seen the candidates attack one another.
spirare	to breathe	respiration *n.*	the act of breathing	His **respiration** was steady, but he remained unconscious.
tendere	to stretch	extend *v.*	to make longer, stretch out	Please **extend** the deadline by two weeks so you can complete the project properly.
verbum	word	verbatim *adv.*	word for word	The student failed because she had copied an article **verbatim** instead of writing her own essay.

▶ Common Greek Word Roots

Many other English words have their origins in the ancient Greek language. The following table shows the Greek words that you have used (whether you know it or not) to create various English words. The Greek words serve as **roots**, providing the core meaning of the words; prefixes, suffixes, and other alterations give each word its distinct meaning. The word roots are listed in alphabetical order.

ROOT	MEANING	EXAMPLE	DEFINITION	SENTENCE
bios	life	biology *n.*	the science of living organisms	He is majoring in **biology** and plans to go to medical school.
chronos	time	chronological *adj.*	arranged in the order in which things occurred	The story is confusing because she did not put the events in **chronological** order.
derma	skin	dermatology *n.*	branch of medical science dealing with the skin and its diseases	She has decided to study **dermatology** because she has always been plagued by rashes.
gamos	marriage, union	polygamy *n.*	the practice or custom of having more than one spouse or mate at a time	Throughout history, certain cultures have practiced **polygamy**, but it is uncommon today.

ROOT	MEANING	EXAMPLE	DEFINITION	SENTENCE
genos	race, sex, kind	genocide *n.*	deliberate extermination of one race of people	The recent **genocide** in Bosnia has created a crisis in orphaned children.
geo	earth	geography *n.*	the study of the Earth's surface; the surface or topographical features of a place.	The **geography** of this region made it difficult for the different tribes to interact
graphein	to write	calligraphy *n.*	beautiful or elegant handwriting	She used **calligraphy** when she addressed the wedding invitations.
krates	member of a group	democrat *n.*	one who believes in or advocates democracy as a principle of government	I have always been a **democrat**, but I refuse to join the democratic party.
kryptos	hidden, secret	cryptic *adj.*	concealing meaning, puzzling	He left such a **cryptic** message on my answering machine that I don't know what he wanted.
metron	to measure	metronome *n.*	device with a pendulum that beats at a determined rate to measure time/rhythm	She used a **metronome** to help her keep the proper pace as she played the song.
morphe	form	polymorphous *adj.*	having many forms	Most mythologies have a **polymorphous** figure, a "shape shifter," who can be both animal and human.
pathos	suffering, feeling	pathetic *adj.*	arousing feelings of pity or sadness	Willy Loman is a complex character who is both **pathetic** and heroic.
philos	loving	xenophile *n.*	a person who is attracted to foreign peoples, cultures or customs	Alex is a **xenophile**; I doubt he'll ever come back to the States.
phobos	fear	xenophobe *n.*	person who fears or hates foreigners or strange cultures, or customs	Don't expect Len to go on the trip; he's a **xenophobe**.
photos	light	photobiotic *adj.*	living or thriving only in the presence of light	Plants are **photobiotic** and will die without light.

ROOT	MEANING	EXAMPLE	DEFINITION	SENTENCE
podos	foot	podiatrist *n.*	an expert in diagnosis and treatment of ailments of the human foot	The **podiatrist** saw that the ingrown toenail had become infected.
psuedein	to deceive	pseudonym *n.*	false name	Was George Eliot a **pseudonym** for Mary Ann Evans?
pyr	fire	pyromaniac *n.*	one who has a compulsion to set things on fire	The warehouse fire was not an accident; it was set by a **pyromaniac**.
soma	body	psychosomatic *adj.*	of or involving both the mind and body	In a **psychosomatic** illness, physical symptoms are caused by emotional distress.
tele	distant	telescope *n.*	optical instrument for making distant objects appear larger and nearer when viewed through the lens	While Galileo did not invent the **telescope**, he was the first to use it to study the planets and stars.
therme	heat	thermos *n.*	insulated jug or bottle that keeps liquids hot or cold	The **thermos** kept my coffee hot all afternoon.

Math and vocabulary
for civil service
exams.

PAPER BINDER

DATE			

**PLEASE
DO NOT WRITE ON THE
PAGES IN THIS BOOK.
MAKE PHOTOCOPIES OF
THE ONES YOU NEED.**